About the book;

The topics in Canada in Crisis cover a broad spectrum of this large and diverse country and its governance. These topics require the knowledge, experience, and skills of many people to properly assess past policies of the government, and to propose new policies. However, any undertaking must begin with one initial step, in the hope that others will take up the challenge. The following analyses and suggested goals serve only to scratch the surface of Canada's past history and future potential. The topics are presented in a strategic perspective, in the hope of encouraging others to expand on this small beginning of an urgent endeavour to achieve a better future for Canada. Please take up the torch . . .

To appreciate this document, one must have a vision of Canada's potential, the path to attain that potential, and the future that Canada deserves to enjoy. Canada is a bountiful country blessed with an abundance of human and material resources, but burdened with excessive government. We must reduce the dead weight of government as a proportion of Canada's Gross Domestic Product and allow the people and the private sector to prosper.

About the author;

Bob and his wife Ruth both grew up in Burlington Ontario. Bob graduated from the University of Toronto in 1959 with a BASc (P Eng), married Ruth, and served eight years in the RCAF in Germany and Alberta from 1958 to 1966. He left the RCAF to earn an MBA from the University of Western Ontario in 1968. After graduation Bob joined the federal government and they moved to Ottawa, where Ruth taught Kindergarten. They have two married sons and three grand-children. Bob retired in 1992.

During his 30 years with the federal government (including the RCAF), Bob worked in 14 different agencies, bureaux, boards, commissions, departments, secretariats, and Crown corporations. These included such agencies as the Department of Industry Trade and Commerce, the Bureau of Management Consultants, the Treasury Board Secretariat, the Anti-Inflation Board, the Audit Services Bureau, the Unemployment Insurance Commission, the Canadian Saltfish Corporation (in Newfoundland), the Department of Indian Affairs, and the Export Development Corporation (as Deputy Chief of Industrial Analysis). In 1992, Bob appeared before the Finance Committees of Parliament and the Senate to advocate that all pensions and life annuities be made optional, portable, and commutable at any time by the employee.

CANADA in CRISIS (1)

An Agenda to Unify the Nation

Order this book online at www.trafford.com
or email orders@trafford.com

Most Trafford titles are also available at major online book retailers.

Printed in Victoria, BC, Canada.

ISBN: 978-1-4269-1897-1 (sc)
ISBN: 978-1-4269-1898-8 (hc)

Library of Congress Control Number: 2009938320

*Our mission is to efficiently provide the world's finest, most comprehensive book publishing
service, enabling every author to experience success. To find out how to publish your book, your
way, and have it available worldwide, visit us online at www.trafford.com*

Trafford rev. 9/27/2010

 www.trafford.com

North America & international
toll-free: 1 888 232 4444 (USA & Canada)
phone: 250 383 6864 ♦ fax: 812 355 4082

To my family:
my wonderful wife Ruth of 50 years,
our two sons and their wives,
Kevin & Erica, and Chris & Teresa,
and our three grandchildren.
Jordan & Amanda, and Cassie

Table of Contents

Prologue

The topics in this book cover a broad spectrum of any country, let alone one as large and diverse as Canada. The topics also require the knowledge, experience, and skills of many persons to properly assess past policies of a government, or to propose new policies. However, any undertaking must begin with one initial step, in the hope that others will take up the challenge. The Canadian author is fortunate to have had a background in engineering (UoT 59 BASc) and business (UWO 68 MBA) from excellent universities in Canada. He has worked in various fields of the federal government, in the RCAF and 14 departments, bureaux, boards, commissions, secretariats, and Crown corporations over a 30 year period, in Canada and in Europe. The following analyses and suggested goals serve only to scratch the surface of Canada's past history and future potential. The topics are presented in a strategic perspective, in the hope of encouraging others to expand on this small beginning of an urgent endeavour to achieve a better future for Canada. Please take up the torch . . .

To appreciate this document, one must have a vision of Canada's potential, the path to attain that potential, and the future that Canada deserves to enjoy. Canada is a bountiful country blessed with an abundance of human and material resources, but burdened with excessive government. We must reduce the dead weight of government as a proportion of Canada's Gross Domestic Product and allow the people and the private sector to prosper.

The author is greatly indebted to Wikipedia for the wealth of knowledge that is made available to everyone these days, the various references cited in Wikipedia and other sources, and the various journalists with

Canadian newspapers for outstanding articles over the past years, and to the authors of such books as 'The Year 2000', 'The Limits to Growth', 'Atlas Shrugged', and others. Thanks are due to a few friends with 50 year memories, for having the patience to read through this work in progress . . . they too shared concerns for the future of Canada. And finally, my deep and everlasting appreciation to my wife, and my friends' wives, for their shared concerns for the future of Canada.

Robert A. Battram

Introduction - Unity

United we stand . . . divided we fall - Aesop

The phrase has been attributed to Aesop, in his fable The Four Oxen and the Lion. The Four Oxen and the Lion. Æsop. (6th century BC) Fables. The Harvard Classics. 1909–14.

A lion used to prowl about a field in which four oxen used to dwell. Many a time he tried to attack them. But whenever he came near they turned their tails to one another, so that whichever way he approached them he was met by the horns of one of them. At last, however, they fell to quarrelling among themselves, and each went off to pasture alone in a separate corner of the field. Then the Lion attacked them one by one and soon made an end of all four.

The American statesman, Patrick Henry used the phrase in his last public speech, given in March 1799, in which he denounced The Kentucky and Virginia Resolutions [to nullify federal laws]. Clasping his hands and waving his body back and forth, Henry declaimed, "Let us trust God, and our better judgment to set us right hereafter. United we stand, divided we fall. Let us not split into factions which must destroy that union upon which our existence hangs."

Unilateral Secession Denied - Abe Lincoln

Decades after the Resolutions were published, during the "nullification crisis" of 1828–1833, South Carolina threatened to nullify a federal law regarding tariffs. Andrew Jackson issued a resounding proclamation against the doctrine of nullification, stating: "I consider . . . the power to annul a law of the United States, assumed by one State, incompatible with the existence of the Union, contradicted expressly by the letter of the Constitution, unauthorized by its spirit, inconsistent with every principle on which it was founded, and destructive of the great object for which it was formed." He also denied the right of secession: "The Constitution . . . forms a government not a league . . . To say that any State may at pleasure secede from the Union is to say that the United States is not a nation." Later, Abraham Lincoln also rejected the compact theory saying the Constitution was a binding contract among the states and no contract can be changed unilaterally by one party.

Unilateral Secession Denied - Jean Chrétien

In 1999, Canadians were concerned by the wording of the question to be posed and the possibility of another referendum on secession. Prime Minister Chrétien referred the matter to the Supreme Court of Canada in December of 1999. The Court ruled that Quebec, with less than 23 percent of Canada's population, could not unilaterally secede, and could accede to sovereignty only if the referendum had a clear majority in favour of a clearly worded question.

Following the Supreme Court's decision, the federal government introduced legislation known as the Clarity Act. That Act set forth the guidelines for any future referendum undertaken by the government of any province on the subject of separation. Ironically, the definition of "clearly worded" and "clear majority" were never given in the bill. Instead, it stated that the federal government would determine "whether the question is clear" and whether a "clear majority" (with a requisite super majority for success being inferred) was attained.

With a majority of the votes supported by all members of the House of Commons, except those of the Bloc Québécois, both houses of the Parliament approved the legislation.

Chapter 1 - Definitions and Goals

Definitions & Goals   *(Definitions are from The Shorter Oxford English Dictionary)*
(Goals are proposed for explicitly legislated Official Status)

One Country: *"the territory of a nation, the land of a person's birth, residence, citizenship"*

Canada: a single, united country (nation) having common goals and values.

One Nation: *"a distinct race or people, characterized by common descent, language or history, usually organized as a separate political state, and occupying a definite territory".*

Canada: a single, united nation (country) having common goals and values.

One Governance: *"the manner of governing, directing and controlling the affairs of a people"*

Canadian: a federal Parliament, provincial Legislatures, and municipal Councils.

One Justice: *"the quality of being morally just or righteous; rectitude".*

Canadian: English common law applied equally to all peoples of the country.

One Economy: *"the art of managing the resources of a people and of its government"; and the "careful management and frugality of labour, money, time etc."*

Canadian: a single economy under federal direction and regulatory structures.

One Religion: *"conduct indicating a belief in, reverence for, and desire to please a divine ruling power; a particular system of faith and worship".*

Christian: official acceptance of Christianity; tolerance of other peaceful religions.

One Language: *"the whole body of words and methods of combining them used by a people, nation, or race".*

English: the education and usage of proper English in all public affairs of the nation, with tolerance of the private use of other languages.

One Culture: *"the training and refinement of mind, tastes and manners; the intellectual side of civilization".*

Canadian: educated, self-reliant, industrious, honest, ethical, tolerant.

One People: *"the persons belonging to a place, constituting a particular concourse, congregation, company, or class; the whole body of enfranchised or qualified citizens considered as the source of power especially in a democratic state".*

Canadian: those devoted to defending and swearing allegiance to a united Canada.

Chapter 2 - One Country (Nation)

(Bibliography: One Country - Canada's Lands & People)
(Bibliography: One Country - The Constitution of Canada)

One Country: *the territory of a nation, the land of a person's birth,*
                residence, citizenship

Canada: a single, united country (nation) having common
                goals and values.

One Country

Canada is a country, mostly north of the 49th parallel and the Great
Lakes of North America, extending from the Atlantic in the east, to
the Pacific in the west, and to the Arctic in the north. It is the world's
second largest country with a total area of 9,984,670 km² of which
almost 9% is water, and shares land borders with the United States to
the south and northwest.

The land occupied by Canada was inhabited for millennia by various
aboriginal peoples. Beginning in the late 15th century, British and
French expeditions explored and later settled the Atlantic coast. In
1763 after the Seven Years' War, France ceded all of its colonies in
North America, except the two small islands of St Pierre and Miquelon
off Newfoundland. In 1867, with the union of three British North
American colonies through Confederation, Canada was formed as a
federal dominion of four provinces. The addition of more provinces
and territories led to increasing autonomy from the United Kingdom,
culminating in the Canada Act in 1982 which severed the last vestiges
of legal dependence upon the British parliament.

A federation now comprising ten provinces and three territories, Canada is a parliamentary democracy and a constitutional monarchy. It is a multicultural country, with both English and French as official languages at the federal level. Technologically advanced and industrialized, Canada maintains a diversified economy that is heavily reliant on its abundant natural mineral and water resources, gold, silver, iron, copper, zinc, molybdenum, diamonds, potash, and especially the oil, gas, and tar sands. It is a member of the G8, NATO, and the Commonwealth of Nations. Canada fought valiantly in World War I (1914- 1918), World War II (1939- 1945), finished that war with one of the largest armed forces in the world, and was one of the first countries to join the UN. Canada fought in Korea 1950- 1953, and is currently serving in many other countries under UN or NATO mandates.

The recent influx of people to Canada began with the French and English settlers in the 1700's. Others soon followed over the centuries, from Portugal, Spain, Iceland, Germany, Poland, Russia, Czechoslovakia, Hungary, Italy, Holland, Belgium, Scandinavia, the Balkans, and other western European countries. These settlers were entirely from Christian religions and European cultures. Following the new Immigration Acts introduced in 1967 and 1976, and official multiculturalism in 1971, waves of non-European immigration changed the face of the country. Peoples from the mid-East, Asia, Africa, and South America joined the previous settlers, primarily in urban centres of Vancouver, Toronto, and Montreal. The variety of religions and cultures, (Christianity, Islam, Hinduism, Buddhism, Judaism, Confucianism, Taoism, Shinto), and governments of the peoples from these countries expanded within a milieu charged with the responsibility of mutual respect and tolerance.

Commentary

The international stature and recognition of any country such as Canada is best defined by its Constitution, its Charter of Rights and Freedoms, and its justice system and laws. Other important criteria of a country must be the international recognition of its territorial claims, and its capacity and willingness to defend and control that territory. An important component of that willingness depends upon the involvement of its people and its government.

The people of any country must share those special bonds which define a nation . . . *"common descent, language or history, political state, and occupying a definite territory"*. Canada is a young country, governed for a mere few centuries rather than millennia. In the early years, Canadian military forces never fought in international wars as a major combatant, but always under the command and control of Great Britain. Only in World War II, did Canada commit its forces of its own accord and by the acts of its own Parliament. At the end of WWII, Canada had established itself as one of the best of countries for its freedom, values and principles. That may have been its finest hour. Those values had been crucial to define itself as a nation and a country, with the military power to defend its claims. Recently, Canada has still ranked in the top ten countries of the world for its qualities of life and liberty.

The arrival of so many different peoples following the end of World War II encouraged the government to introduce the Canadian Multiculturalism Act (Bill C-93) in 1988. Subsequently, a major consequence of rapid increases in immigration from regions beyond western Europe and the policy of multiculturalism has been a loss of Canadian identity. It has become more difficult to define ourselves. What is a Canadian in the 21 st century? The lost sense of identity has become more troubling as many later arrivals changed our society by bringing old customs and quarrels into the land. Many older Canadians have begun to challenge the loss of their culture, their values, and their identity. At the end of World War II, Canada had established itself internationally as a significant member of the western world. That reputation and that status have been changed through diversification to the point where we no longer know who we are, or where we stand.

Through our lost adherence to common values and principles, we risk becoming less understood and recognizable, and less significant as a nation. There is a need for a new Constitution to properly define our culture, morals, principles, and laws. The Charter of Rights and Freedoms of 1982 was enshrined in the Constitution Act but is failing us now, and these articles must be revised to redefine and clearly state our values.

Prime Minister Diefenbaker enacted a Bill of Rights in 1960, sanctioned only by Parliament. Other documents of supreme importance were the repatriation of the Constitution from Britain, and the Charter of Rights and Freedoms enacted by Prime Minister Trudeau in 1982. These were sanctioned by the federal Parliament and all provincial governments (except Quebec).

The crucial distinction between Diefenbaker's Bill of Rights, and Trudeau's Charter of Rights and Freedoms lies in the failure of the latter to protect personal property. The Bill of Rights granted the protection of personal property, while the Charter failed to do so. Unfortunately, the Charter prevailed in law for many years, having been sanctioned by the provinces, while the Bill of Rights had not been accorded that legitimacy. To the credit of the Supreme Court of Canada, more recognition has been given recently to the Bill as providing for gaps and omissions in the Charter, although only on a case by case basis. There are at least four major issues where the Charter fails to provide protection to the people.

Suggestions and Proposals

The Constitution should guarantee and protect the rights of its peoples to the peaceful enjoyment of their property and business affairs.

The Constitution should ensure that the rights of society prevail over the rights of the individual where the culture and security of the peoples and the nation are concerned.

The Constitution should provide clear distinctions between the rights and privileges of its peoples, and the duties, obligations, and loyalties of those peoples.

The Charter of Rights and Freedoms should be amended to subordinate the right to freedom of religion to all other rights under the Charter, to ensure that the transgressions of any other rights are not permitted, excused, or condoned by pretentious claims of freedom of religion.

Canada should revise the Constitution to benefit the peoples rather than the government. The issue is one of propriety at the highest level: whether the Constitution should protect the rights of the government . . . or the rights of the people.

To quote Cicero, (106– 43 BC), a Roman statesman, lawyer, political theorist, and constitutional expert . . . *"The peoples' good is the highest law".* Until the political situation permits the Constitution and the Charter to be amended, Canada shall remain a lesser country than its potential warrants.

Chapter 3 - One Nation (Country)

(Bibliography: One Nation - Canada **is** the Nation)

One Nation: *a distinct race or people, characterized by common descent, language or history, usually organized as a separate political state, and occupying a definite territory*

Canada: a single, united nation (country) having common goals and values

One Nation

A nation is a territory or country as a political entity or a grouping of people who share real or imagined common history, culture, language or ethnic origin, often possessing or seeking its own government. The concept and the development of a nation is closely related to the development of modern industrial states and nationalist movements in Europe in the eighteenth and nineteenth centuries, although nationalists would trace nations into the past along uninterrupted lines of historical narrative. Benedict Anderson argued that nations were "imagined communities" because "the members of even the smallest nation will never know most of their fellow members, meet them, or even hear of them, yet in the minds of each lives the image of their communion". Although "nation" is also commonly used in informal discourse as a synonym for state or country, a nation is not identical to a state. Countries where the social concept of "nation" coincides with the political concept of "state" are called nation states.

The concept of a national identity refers both to the distinguishing features of the group, and to the individual's sense of belonging to it.

8

All of the characteristics may be disputed, and opposition to secessionist nationalism often includes the denial that a separate nation exists. Almost all nationalist movements make some claim to shared origins and descent, and it is a component of the national identity in most nations. The fact that the ancestry is shared among the members of the nation unites them, and sets them apart from other nations, which do not share that ancestry. A language is the primary ingredient in the making of a nation. Without a common language a nation cannot evolve. A common culture and a common history is dependent on language.

Also dealing with everyday affairs within a group of people living in a specified boundary needs a common mean of communication to trade and socialize. Many nations are constructed around the idea of a shared culture, the national culture. The national culture may be assumed to be shared with previous generations, and includes a cultural heritage from these generations. As with the common ancestry, this identification of past culture with present culture may be largely symbolic. A nation may be constructed around a common history or chronologically recorded events in the past, which their ancestors have endured. Religion is sometimes a defining factor for a nation, although some nationalist movements such as those in Ireland de-emphasize it as a divisive factor.

A state which identifies itself explicitly as the home of a cultural nation is a nation state. Many modern states try to legitimize their existence in this way, although there might be disputes as to the appropriateness of this. Because so many of the states are nation states, the words "nation", "country", and "state" are often used synonymously.

Commentary

Almost all nations are associated with a specific territory, the national homeland. Some live in a historical diaspora, that is, scattered or sown outside the national homeland. A state which explicitly identifies itself as the homeland of a particular nation is a nation state, and most modern states fall into this category, although there may be disputes about their legitimacy. In Canada the term "First Nations" is used for groups which share an aboriginal culture, and have official recognition or partial autonomy.

Note that Canada is a country which accepted and authorized the use of the phrase "First Nations", although Canada itself is recognized throughout the world as a nation. The failure to repudiate the practice by so-called nations within Canada when the phrase was first used may be attributed to political opportunism. The government of Canada should never have pandered to a minority of its people over the fantasy of recognition as a separate nation within the nation of Canada. Such minorities may become nations only when they conjure up the authority, courage, and will to lawfully separate from the parent nation and defend a definite territory.

Recall the Oxford definitions of these two key words country and nation, just after the Chapter title. From those definitions, one should appreciate that the concept of a "nation" within another nation is merely the first step in a stratagem for separatism. Such pretension is logically inadmissible within any endeavour toward the unification of Canada. The claim by aboriginal or other peoples to be a nation within Canada is an odious pretense that should be repudiated in the strongest terms.

Without question, both Sweden and Switzerland are recognized internationally as neutral countries. They are also nations having defined histories, cultures, languages, and territories. Their status as independent countries is based on historical claims to their territories, and their willingness to defend those claims. Their neutrality is respected, based on their capacity to defend those territorial claims by force of arms.

Are Liechtenstein and Monaco nations? No, they are defined as principalities governed by Princes, subordinate to Switzerland and France for currency, defence, and foreign affairs. Neither is able to defend its claims to its territories without reliance on its benefactors.

Are the Aboriginal peoples of the North American continent nations? They claim to be First Nations of Canada, yet they are reliant on Canada for their daily survival. The federal government is recognized internationally under English common law as a legal Trustee for the Aboriginal peoples. Those peoples have very separate and diverse languages, histories, territories, cultures and customs, governments and laws. They are more properly described as bands, as stated in the Indian Act.

Are the people of Quebec a nation? In 2006, the Canadian House of Commons passed a symbolic motion recognizing the "Québécois as a nation within a united Canada."

The Secession of Quebec from Canada

For almost three decades, the issue of Quebec's separation from Canada has been vehemently proposed by a large portion of the population of that province. The issue has almost torn the country asunder with its complexities. A major concern is that many of the people currently resident in the province of Quebec do not wish to secede from Canada. Another thorny issue which is not often raised is whether the nation would permit a secessionist Quebec to take with it all of the lands currently known as Quebec. A good example of a contentious portion of those land is the northern area formerly known as Rupert's Land. The majority of the people there are the indigenous Cree, who have twice voted not to join Quebec if it separates from Canada. The majority of the population in Quebec west of a north - south line through Ottawa/ Gatineau would also rebel and refuse to leave Canada. There are similar concerns about the lands south of the St. Lawrence River which currently provides the only land corridor to the Atlantic provinces of New Brunswick, and Newfoundland & Labrador on the mainland east of Quebec.

The formation of political parties at both the provincial (la partie nationale, PQ) and federal (le Bloc Quebecois, BQ) levels has further incensed the situation. The Bloc cares not a whit about the future of Canada, yet currently holds 48 seats (2010) in the federal Parliament in Ottawa. A united Canada with one party advocating the separation of a part of Canada is simply an oxymoron. Rex Murphy, a journalist for the National Post but originally from Newfoundland, wrote and an article was entitled "The Absurdity of the Bloc". In that article he stated that, "The "sovereignist" presence in federal elections impedes the formation of real national governments." Some might have suggested that to permit any separatist to sit in Parliament would be "The Epitome of Ludicrosity".

There is no logical argument as to why the Canadian taxpayer should be obliged to tolerate the presence of a separatist party in Parliament. The qualifications for eligibility for residents of Canada to hold parliamentary office already exclude those with previous criminal records either in Canada or any other country in the world. To that list should be added those who openly or covertly seek the dissolution of Canada, or the secession of any part of Canada to become a separate nation.

All of these changes would require a strong majority government with strong leadership. If and when such a situation should arise, serious consideration must be given to revisions to the Constitution and the structure of Parliament itself.

A large portion of northern Quebec was originally Rupert's Land under the British Government of the day. Rupert's Land was ceded to the Hudson Bay Company by the British Crown in 1670. The Rupert's Land Act of 1868 empowered the surrender of all its lands and privileges of the Company, and provided for the admission of Rupert's Land and the North- western Territory into the Dominion of Canada. The Act stipulated that the peoples of Rupert's Land remained under the trust of the federal government, just as other aboriginal peoples of Canada. That portion of Rupert's Land in Quebec lies roughly north of the Laurentians and west of Labrador, and constitutes 85% of the current provincial land mass. The Inuit of Nunavik will not be part of an independent Quebec, and confirmed this in two referenda (1980, 1995). The Inuit and Cree are almost the entire population of Rupert's Land, and remain wards of the federal government. Quebec has no legal power to unilaterally separate from Canada. If Quebec were to persist in secession from Canada, the federal government would be obliged to deny those lands to Quebec, to protect its wards and their traditional lands.

The concept of Indian bands, the people of Quebec, the province of Quebec, or any other political or territorial group or organization, as nations within Canada is clearly nonsense. It is nothing more than semantic puffery for political appeasement, and a nightmare for the rest of Canada. What would be next . . . the granting of nationhood to the western provinces, or the Acadians in the Atlantic, or the Métis, or the Empire Loyalists, the Doukhobors, or the union of pipe-fitters and blacksmiths? A slippery slope indeed, when once begun.

Suggestions and Proposals

All legislation and official sanctions by government which recognize any group of people, or any organization, or any territory, as a nation within Canada should be rescinded.

Chapter 4 - One Governance

(Bibliography: One Governance - Canada's Governance)

One Governance: *the manner of governing, directing and controlling the affairs of a people*

    Canadian: a federal Parliament with provincial Legislatures

The Crown of Canada

As per the Constitution Act, 1867, Canada is a constitutional monarchy, wherein the role of the reigning sovereign is both legal and practical. The Crown is regarded as a corporation, with the monarch, vested as she is with all powers of state. The Crown has thus been described as the underlying principle of Canada's institutional unity.

The Monarchy

The Canadian monarchy is a federal one in which the Crown is unitary throughout all jurisdictions in the country, with the head of state being a part of all equally. As such, the sovereignty of the federal and provincial regions is passed on not by the Governor General or the federal parliament, but through the overreaching Crown itself. Though singular, the Crown is thus "divided" into eleven legal jurisdictions, or eleven "Crowns"; one federal and ten provincial. Lieutenant Governors serves as the Queen's representative in all provinces, carrying out all the monarch's constitutional and ceremonial duties of state on her behalf, neither the federal government's nor the Governors' General.

Executive Powers

The government is defined by the constitution as the Queen acting on the advice of her Privy Council. However, the Privy Council, comprised mostly of former members of parliament, Chief Justices of the Supreme Court, and other elder statesmen, rarely meets in full. Responsible government requires that those who directly advise the Monarch and Governor General how to exercise the Royal Prerogative be accountable to the elected House of Commons. The day to day operation of government is guided only by a sub-group of the Privy Council made up of individuals who hold seats in parliament. This body of Ministers of the Crown is known as the Cabinet.

One of the main duties of the Crown is to "ensure that a democratically elected government is always in place," which means appointing a prime minister, presently Stephen Harper, to head the Cabinet. By convention, the Governor General must appoint as Prime Minister the person who holds the confidence of the House of Commons. In practice, this is typically the leader of the political party that holds more seats than any other party in that chamber, currently the Conservative Party. Should no party hold a majority in the Commons, the leader of one party, either the one with the most seats or one supported by other parties, will be called by the Governor General to form a minority government. Once sworn in by the viceroy, the Prime Minister holds office until he resigns or is removed by the Governor General, either after a motion of no confidence or after his party's defeat in a general election.

The Parliament of Canada

Canada's bicameral legislature, located on Parliament Hill in the national capital of Ottawa, consists of the sovereign, the House of Commons, and the appointed Senate. The Governor General summons and appoints each of the 105 members of the upper house on the advice of his or her Prime Minister, while the 308 members of the lower house are directly elected by eligible voters in the Canadian populace, with each Member of Parliament representing a single electoral district for a period of not more than four years. By democratic tradition, the House of Commons is the dominant branch of parliament, the Senate and Crown rarely opposing its will. The Senate, thus, reviews legislation from a less partisan standpoint, and the monarch and viceroy provide the necessary Royal Assent to make bills into law and summon, prorogue, and dissolve parliament to call an election, and read the Throne Speech.

The Constitution Act 1867, directs that the Governor General alone is responsible for summoning parliament. A parliamentary session lasts until a prorogation, after which both chambers of the legislature cease all legislative business until the Governor General issues another royal proclamation to open a new session. After a number of such sessions, each parliament comes to an end via dissolution. As a general election typically follows, the timing of a dissolution is usually politically motivated with the Prime Minister selecting a moment most advantageous to his or her political party. The end of a parliament may also be necessary if the majority of Members of Parliament revoke their confidence in the Prime Minister's ability to govern, or the legally mandated four year maximum is reached; no parliament has been allowed to expire in such a fashion.

Canadian Federalism

The powers of the parliament of Canada are limited by the constitution, which divides legislative abilities between the federal and provincial governments; in general, provincial legislatures may pass laws relating only to topics explicitly reserved for them by the constitution, such as education, provincial officers, municipal government, charitable institutions, and "matters of a merely local or private nature". Any matter not under the exclusive authority of the provincial Legislatures is within the scope of the federal parliament's power. Thus parliament alone may pass laws (amongst other things) relating to the postal service, the census, the military, navigation and shipping, fishing, currency, banking, weights and measures, bankruptcy, copyrights, patents, First Nations, and naturalization. In some cases, however, the jurisdictions of the federal and provincial parliaments may be more vague. For instance, the parliament in Ottawa regulates marriage and divorce in general, but the solemnization of marriage is regulated only by the provincial legislatures. Other examples include the powers of both the federal and provincial parliaments to impose taxes, borrow money, punish crimes, and regulate agriculture.

Commentary

Four parties elected representatives to the federal parliament in the 2008 elections: the Conservative Party of Canada (the minority Governing Party), the Liberal Party of Canada (the Official Opposition), the New Democratic Party (NDP) and the Bloc Québécois (BQ).

Canada's federalist structure divides the responsibilities of government between the federal and the ten provincial governments. Unicameral provincial legislatures operate in parliamentary fashion similar to the House of Commons. Canada's three territories have legislatures, but with fewer constitutional responsibilities than the provinces, and with some structural differences. Most notable is the Legislative Assembly of Nunavut in the far central north which has no political parties and operates on a consensual basis.

The Prime Minister is normally the leader of the party that holds the confidence of the House of Commons. The Cabinet is made up of Ministers usually selected from the House of Commons and appointed by the Prime Minister. The Prime Minister's Office (PMO) is one of the most powerful institutions in government, proposing most legislation for parliamentary approval, and suggesting the appointment of Cabinet members, Senators, federal court judges, heads of Crown corporations, and the Governor General for approval by the Prime Minister. Madame Michaëlle Jean has served as Governor General since 27 September 2005; the Right Honourable Stephen Harper, leader of the Conservative Party, has been Prime Minister since 6 February 2006.

As stated before, Canada is a federation composed of ten provinces and three territories. The three northern territories are the Yukon, the Northwest Territories, and Nunavut. Provinces have more autonomy than territories. The provinces are responsible for most of Canada's social programs such as health care, education, and welfare, and together collect more revenue than the federal government. By using its spending powers, the federal government can initiate national policies in provincial areas, such as the Canada Health Act. In practice, the provinces rarely refuse to participate in federally funded programs. The federal government makes equalization payments to ensure reasonably uniform standards of services and taxation between the richer and poorer provinces.

The responsibilities of each level of government are still taken as those originally in the British North American Act (BNA). Certain fields of endeavour are crucial to the federal level of government, while others are the proper ambit of the provinces. The foremost of these federal endeavours are the justice system and law enforcement, national security including military and police forces, transportation and communication systems, finance and banking, immigration, and most importantly the assurance of freedom in all economic activities. All of these powers extend across the entire expanse of the nation's lands. The provincial governments are responsible for certain other remaining fields of endeavour within their own regions as specified under the BNA Act and its amendments. Foremost among these are resources, education, health, labour, regional transportation, welfare and social programs, and municipal governance.

In practice, many aspects of these endeavours overlap the two levels of government. The federal government in particular has tended to use various means to intercede in some areas better left to the provincial governments. The fault lies essentially in the Constitution. Although repatriated with great fanfare from the British government, further reforms are needed. The federal government still has a parochial and omniscient attitude, believing that it must provide single solutions (one size fits all) to satisfy all of the peoples in the country.

We should heed the warning of a distinguished former president of the United States, Thomas Jefferson: *"A government big enough to give you everything you want, is big enough to take away everything you have."*

Politics, Parliaments, and Legislatures

More important than the division of responsibilities among the levels of governance, is the organizational structure within each level of governance itself . . . the British parliamentary model. The democratic system and parliamentary principles have been admired and replicated throughout many countries of the world. However, any knowledgeable and sensible observer will concede that the organizational structure affecting the management of our entire country is both archaic and awesomely inefficient. To be quite blunt, a common expression springs to mind . . . "A roomful of monkeys could do it better".

Why do the rules refuse to allow the television cameras to scan the entire House of Commons while in session? Why are Members permitted to heckle and shout, while another Member of Parliament has the floor with the permission of the Speaker of the House. Why is there such an adversarial atmosphere? Does it derive from the feudal days of Europe, where feudal kingdoms strove to dominate others over the centuries? Why are so many Members lawyers, who characteristically thrive on the challenges and confrontations of litigation?

The last question is the crucial key, and thereby provides a possible answer to the other questions. It has been assumed that only lawyers have the capacity to draft and pass complex legislation. Yet when asked for legal opinions, any self respecting lawyer will generally first ask, "Which answer do you wish to hear?" Few lawyers have been accused of leadership, or of wide ranging visions of the future potential of a country and its peoples. The country might be better served to have more of the latter and fewer of the former. The country would also be better served if governance were consensual rather than confrontational. Even Barack Obama, President of the United States is desperately trying to garner bipartisan support for his initiatives in governing. But is that possible?

Consensual Parliaments and Legislatures

There are other structures for governance that deserve consideration such as the consensual councils governing all municipalities in Canada.

Another outstanding example is right under our very noses . . . the unicameral legislature of Nunavut (*Our Land*) which functions not along political party lines, but rather by consensus. To put that in a very relevant perspective, which would you prefer to lead you to your goals; bands of partisan monkeys all jabbering at once and tearing off in different directions, or a competent, purposeful, and dedicated team of huskies pulling your sled? A cohesive corporate structure, such as the Royal Bank of Canada, or Encana, would be far more effective as managers of Canada than the existing confrontational and party based political structure.

One must admire the northern peoples of Nunavut who have survived under extremely adverse conditions for thousands of years in harmony with each other. Common sense rules their day, with courteous discussion, in the best interests of their people. The same members of a consensual legislature may not always agree on different issues, so the only path to success is to respect all members, any of whom may be your allies on future issues for decision. Proper decorum would prevail. For Canada, a unicameral and consensual government (without a Senate), would be more effective than the current bicameral and partisan government.

The House of Commons is governed by unwritten conventions and traditions and by its 'statute law', the standing orders. These special statutes have a constitutional aspect. They set out some of the rights of the minority parties in the House of Commons versus the majority party, and the rights of all backbenchers versus the executive. The standing orders may be amended by a simple majority (unlike most constitutional documents), but are regarded as a matter for the whole House to determine.

Referenda by the People

There is another decision making process that deserves more attention; the referendum. The current process of political parties has created laws and legislation that are proposed and approved by the party of the government (or parties of a coalition). Decisions made by political parties are not always those that would be made by a simple majority of the people. Hence, the political party structure does not properly reflect an open and free democracy, despite Canada's proud claim to be such a democracy. There are at least two potential influences to cause that failure.

The first influences confronting a party in government are historic party positions or lobbying by industry, which may cause it to legislate against the best interests of the people. An example is the long standing prohibition instigated by the life insurance industry that life annuities may not be commuted or transferred. *(Author's Note: after many years, the prohibition was rescinded, but without any obligations to provide commutation and transfer: thus, no prohibition against such transfers, but alas no obligation to provide such transfers).*

The second influences confronting a party in government, which are not in the best interests of the people, are the fears of offending some small but vocally significant portion of the voting public. This inevitably leads to the persistent retention of previous bad legislation. An example of that was the long delay in legislating the reversal of the government's position on the transfer of pensions. A politician's worst nightmare is alienating a strong lobby or a significantly vocal portion of the public, with the consequent loss of support in the next election.

Consider the likely affect of a referendum on recent policies and legislation of the government of Canada; the bilingualism policy, the endless appeal process for immigrants, the destruction of the A. V. Roe Aircraft company's CF105 Avro Arrow, the cancellation of contracts at a loss of $500 million for desperately needed helicopters (partisan politics at its very worst), and the subordination of the rights of society to the rights of individuals under the Charter. Would these policies be continued if Canadians were allowed to determine their fate by referendum? Would they even be implemented by a consensual government in the first place? The Constitution should be amended in the interests of true democracy to permit referenda on major issues and policies by the people of Canada. To quote again from Cicero, *"The peoples' good is the highest law"*.

Suggestions and Proposals

The British North America Act and the Constitution should be amended (or rescinded and a new Constitution established) with the division of responsibilities between federal and provincial levels of government revised to better accord with the 21 st century political climate and the people's wishes.

The structures of politics, parliament, and legislatures should be reviewed to determine whether they are relevant and the best suited for modern management of a country such as Canada.

The Constitution should be amended to deny eligibility for election to Parliament to any person who has a criminal record in Canada or abroad, or advocates the dissolution of Canada or the separation or secession of any part of Canada.

The Constitution should be amended to abolish the Senate and create a unicameral Parliament.

The Constitution should be amended to abolish political parties at the federal level to permit the formation of a consensual federal parliament.

The Constitution should be amended to require referenda on issues of national importance in the interests of true democracy to protect the rights of the people of Canada.

Chapter 5 - One Justice

(Bibliography: One Justice - Canada's Justice System)

One Justice: *"the quality of being morally just or righteous; rectitude"*
Canadian: English common law applied equally to all
citizens of the country.

The Justice System of Canada

The Supreme Court of Canada

The sovereign is responsible for rendering justice for all her subjects, and is thus traditionally deemed the fount of justice. However, she does not personally rule in judicial cases; instead the judicial functions of the Royal Prerogative are performed in trust and in the Queen's name by Officers of Her Majesty's Court.

The Supreme Court of Canada, the country's court of last resort, has nine justices appointed by the Governor General and led by the Chief Justice of Canada. The Supreme Court hears appeals from decisions rendered by the various appellate courts from the provinces and territories. Below this is the Federal Court, which hears cases arising under certain areas of federal law, and works with the Federal Court of Appeal and Tax Court of Canada.

The Constitution Act, (England) 1867

This was an Act of the British Parliament, originally called the British North America Act 1867, that created the Dominion of Canada out of three separate provinces in British North America (Province of Canada, New Brunswick, and Nova Scotia) and allowed for subsequent provinces and colonies to join this union in the future. It outlined Canada's system of government, which combines Britain's Westminster model of parliamentary government with division of sovereignty (federalism). Although it is the first of twenty British North America Acts, it is still the most famous of these and is understood to be the document of Canadian Confederation (i.e. union of provinces and colonies in British North America). With the patriation of the Constitution in 1982, this Act was renamed Constitution Act, 1867. In recent years, the Constitution Act, 1867 has mainly served as the basis on which the division of powers between the provinces and federal government have been analyzed.

The Constitution Act, (Canada) 1982

The Constitution of Canada (La Constitution du Canada) is the supreme law in Canada; the country's constitution is an amalgamation of codified acts and uncodified traditions and conventions. It outlines Canada's system of government, as well as the civil rights of all Canadian citizens. Interpretation of the Constitution is called Canadian constitutional law.

The composition of the Constitution of Canada is defined in subsection 52(2) of the Constitution Act 1982 as consisting of the Canada Act 1982 (including the Constitution Act 1982), all acts and orders referred to in the schedule (including the Constitution Act 1867, formerly the British North America Act), and any amendments to these documents. The Supreme Court of Canada held that the list is not exhaustive and includes unwritten components as well.

The patriation of the Canadian Constitution was achieved in 1982 when the British and Canadian parliaments passed parallel acts, the Canada Act 1982 in London, and the Constitution Act 1982 in Ottawa. Thereafter, the United Kingdom was formally absolved of any responsibility or jurisdiction over Canada; and Canada became responsible for her own destiny. In a formal ceremony on Parliament Hill in Ottawa, the Queen signed both acts into law on April 17, 1982.

The Canada Act/ Constitution Act included the Canadian Charter of Rights and Freedoms. Prior to the Charter, there were various statutes which protected an assortment of civil rights and obligations, but nothing was enshrined in the Constitution until 1982. The Charter has thus placed a strong focus upon individual and collective rights of the people of Canada.

Amendments to the Constitution Act, 1982

With the Constitution Act, 1982, amendments to the constitution must be made in accordance with Part V of the Constitution Act, 1982 which provides for five different amending formulas. Amendments may be brought forward under section 46(1) by any province or either level of the federal government. The general formula is set out in section 38(1), known as the "7/50 formula", requires: (a) assent from both the House of Commons and the Senate; (b) the approval of two-thirds of the provincial legislatures (at least seven provinces), representing at least 50% of the population (effectively, this would include at least Quebec or Ontario, as they are the most populous provinces). This formula specifically applies to amendments related to the proportionate representation in Parliament, powers, selection, and composition of the Senate, the Supreme Court and the addition of provinces or territories. The other amendment formulas are for exceptional cases as provided by in the Act:

- In the case of an amendment related to the Office of the Queen, the number of senators, the use of either official language (subject to section 43), the amending formula, or the composition of the Supreme Court, the amendment must be adopted by unanimous consent of all the provinces in accordance with section 41.

- However, in the case of an amendment related to provincial boundaries or the use of an official language within a province alone, the amendment must be passed by the legislatures affected by the amendment (section 43).

- In the case of an amendment that affects the federal government alone, the amendment does not need approval of the provinces (section 44). The same applies to amendments affecting the provincial government alone (section 45).

English Common Law

All provinces and territories within Canada, excluding Quebec, follow the common law legal tradition. Equally, courts have power under the provincial Judicature Acts to apply equity.

As with all common law countries, Canadian law adheres to the doctrine of "stare decisis". Lower courts must follow the decisions of higher courts by which they are bound. For instance, all Ontario lower courts are bound by the decisions of the Ontario Court of Appeal and, all British Columbia lower courts are bound by the decisions of the British Columbia Court of Appeal. However, no Ontario court is bound by decisions of any British Columbia court and no British Columbia court is bound by decisions of any Ontario court. Nonetheless, decisions made by a province's highest court (provincial Courts of Appeal) are often considered as "persuasive" even though they are not binding on other provinces.

Only the Supreme Court of Canada has authority to bind all courts in the country with a single ruling. The busier courts, such as the Court of Appeal for Ontario, for example, are often looked to for guidance on many local matters of law outside the province, especially in matters such as evidence and criminal law.

Quebec Civil Law

For historical reasons, Quebec has a hybrid legal system. Private law follows the civil law tradition, originally expressed in the Coutume de Paris as it applied in what was then New France. Today, the jus commune of Quebec is codified in the Civil Code of Quebec. As for public law, it was made that of the conquering British nation after the fall of New France in 1760, that is the common law. It is important to note that the distinction between civil law and common law is not based on the division of powers set out in the Constitution Act, 1867. Therefore, legislation enacted by the provincial legislature in matters of public law, such as the Code of Penal Procedure, should be interpreted following the common law tradition. Likewise, legislation enacted by the federal Parliament in matters of private law, such as the Divorce Act, is to be interpreted following the civil law tradition and in harmony with the Civil Code of Quebec. Because of Quebec's unique legal system, lawyers trained in either common law or civil law may not practice in Quebec without undergoing further training in one or the other legal system.

The Powers of the Federal Government

The Constitution Act of 1982 added the Canadian Charter of Rights and Freedoms, which guaranteed basic rights and freedoms usually not overridden by any level of government. The exception was a "Notwithstanding" clause allowing parliament and provincial legislatures to override certain sections of the Charter for a period of five years, and an added constitutional amending formula. The federal government has power "to make laws for the peace, order and good government of Canada", except where the provinces are given exclusive powers.

The federal government has many exclusive powers among which are: trade and commerce, post office, the census, national defence, citizenship, money and banking, copyrights, criminal law, employment insurance, and foreign policy.

Through their legislatures, the provincial governments have the power to enact or amend laws and programs related to the following: hospitals, social services, natural resources, the environment, education, administration of justice, provincial property and civil rights. The provinces directly fund or transfer money to institutions to ensure the delivery of these important responsibilities, as well as funding provincial highways, culture and tourism, prisons, post-secondary education, and other services. The provincial legislatures also have power over all municipal institutions in the provinces.

In civil law, special condition may apply for certain religious or ethnic groups. For instance family law for Jewish and Catholic adherents follows certain religious principles, while custom or traditional practices may be applied for aboriginal peoples of Canada. Recent initiatives to include the principles of Sharia law in Ontario were found not acceptable to most people of that province, especially Muslim women, for a lack of respect for the status of absolute equality of women with men. There have been many laws that may have seemed appropriate at the time of their passage, but which have become intolerable in the current society of Canada and the western world. Some examples follow.

Abolition of Slavery in Canada
　　　　　　　　(Bibliography: One Justice - Slavery in Canada)

Slavery in what now comprises Canada existed from prehistoric times to the 1830s, when slavery was officially abolished. Some slaves were of African descent, while others were aboriginal (typically called panis, likely a corruption of Pawnee). It should be noted that Canada was created on July 1st 1867, and thus no slavery has ever existed in Canada as a nation. Slavery was practised within Canada's current geography, and was practised primarily by Aboriginal groups and the French Empire. Moreover, free and enslaved Blacks who fled the United States after the American Revolution had their freedom guaranteed upon arrival. Canada was also the final destination for thousands of enslaved Blacks who came to freedom in Canada, via the Underground Railroad. Slavery was practised by some aboriginal nations, who routinely captured slaves from neighbouring tribes.

African slaves were forcibly brought as chattel by Europeans to the Canada. Chattel slavery, a form of hereditary slavery, was established by European colonization and settlement of Canada during the 17th century. Legally, slaves were regarded as movable possessions and

28

private property. Large scale plantation slavery of the sort that existed in warmer parts of the New World never existed because there were no plantations. Most of the slaves in Canada were domestic house servants, although some performed agricultural labour. Although Canada has a history of slavery, it is often overshadowed by the more tumultuous kind featured in the Americas. Afua Cooper states that slavery is, "Canada's best kept secret, locked within the National closet."

Slavery in New France

By 1688, New France's population was 11,562 people, made up primarily of fur traders, missionaries, and farmers settled along the St. Lawrence Valley. To help overcome its severe shortage of servants and labourers, King Louis XIV granted New France's petition to import black slaves from West Africa. While slavery was prohibited in France, it was permitted in its colonies as a means of providing the massive labour force needed to clear land, construct buildings and work sugar plantation in the Caribbean colonies. New France soon established its own 'Code Noir,' defining the control and management of slaves. The Code in 1685 set the pattern for policing slavery. It required that all slaves be instructed as Catholics and not as Protestants. It concentrated on defining the condition of slavery, and established harsh controls. Slaves had virtually no rights, though the Code did enjoin masters to take care of the sick and old. The blacks were usually called "servants," and the harsh gang system was not used. Death rates among slaves were high.

Slavery Under British rule

After 1783, about 3,500 free blacks immigrated to Canada, mostly persons who had won their freedom by supporting the British by taking up arms during the U.S. War of Independence. Many Loyalists from the United States brought their slaves with them to Canada after the American Revolution. Some slaves fled Upper and Lower Canada to free states in America such as Massachusetts, Maine, Vermont, and Pennsylvania. The Imperial Act of 1790 assured prospective immigrants that their slaves would remain their property.

Canadian First Nations also owned or traded in slaves. Shawnee, Potawatomi, and other western tribes imported slaves from Ohio and Kentucky and sold them to Canadian settlers. Thayendenaga (chief Joseph Brant) used blacks he had captured during the American Revolution to build Brant House at Burlington Beach and a second home near Brantford. In all, Brant owned about forty black slaves.

By 1790 the abolition movement was gaining credence in Canada and the ill intent of slavery was evident. Under the auspices of Simcoe, "The Slave Act of 1793," was legislated. The compromise Slave Act of 1793 stands as the only attempt by any Canadian legislature to act against slavery. This legal rule ensured the eventual end of slavery in Upper Canada, although as it diminished the sale value of slaves within the province it also resulted in slaves being sold to the United States.

By 1797, courts began to rule in favour of slaves who complained of poor treatment from their owners. These developments were resisted in Lower Canada until 1803, when Chief Justice William Osgoode ruled that slavery was not compatible with British law. This historic judgment, while it did not abolish slavery, set free 300 slaves and resulted in the rapid decline of the practice of slavery. However, slavery remained in Upper and Lower Canada until 1834 when the British Parliament's Slavery Abolition Act ended slavery in all parts of the British Empire.

Proclamation of Womens' Rights in Canada
(Bibliography: One Justice - Womens' Rights)

Women's suffrage is the right of women to vote, and historically includes the economic and political reform movement aimed at extending suffrage to women, on an equal basis to those for men and without any restrictions or qualifications such as property ownership, payment of tax or marital status. In Sweden, during the age of liberty between 1718 and 1771, women were permitted to vote if they were tax paying guild members. Of currently existing independent countries, New Zealand was the first to give women the right to vote in 1893. However. At that time New Zealand was a self overning British colony, not a country in the sense of an independent nation state.

Appeal to the Supreme Court of Canada

For years women's groups in Canada signed petitions and appealed to the federal government to open the Senate to women. By 1927, Emily Murphy decided to appeal to the Supreme Court of Canada for clarification. She and four other prominent Alberta women's rights activists, now known as the Famous Five, signed a petition to the Senate. The question asked was "Does the word "persons" in Section 24, of The British North America Act, 1867, include female persons?"

On April 24, 1928, the Supreme Court of Canada answered "no." The court decision said that in 1867 when the BNA Act was written, women did not vote, run for office, nor serve as elected officials; only male nouns and pronouns were used in the BNA Act; and since the British House of Lords did not have a woman member, Canada should not change the tradition for its Senate.

British Privy Council Decision

With the help of Canadian Prime Minister Mackenzie King, the Famous Five appealed the Supreme Court of Canada decision to the Judicial Committee of the Privy Council in England, at the time the highest court of appeal for Canada.

On October 18, 1929, Lord Sankey, Lord Chancellor of the Privy Council, announced the British Privy Council decision that "yes, women are persons . . . and eligible to be summoned and may become Members of the Senate of Canada." Lord Sankey, Lord Chancellor of the Privy Council also said, "that the exclusion of women from all public offices is a relic of days more barbarous than ours. And to those who would ask why the word "persons" should include females, the obvious answer is, why should it not?"

Abolition of the Chinese Head Tax
(Bibliography: One Justice - Chinese Head Tax)

In 1885 the Chinese Immigration Act authorized a fixed fee head tax for each Chinese person entering Canada to discourage Chinese immigration after completion of the Canadian Pacific Railway. The head tax was ended by the Chinese Immigration Act of 1923, which stopped Chinese immigration except for business people, clergy, educators, and students.

In 1993, Prime Minister Jean Chrétien refused to provide an apology or redress for the wrongs of the Chinese head tax. On June 22, 2006, Prime Minister Stephen Harper offered an apology and compensation only for the head tax once paid by Chinese immigrants. Survivors or their spouses will be paid approximately $20,000 CAD in compensation. There are only an estimated 20 Chinese Canadians who paid the tax still alive in 2006.

Currently, the major issues revolve around the content of any future settlement, with the leading groups demanding meaningful redress, not only for the handful of surviving "head tax" payers and widows/spouses, but first generation sons/daughters who were direct victims. Some have proposed that the redress be based on the number of "Head Tax" Certificates (or estates) brought forward by surviving sons and daughters who are still able to register their claims, with proposals for individual redress, ranging from $10,000 to 30,000 for an estimated 4,000 registrants.

Rejection of Sharia Law in Ontario
(Bibliography: One Justice - Sharia Law)

Premier Dalton McGuinty said today Ontario will reject the use of Shariah law and will move to prohibit all religious based tribunals to settle family disputes such as divorce. His announcement comes after hundreds of demonstrators around the world this week protested a proposal to let Ontario residents use Islamic law for settling family disputes. Ontario Premier Dalton McGuinty was reacting to a recommendation, by former NDP attorney general Marion Boyd, to allow Muslims to establish Shariah based tribunals similar to Jewish and Catholic arbitration bodies.

"We will not tolerate the interference of religion in our justice system," said Homa Arjomand, who organized a protest in Toronto that drew hundreds of people Thursday. The protests were generally peaceful, but on the outskirts of the Toronto demonstration, pro-Shariah activist Mubin Shaikh and his wife, Joanne Sijka, verbally sparred with protesters. Shaikh said the misuse of Shariah doesn't mean it should be excluded from Canadian civil law. "Abuse of the process is not a proof against a process, just as people wrongfully imprisoned is not a proof against Canadian law," Shaikh said.

In Montreal around 100 people gathered Thursday to protest the tribunals. In Ottawa more than 100 others, mostly women, protested in the rain in front of the parliament building. And in the western German city of Dusseldorf, about 25 people protested at the Canadian consulate. "If the Shariah is used in Canada, I also feel threatened here," said protester Nasrin Ramzanali, who said there should be a clear separation of church and state. Other protests were planned this week in Waterloo and Victoria, and in Europe in Amsterdam, Dusseldorf, Stockholm, Goteborg, London, and Paris.

Ontario has allowed Catholic and Jewish faith based tribunals to settle family law matters on a voluntary basis since 1991, but the practice got little attention until Muslim leaders demanded the same rights. According to the latest census in 2001, some 600,000 Muslims live in Canada, just over 100,000 of them in Quebec.

Revision of Quebec Civil Law
(Bibliography: One Justice - Quebec Civil Law)

The Civil Code of Quebec (French: Code civil du Québec) is the civil code in force in the province of Quebec, Canada. The Civil Code of Quebec came into effect on January 1, 1994, except for certain parts of the Law of the Family which were adopted by the National Assembly in the 1980s. It replaced the Civil Code of Lower Canada (French: Code civil du Bas- Canada) enacted by the Legislative Assembly of the Province of Canada in 1865, and which had been in force since July 1, 1866.

The Government of Canada undertook a review of all federal laws that dealt with private law to ensure that they took into consideration the terminology, concepts, and institutions of Quebec civil law. On January 31, 2001, it tabled a Bill entitled "A First Act to Harmonize Federal Law with the Civil Law of the Province of Quebec" and to amend certain Acts to ensure that each language version takes into account the common law and the civil law.

The reform process that led to the replacement of the Civil Code of Lower Canada by the Civil Code of Quebec was one of the largest legislative re-codification undertakings in any civil law jurisdiction. The Civil Code of Quebec was a complete restatement of the civil law in Quebec as of the date of its adoption, including judicial interpretation of codal provisions that include broad privacy rights protection and the adoption of a section on the patrimony of affectation.

Abolition of Apartheid in South Africa
(Bibliography: One Justice - Apartheid in South Africa)

Apartheid (Afrikaans equivalent to English "apart+hood") was a system of legal racial segregation enforced by the National Party government in South Africa between 1948 and 1994. The rights of the majority black inhabitants of South Africa were curtailed and minority rule by whites was maintained.

Racial segregation in South Africa began in colonial times, but apartheid as an official policy was introduced following the general election of 1948. New legislation classified inhabitants into racial groups ("black", "white", "coloured", and "Indian"), and residential areas were segregated by means of forced removals. From 1958, Blacks were deprived of their citizenship, legally becoming citizens of one of ten tribally based self governing homelands called Bantustans, four of which became nominally independent states. The government segregated education, medical care, and other public services, and provided black people with services inferior to those of whites.

Apartheid sparked significant internal resistance and violence as well as a long trade embargo against South Africa. A series of popular uprisings and protests were met with the banning of opposition and imprisoning

34

of anti-apartheid leaders. As unrest spread and became more violent, state organizations responded with increasing repression and state sponsored violence. Reforms to apartheid in the 1980s failed to quell the mounting opposition, and in 1990 President Frederik Willem de Klerk began negotiations to end apartheid, culminating in multi-racial democratic elections in 1994, which were won by the African National Congress under Nelson Mandela. The vestiges of apartheid still shape South African politics and society.

Submission to Apartheid Law in Canada
(Bibliography: One Justice - Apartheid Law in Canada)

The Indian Act is a statute that concerns registered Indians, their bands, and the system of Indian reserves. The Act was enacted in 1876 by Parliament under the provisions of Section 91(24) of the Constitution Act 1867, which gives the federal government exclusive authority to legislate regarding "Indians and Lands Reserved for Indians". The Indian Act is administered by the Minister of Indian Affairs and Northern Development.

The Act defines who is an "Indian" and contains certain legal disabilities and legal rights for registered Indians. The rights exclusive to Indians in the Indian Act are beyond legal challenge under of the Canadian Charter of Rights and Freedoms. Section 25 of the Canadian Charter of Rights and Freedoms provides that the charter shall not be interpreted as negating specific aboriginal treaties and their corresponding rights and freedoms. Section 35 of the Constitution Act, 1982 also recognizes and affirms the legal validity of aboriginal treaties.

An Indian whose name was in the Indian Register established by the act was said to have Indian status or treaty status. An Indian who was not registered was said to be a non- status Indian. Prior to 1985, Indians could lose status in a variety of ways, including:

* marrying a man who was not a Status Indian
* enfranchisement (until 1960, Indians could vote only by renouncing Indian status)

- having a mother and paternal grandmother who did not have status before marriage
- being born out of wedlock to a mother with status and a father without.

In Attorney General of Canada v. Lavell (1974), these laws were upheld despite arguments made under the Canadian Bill of Rights. The Indian Act was amended in 1985 (Bill C-31) to restore status to people who had lost it in one of these ways, and to their children.

Commentary

Criticism of the Indian Act and Apartheid

The Act was extensively amended after 1945, and was again under study in the mid-1960's. The Hawthorne Report vividly portrayed the Indian situation in Canada. After a national consultation with chiefs, the government advanced the 1969 White Paper Policy to abolish Indian status, Indian reserves, Indian Treaties, the Indian Department, and the Indian Act.

Indian resistance to this initiative and favourable court decisions forced government to revise its policies. In 1973, the White Paper was withdrawn and government began to deal seriously with land claims but its resistance to such claims was apparent. In the Guerin case of 1984, the government denied legal responsibility for leasing reserve lands on terms much less favourable than those discussed with a band. However, the Supreme Court of Canada disagreed, and confirmed the fiduciary duties of the Crown deriving from the nature of Indian legal title and the Indian Act, and held Canada liable for its breach of duty as a Trustee.

The Indian Act is an anachronism in Canadian law. It singles out a segment of society on the basis of race. It gives the Minister of Indian Affairs discretion that is intrusive and frequently offensive. The Act has been roundly criticized even by persons who tend to be non-Aboriginal. There is discrimination between Indians who reside on reserve and those who reside elsewhere. Most telling of this attitude was the definition of "person" which was in the statute until 1951 as: "an individual other than an Indian". Indians could become persons and be enfranchised either voluntarily by renouncing their Indian status, or involuntarily by certain other circumstances according to the Act.

The modern global economy is driven by cities, with industries, transportation networks, and skilled workers. Rural economies have been dying since World War II. No government would pay anyone except Indians to confine themselves to the jobless outback, hundreds of miles from universities and job centres. Yet that is exactly the treatment of Indians on reserves.

One of the great lessons of the 20th century was that collective land ownership is a recipe for economic disaster. Behind the Iron Curtain, agricultural productivity exploded once people were given the rights to their own land and to sell the proceeds for profit. Denying land title to slum dwellers is the main impediment to prosperity in poor societies. Yet the reserves are still run like Marxist workers' collectives. Criticisms are often made about the poor housing. But who would pay his own money to care for a house the government would rebuild for free?

A recent study by the Environics Institute and released to the CBC showed that a majority of registered status Indians have migrated away from the reserves, and actually seem to prefer living in cities with the rest of Canadians. Their goals are greater opportunities for education, employment, and a life style with contemporary society, even though assimilation and acceptance is occasionally difficult due to enduring racism and perceptions of Indians as being indolent and expensive wards of the state.

Today, aboriginal business elites are the Indians who gained wealth and power through their involvement with the Indian Act. Much of the Indian elite's wealth comes from government funding and corporations. Many band councils manage million dollar budgets as Indian corporations in many diverse businesses such as logging, mining, and leasing of reserve land. Yet a century ago bands were directly administered by the government and its Indian Agents. Today, the government's annual budget for the Indian program and its own overhead is about $8-10 billion. This situation will continue forever, unless it is halted. The situation is a mug's game *("a futile or unprofitable endeavour"),* and the Canadian taxpayers are the mugs. The White Paper of 1969 had the proper approach. Perhaps the political time was not right.

There is a justice system for non-Indian Canadians, and a different and discriminatory justice system for Indians. The Indian Act, the treaties, the fiduciary duties, and the presence of Apartheid in Canada will persist into the future forever unless the government takes bold action. The government has made many errors in the past either by the omission or commission of misguided legislation. Eventually, the government has corrected such egregious legislation as the support for slavery, the imposition of the Chinese Head Tax, and the failure to recognize women as persons. The abolition of these archaic discriminations against certain peoples of Canada were finally legislated, despite setting international precedents.

The rescission of the Indian Act, and the abrogation of the treaties and trusts, would be no different. Those actions would have ramifications around the world, as did the Guerin case in 1984. That ruling by Canada's Supreme Court has been respected all over the world, and constitutes a legal precedent for those countries which espouse English common law. The ruling confirms that the Crown is indeed a trustee for aboriginal peoples in North America, Australia, New Zealand, many countries in Africa, and some in Asia. Yet rescission of the Indian Act and abrogation of the treaties and trusts would be seen as a courageous step by Canada to re-define itself as a modern country with the highest of moral values and principles.

Suggestions and Proposals

There is a justice system for the vast majority of Canadians, and a different justice system and special restrictions for Indians. If action is not taken, the Indian Act and the English common law of treaties and trusts will persist into the future in the maintenance of Apartheid in Canada.

The government should rescind the Indian Act to abolish Indian status and the Indian reserves, and should abrogate the Indian treaties, the trusts, and fiduciary duties, and the discrimination that those entail. Better abrogation once . . . than discrimination forever!

The government should provide compensation to each individual Indian at the time of abolition. First, the lands and trust funds could be disbursed (or compensation given) or returned to all status Indians on a per capita basis. To provide time for reasonable assimilation into the mainstream of society in Canada, the federal government should provide some form of annual income for some length of time, even as long as a generation. Assuming the annual administration budget remains at $8,000,000,000 and there are about 400,000 status Indians on reserves, the annual tax free direct income payments should amount to some $20,000 per person. The monies due to minors should be held, with interest, by the government until the age of their majority. Assistance with education including Bachelor level at university should be considered, but subject to academic qualification and financial need and not as a right. And, finally, the existing land claims must also be resolved in addition to these changes.

After the assimilation period, there should be a complete termination of the assimilation payments. Of greatest importance, should be a complete termination of the treatment of Indians as second class citizens under the system of Apartheid. The aboriginal peoples of Canada may then be able to hold their heads high as distinguished Canadians, much as do the Maori people of New Zealand, and the Sami people of Finland, Sweden, and Norway.

Chapter 6 - One Economy

(Bibliography: One Economy - The Economy of Canada)
(Bibliography: One Economy - Mark Steyn and Canada)
(Bibliography: One Economy - Electrical Power & the BNA)

One Economy: *"the art of managing the resources of a people and of its government"; and the "careful management, frugality of labour, money, time etc."*

Canadian: a single economy under federal direction and regulatory structures.

The Economy of Canada

Canada has the tenth largest economy in the world (measured in U.S. dollars at market exchange rates) is one of the world's wealthiest nations, and a member of the Organization for Economic Co-operation and Development (OECD) and Group of Eight (G8). As with other developed nations, the Canadian economy is dominated by the service industry, which employs about three quarters of Canadians. Canada is unusual among developed countries in the importance of the primary sector, with the logging and oil industries being two of Canada's most important. Canada has a sizable manufacturing sector centred in Central Canada, with the automobile industry especially important.

Canada has one of the highest levels of economic freedom in the world. Today Canada closely resembles the U.S. in its market oriented economic system, and pattern of production. As of June 2009, Canada's national unemployment rate stood at 8.6% as the effect of the world economic crisis settled in and more people looked for work. Provincial

40

unemployment rates vary from a low of 3.6% in Alberta to a high of 15.6% in Newfoundland and Labrador; however, Newfoundland and Labrador was the only province with employment gains in June of 2009, up 2,500. At the same time, the unemployment rate edged up to 15.6% from previous lows as more people entered the labour force. According to the Forbes Global 2000 list of the world's largest companies in 2008, Canada had 69 companies in the list, ranking 5th next to France. As of 2008, Canada's total government debt burden is the lowest in the G8.

International trade makes up a large part of the Canadian economy, particularly of its natural resources. The United States is by far its largest trading partner, accounting for about 76% of exports and 65% of imports as of 2007. Canada's combined exports and imports ranked 8th among all nations in 2006.

Economic sector: Canada has considerable natural resources spread across its varied regions. In British Columbia, the forestry industry is of great importance, while the oil industry is important in Alberta and Newfoundland and Labrador. Northern Ontario is home to a wide array of mines, while the fishing industry has long been central to the character of the Atlantic provinces, though it has recently been in steep decline. Canada has mineral resources of coal, copper, iron ore, and gold.

These industries are increasingly becoming less important to the overall economy. Only some 4% of Canadians are employed in these fields, and they account for less than 6% of GDP. They are still paramount in many parts of the country. Many, if not most, towns in northern Canada, where agriculture is difficult, exist because of a nearby mine or source of timber. Canada is a world leader in the production of many natural resources such as gold, nickel, uranium, diamonds and lead. Several of Canada's largest companies are based in natural resource industries, such as EnCana, Potash, Cameco, Goldcorp, and Barrick Gold. The vast majority of these products are exported, mainly to the United States. There are also many secondary and service industries that are directly linked to primary ones. For instance one of Canada's

41

largest manufacturing industries is the pulp and paper sector, which is directly linked to the logging industry.

The relatively large reliance on natural resources has several effects on the Canadian economy and Canadian society. While manufacturing and service industries are easy to standardize, natural resources vary greatly by region. This ensures that differing economic structures developed in each region of Canada, contributing to Canada's strong regionalism. At the same time the vast majority of these resources are exported, integrating Canada closely into the international economy. Howlett and Ramesh argue that the inherent instability of such industries also contributes to greater government intervention in the economy, to reduce the social impact of market changes.

Such industries also raise important questions of sustainability. Despite many decades as a leading producer, there is little risk of depletion. Large discoveries continue to be made, such as the massive nickel find at Voisey's Bay. The far north remains largely undeveloped as producers await higher prices or new technologies as many operations in this region are not yet cost effective. In recent decades Canadians have become less willing to accept the environmental destruction associated with exploiting natural resources. High wages and Aboriginal land claims have also curbed expansion. Instead many Canadian companies have focussed their exploration and expansion activities overseas where prices are lower and governments more accommodating. Canadian companies are playing important roles in Latin America, Southeast Asia, and Africa.

It is the renewable resources that have raised some of the greatest concerns. After decades of escalating overexploitation the cod fishery all but collapsed in the 1990s, and the Pacific salmon industry also suffered greatly. The logging industry, after many years of activism, have in recent years moved to a more sustainable model.

Canada is one of the few developed nations that is a net exporter of energy. Most important are the large oil and gas resources centred in Alberta and the Northern Territories, but also present in neighbouring

British Columbia and Saskatchewan. The vast Athabasca Tar Sands give Canada the world's second largest reserves of oil after Saudi Arabia according to USGS (the United States Geological Survey). In British Columbia and Quebec, as well as Ontario, Saskatchewan, Manitoba and the Labrador region, hydroelectric power is an inexpensive and relatively environmentally friendly source of abundant energy. In part because of this, Canada is also one of the world's highest per capita consumers of energy. Cheap energy has enabled the creation of several important industries, such as the large aluminum industry in Quebec, Alberta and British Columbian.

Historically, an important issue in Canadian politics is that while Western Canada is one of the world's richest sources of energy, the industrial heartland of Southern Ontario has fewer sources of power. It is, however, cheaper for Alberta to ship its oil to the western United States than to eastern Canada. The eastern Canadian ports thus import significant quantities of oil from overseas, and Ontario makes significant use of nuclear power.

In times of high oil prices the majority of Canada's population suffers, while the West benefits. The National Energy Policy of the early 1980s attempted to force Alberta to sell low priced oil to eastern Canada. This policy proved deeply divisive, and quickly lost its importance as oil prices collapsed in the mid-1980s. One of the most controversial sections of the Canada - United States Free Trade Agreement of 1988 was a promise that Canada would never charge the United States more for energy than fellow Canadians.

Government Operations

Effectiveness of Government

For the past 20 years of more, the government has instituted performance measures in such diverse areas as the Export Development Corporation and the Reserves and Trusts Branch of the Department of Indian Affairs. The performance measures for those organizations were both quantitative and qualitative, based on economic cost and benefit principles, and well done. However, such measures are usually reduced to time and motion studies of easily measured functions at the lower levels of operations, i.e. for technicians, clerks, and secretaries. In the interests of greater effectiveness, the government should ensure that both quantitative and qualitative measures of performance are determined based on cost and benefit analyses at the highest levels of the organizations, rather than time and motion studies at lower levels. Only then can senior departments such as Finance and the Treasury Board Secretariat determine if the conduct of those departments is actually in the best interests of tax paying Canadians.

To place greater control over the unprecedented costs of government salaries, and to operate in a competitive environment, the government should abolish all unions in the employ of the federal civil service. All government services should either be essential to the economy of Canada, or be candidates for privatization.

Mobility of Professionals & Tradesmen

When it comes to international trade, the government is involved with negotiations and trade treaties. These are designed to prevent undue trade practices with goods and services with foreign countries. If unfair practices are perceived, trade barriers are quickly erected to prevent cheap or shoddy goods from being imported into Canada. If Canadian export goods are perceived as having improper barriers raised against their importation into foreign markets, Canada will seek the removal of those improper barriers to free trade.

Yet within Canada, there are similar interprovincial barriers against trade in the services of professional persons such as lawyers, doctors, engineers, dentists, and accountants, as well as tradesmen such as electricians, plumbers, carpenters, general contractors and others. For example, tradesmen living in Gatineau, Quebec seek work in the city of Ottawa, Ontario without having to be re-certified. Yet tradesmen from Ontario cannot work in Gatineau without being re-certified in a unilingual French province. This re-certification requirement is simply a barrier to protect the jobs of the Quebec tradesmen in their home province.

For professional persons such as doctors and dentists, there are excuses to disallow trained professionals unless they retake their professional examinations, even though fully qualified in other jurisdictions. With a critical shortage of doctors and others in Canada, that is reprehensible action on the part of these self governing occupational professions.

While some modest actions have been taken to remove unreasonable barriers, not enough has been done. Greater efforts must be made to alleviate the shortages of critical employees and workers. For example, professionals (e.g. doctors) fully qualified in other jurisdictions or other countries could be given "associate" accreditation. After five years of qualified work experience and/ or language improvement, they could then be granted "full" professional accreditation.

Communications

Canada is fortunate to have one of the most modern and well managed communication systems in the world. The government's management of its radio spectrum and leasing policies to the private sector has been excellent. Progress is still needed in recent developments of the internet such as speed and access for all, but Canada's expertise in the field of satellite communications should provide a high standard of service to the people.

Transportation

Canada has one of the world's longest coastlines and land borders with its neighbouring country, the United States of America. The land borders and the coastlines have been undefended for the last century of the nation's history, due to the amicable relations with its neighbour. In the last decade, threats have arisen not from its neighbour, but from nationals from other countries or third parties who seek to damage both Canada and the United States. The various ports of Canada, those of air, sea, and land will require greater prudence in their management to ensure the security and safety of Canada. Mutual cooperation with the United States will be required to attain suitable levels of security, or face restricted access for trade with our southern neighbour. The governments of both countries are aware of the potential threats, and are in the process of enhancing security of the borders and coastlines.

Highways and Roads

One of Canada's biggest problems lies in the combination of its enormous size and small population. To provide good roads, highways, and bridges under those constraints is a challenge. Canada has not fared well in the face of this challenge, when one compares its national highway system to those of the United States, Germany, France, Italy and other western European nations. The roads, highways, and bridges of Canada are in serious trouble. With rare exception, Canada's highways are well below international standards for western countries. For example, while an Act was passed in 1949 to construct the Trans- Canada Highway to standards equal to the American Interstate Highways, the Autobahnen of Germany, the Autostrada of Italy, or the Autoroutes of France, the Trans Canada is still incomplete in 2009 after 60 years. As highways are crucial to the economic performance of the country, current and future governments at the federal and provincial levels will be forced to place emphasis on the development and timely maintenance of better highways.

Energy and Power

The Generation of Electrical Power

Electrical power is a reasonably efficient and convenient form of power for many purposes. That power may be generated from various sources, including both renewable and non-renewable sources. The major sources of the former include water, wind, solar systems, while the latter include oil, gas, coal, and uranium. The majority of generating stations currently use either oil or gas, both of which create unwanted by products in the generation of the electrical power. Both Canada and the United States have recently been fortunate to have discovered immense quantities of gas in easily accessed deposits, and also in shale rock for which new technologies permit extraction at reasonable costs.

The replacement of older oil and coal fired generating stations with water, nuclear or other generating systems would likely be slow and costly. However, the conversion of those older oil and coal fired stations to gas fired stations might not be nearly as slow or costly. Both oil and coal are non-renewable sources of energy, as well as creating undesirable by products during their combustion. On the other hand, gas is plentiful in Canada and the United States, and a far cleaner burning fuel for the generation of electrical power.

In his recent book "Why your world is about to get a whole lot smaller," Jeff Rubin (former chief economist with the Canadian Imperial Bank of Commerce) provides reasonable evidence that the world's supply of oil may rapidly increase in cost and diminish in supply. This makes the conversion of Canadian oil fired generating stations to gas fired stations seem a prudent strategy over the next decade.

There is another aspect which makes the conversion from oil to gas very desirable. Currently, a major portion of the world supply of oil comes from the mid-east countries such as Saudi Arabia, Iraq, and Iran. Canada is fortunate to have reserves of gas and oil in conventional deposits, shale deposits, and oil sands which nearly equal those in Saudi Arabia. The conversion of oil fired stations to gas fired stations by Canada, the United States, and Europe (where gas is available from Russia) could greatly relieve the need for these countries to purchase oil from the mid-east countries. Indirectly, this would reduce the supply of funds to the operations of terrorists operating from some mid-east countries. It might also reduce the need for western influence and presence in the mid-east.

The Transmission of Electrical Power

From the BNA Act 92A (1) c), in each province, the legislature may exclusively make laws in relation to the development, conservation and management of sites and facilities in the province for the generation and production of electrical energy. In sub- section (2), the legislature may make laws in relation to the export from the province to another part of Canada of the production from facilities in the province for the generation of electrical energy, but such laws may not authorize or provide for discrimination in prices or in supplies exported to another part of Canada. And in sub- section (3), nothing in subsection (2) derogates from the authority of Parliament to enact laws in relation to the matters referred to in that subsection and, where such a law of Parliament and a law of a province conflict, the law of Parliament prevails to the extent of the conflict.

From the above, there is no specific mention of the transfer of the electrical power from the generating facility to the market place; ie the transmission of the electrical power over the electrical transformers, towers, and lines which constitute the grid. As there is no specific mention of the transmission system as falling exclusively under the purview of the provinces, the federal government may legally assume management authority over the transmission of the electrical power on the grid system.

In practice, electrical power is shared across the provinces, and even across the north American continent according to demand by consumers. That sharing takes place in the event of natural disasters such as the ice storm in Quebec and eastern Ontario in 1998, loss of local generating facilities, or terrorist attacks. In the interest of national security, the federal government would seem the logical body to have absolute authority to manage the transmission of electrical power over the electrical transmission grid in all provinces and territories of the nation. This need not include the actual purchase, ownership, or maintenance of such transmission grids, only their location and use for the transfer of electrical power.

National Defence

The recent threats of international terrorism have and will place greater burdens on the military and police forces of Canada. For the last 40 years, the military has been slowly reduced to a far less significant fighting force than it had been. Both equipment and serving members of the forces have been reduced to the point of virtual incapacity to act in a meaningful manner. Front line equipment, weaponry, ships, aircraft, tanks etc, and training and logistic capabilities had been well past their "best before dates". Fortunately that situation has markedly improved over the last few years as increased military spending has provided more modern and capable equipment to strengthen the forces. National police forces have also been under review to improve their capabilities, and to focus their attention on the internal security of the nation.

Banks & Brokerages

(Bibliography: One Economy - Banks & Brokerages in Canada.wpd)
(Bibliography: One Economy - Security Exchanges & Commissions)
(Bibliography: One Economy - Islamic Banking & Canadian Banks)

Canada is fortunate in having a banking system dominated by what is known as "The Big Six" banks where most business is conducted. The banks are well managed, well regulated, and well capitalized. Canada was also fortunate to avoid most of the damage from the financial crisis of 2008 - 2009. As stated by the World Economic Forum, "The Canadian financial sector is among the world's most highly developed, and offers many examples of best practice." Canadians may rely on their banking system to provide a secure and stable depository for the management of their cash savings and other financial needs such as investments, mortgages, insurance, and credit cards.

Canadian retail operations of the Big Five comprise other activities that do not need to be operated from a regulated bank. These other activities include brokerage activities, mutual funds, insurance, and credit cards. In addition, they have large international subsidiaries. The Canadian banking operations of the Big Five are largely conducted out of each parent company, unlike U.S. banks that use a holding company structure for their primary retail banking subsidiaries.

Islamic Banking & Canadian Banks

The concept of Islamic banking has arrived abruptly on the door step of Canada's banks, and some government institutions such as CMHC (the federal Canadian Mortgage and Housing Corporation). As some Muslims themselves have disclosed, the rush to pander to the alleged needs of the Muslim community are hasty and ill conceived. There are at least three dominant factors negating the propriety of Islamic banking.

First, the Qur'an does not forbid the payment of interest on loans, mortgages, credit cards, or similar vehicles. The Qur'an does forbid usury or excessive rates of interest (the Arabic "riba" always has been and is properly translated as usury, not interest). The laws of all western nations, including Canada, have themselves always forbidden usury.

To quote from the reference in the Bibliography, "Every English language translation of the Koran has translated the Arabic word "riba" as usury, not interest. Yet, Islamists have deliberately portrayed bank interest as usury and labelled the current banking system as un-Islamic. Instead, these Islamists have created exotic products with names that are foreign to much of the world's Muslim population. This is where they mask interest under the niqab of Mudraba, Musharaka, Murabaha, and Ijara."

Second, highly respected Muslim bankers and academics have stated that Islamic banking is a sham which provides a convenient pretext for advancing broad Islamic objectives and for lining the pockets of religious officials. Muhammad Saleem is a former president and CEO of Park Avenue Bank in New York. In his book, Islamic Banking, "*A $300 Billion Deception*", Mr. Saleem not only dismisses the founding premise of sharia and Islamic banking, he says, "Islamic banks do not practise what they preach: they all charge interest, but disguised in Islamic garb. Thus they engage in deceptive and dishonest banking practises." And two New Zealand business professors, Beng Soon Chong and Ming-Hua Liu of Auckland University in October, 2007 conducted a study which provided new evidence, showing that, in practice, Islamic deposits are not interest free." They concluded that the rapid growth in Islamic banking was "largely driven by the Islamic resurgence worldwide."

Third, an organization such as the CMHC seems oblivious to the fact that almost all Muslim Canadians currently have home mortgages through banks and don't feel they are living in sin. If so, then there is no need what so ever to permit Canadian banks and other similar financial institutions from providing services for Islamic banking. There seems to be sufficient evidence to show that such financial services are not be in the best interests of the people or the nation.

Security Exchanges & Commissions

Canadian securities regulation is managed through laws and agencies established by Canada's 13 provincial and territorial governments. Each province and territory has a securities commission or equivalent authority. Canada is the only western developed nation to have more than one Securities and Exchange Commission, even though its markets are the sixth largest in the world.

Federal Finance Minister Jim Flaherty was reported in July 2008 to say that he was certain that Canada would soon have a single securities regulator. However, there is still no agreement from provinces other than Ontario. The Quebec National Assembly passed a unanimous resolution in October 2007 asking the federal government to abandon the single regulator project. The Quebec government has said it will never agree to it. The Expert Panel on Securities Regulation released its report in January 2009.

The largest of the provincial regulators is the Ontario Securities Commission. Other significant provincial regulators are the British Columbia Securities Commission and Alberta securities commissions, and the Autorité des marchés financiers (Québec). The provincial and territorial regulators work together to coordinate and harmonize regulation of the Canadian capital markets through the Canadian Securities Administrators (CSA). The major provincial securities regulators also participate in various international cooperative organizations and arrangements.

New Tax Free Savings Accounts (TFSAs)

The federal Minister of Finance, Jim Flaherty, has issued new directives for Designated Stock Exchanges, and new Tax Free Savings

Accounts (TFSAs). Later parts of this chapter propose the creation of a new system of retirement saving accounts entitled Twin TFSAs. The proposal includes one restricted TFSA solely for retirement and other income to replace employer pensions and CPP, employment insurance, and health insurance; and a second unrestricted TFSA for mortgages, education, vacations, extra retirement income, or any other purpose. Following acceptance of that proposal by the federal government, it seems reasonable that provincial governments, municipalities, and most corporations would adopt the Twin TFSAs for their employees as well. The Twin TFSAs will be seen to be ideal for all Canadians.

For greater stability of the proposed Twin TFSAs, a new Savings Exchange is also proposed in this chapter, with restrictions suggested to lessen the volatility of trading and prices and their adverse affects on the retirement savings of Canadians. On reflection, one must realize that the stock markets as currently structured do not appear to be designed for the benefit of individual Canadians who own the stocks, whether employed or retired. Instead, the current exchange markets seem structured to accommodate those in the administrative industry; the brokers, agents, mutual fund managers, investment bankers, and other investment managers. Consideration should be given to a Savings Exchange where retirement monies may be invested without unnecessary and undesirable volatility.

British North America Act
(Bibliography: One Economy - The British North America Act (BNA))

This Act empowered the federal government to pass legislation concerning Old Age Pensions while recognizing the similar right of provincial legislatures. In 1927, Parliament instituted an Old Age Pension administered by the provinces and jointly funded by them. This amendment allowed the federal government to administer its own pension plan and to pass the Old Age Security Act. The British North America Act 1964 expanded the federal government's jurisdiction over pensions to include survivor benefits and disability benefits.

This amendment to the BNA Act made the Canada Pension Plan possible.

The Progressive Conservative Party of Canada under both Clark and Mulroney favoured devolution of powers to the provinces. The new Conservative Party of Canada under Stephen Harper has continued the same practice. After the 1995 Quebec referendum on Quebec sovereignty, one of several actions by Jean Chrétien had been to limit the ability of the Government of Canada to spend money in matters of provincial jurisdiction. Thus in 1999, the federal government and all provincial governments except Quebec agreed to the Social Union Framework Agreement, which promoted common standards for social programs across Canada. Paul Martin later used the term asymmetrical federalism to describe this arrangement.

There is a popular anecdote in Canada, that the Constitution isn't intended to solve the problems between the government and the people, but between the different levels of government, namely federal and provincial. Historically, the regulation of market conduct has been a concern of provincial governments. Some believe that common disclosure rules must apply to both federal and provincial financial institutions, and that the federal government and provincial governments should collaborate to establish common disclosure standards. Some also believe that the Joint Forum on Market Regulation is the appropriate vehicle to develop disclosure standards. Such standards need to be flexible to allow for the evolution of new products and processes.

In 1939 the Canadian governments (federal, provincial and municipal) consumed 19.5% of Canada's Gross National Product (See Bibliography - Canada's GNP 1939); in 1948, the Canadian governments consumed 24.6% of Canada's GNP. By 1957, the Canadian governments consumed 24.5% of Canada's GNP. The estimates of the year 2007 show that governments account for 43% of the country's Gross Domestic Product (GDP). *(Note: GDP is now the preferred reference.)* Since the start of World War II, the role of all governments in the Canadian economy has increased dramatically. One may justifiably say that Canada currently has an excess of government.

In the National Post, 2010/02/11, Maxime Bernier, (Conservative Member of Parliament for Beauce, Quebec and former Industry Minister) suggested that the best way to control the growth and intrusion of government into the lives of Canadians would be to legislate zero growth budgets (See Bibliography, Zero Growth Budgets). Perhaps then we could return to the days of the governments' participation at levels closer to 20% of GDP in the nation's economy. Better a return to our former pioneering strengths and self reliance, than the current socialist state. As Thomas Jefferson once said; *'A government big enough to give you everything you want, is big enough to take away everything you have.'*

Participation in Pensions & Insurance
(Bibliography: The Economy - Participation in Pensions & Insurance)

Employment Insurance (EI)

The employment insurance program is an important component of the economic safety net provided by government. To receive employment insurance benefits, applicants must show that they were previously employed between 420 and 700 hours, depending on the local unemployment rate. Following a waiting period of 2 weeks, individuals are eligible to receive 55% of average weekly insured earnings up to a maximum of $447 per week in 2009. The number of weeks for which benefits may be claimed depends on the length of previous employment, previous claims, and the national and regional unemployment rate in 58 regions.

Many economists believe that specific features of the existing system may actually create unemployment. Unemployment is often higher than it should be among those employed in seasonal industries, because it is easier and simpler to collect benefits than to find work in the off season *(aka: "the moral disadvantage")*. EI is also a byzantine system with different rules for different workers. Where unemployment is below 6%, 18 weeks (700 hours) of work is necessary for entitlement to EI assistance. Where unemployment is above 13%, 10.5 weeks (420 hours) is sufficient to receive assistance. Canada has 58 regions with different rates and conditions of entitlement to EI. Such discrepancies reduce the incentives for unemployed workers to move to regions where work is available. If Canada's Employment Insurance program were made more generous, a greater increase would occur in unemployment rates. It is clear that EI should be reformed. And that applies to many other government programs.

Public Service Pension Plan (PSPP)

The Public Service Superannuation Act provides pensions for public service employees, and has been in effect since January 1, 1954. Part II of the Act, the Supplementary Death Benefit Plan, which provides decreasing term life insurance coverage to pension plan contributors, was added a year later. Since then, both the Act and its supporting regulations have been amended many times to respond to changes in the employees' and the employer's needs and to reflect changes in other federal and provincial laws. This booklet includes amendments up to January 1, 2008.

The Canada Pension Plan (CPP)

The Canada Pension Plan (CPP) is a contributory, earnings related social insurance program. It forms one of the two major components of Canada's public retirement income system, the other component being Old Age Security (OAS). Other parts of Canada's retirement system are private pensions, either employer sponsored or from tax deferred individual savings (known in Canada as a Registered Retirement Savings Plan (RRSP)).

The CPP program mandates all employed Canadians who are 18 years of age and over to contribute a prescribed portion of their earnings income to a nationally administered pension plan. The plan is administered by Human Resources and Social Development Canada on behalf of employees in all provinces and territories except Quebec, which operates an equivalent plan, the Quebec Pension Plan (QPP).

The CPP is a hybrid between a fully funded plan and a "pay as you go" plan. In other words, assets held in the CPP fund are insufficient to pay for all future benefits. Following public consultation, the total annual CPP contribution rates (employer and employee) were increased from 6% to 9.9% (4.95% each) of pensionable earnings in 2003.

Public Service Health Care Plan (PSHCP)

The purpose of the PSHCP is to reimburse Plan participants for all or part of costs they have incurred for eligible services and products, as identified in the Plan Document, only after they have taken advantage of benefits provided by their provincial/ territorial health insurance plan or other third party sources of health care expense assistance to which the participant has a legal right. Unless specified in the Plan Document, all eligible services and products must be prescribed by a physician or a dentist who is licensed in accordance with the applicable law, to practice in the jurisdiction in which the prescription is made.

Contributions to Pensions & Insurance
(Bibliography: The Economy - Contributions to Pensions & Insurance)

Employment Insurance (EI) Contributions 2009

Employee and employer contributions to Employment Insurance (EI) are based on all eligible earnings from the first pay each January, and cease once the maximum contributions are reached. EI Deduction rates effective January 1, 2009 were 1.73%;

Annual Employee Maximum Insurable Earnings	$42,300.00
Annual Employee Maximum Contributions	$731.79
Annual Matching Employer Insurable Earnings	$42,300.00
Annual Matching Employer Maximum Contributions	$731.79
Annual Total Joint Contributions	$1463.58

Public Service Pension Plan (PSPP) Contributions 2009

For an employee earning $80,000 per year in 2009:

Annual Employee Contributions up to CPP max ($46,300*0.052)	$ 2,407.60
Annual Employee Contributions over CPP max ($33,700*0.084)	$ 2,830.80
Annual Employee Total Contributions	$ 5,238.40
Annual Employer Matching Contributions	$ 5,238.40
Annual Total Joint Contributions	$10,476.80

Canada Pension Plan (CPP) Contributions 2009

The Canada Revenue Agency announced that the maximum pensionable earnings under the Canada Pension Plan for 2009 would be $46,300. The employee and employer contribution rates for 2009 will remain unchanged at 4.95%.

Annual CPP Employee Maximum Pensionable Earnings	$46,300.00
Annual CPP Employee Maximum EI Contribution	$2,118.60
Annual CPP Employer Maximum Pensionable Earnings	$46,300.00
Annual CPP Employer Maximum EI Contribution	$2,118.60
Annual CPP Total Joint Contributions	$4,237.20

Public Service Health Care Plan (PSHCP) Contributions 2009

Monthly PSHCP Employee Contributions, Family Level 2	$3.52
Annual PSHCP Employee Contributions, Family Level 2	$42.24
Monthly PSHCP Employer Contributions, Family Level 2	$95.13
Annual PSHCP Employer Contributions, Family Level 2	$1,141.56
Annual PSHCP Total Joint Contributions	$1,183.80

Total Annual Contributions of Pension, Health & Employment Insurance

Annual Employment Insurance Joint Contributions	$ 1,463.58
Annual Public Service Pension Plan Joint Contributions	$ 10,476.80
Annual Canada Pension Plan Joint Contributions	$ 4,237.20
Annual Public Service Health Care Plan Joint Contributions	$ 1,183.80
Annual Total of Joint Pension & Insurance Contributions	$ 17,361.27

Commentary

Retirement Savings & Income Plans

Currently, under the British North America Act, the administrative responsibility for pensions, life annuities, and locked- in accounts (LIFs) derived from pensions lies with the provinces (excluding federally regulated public service and corporations), while responsibility for RRSPs, RRIFs, TFSAs, etc lies with the federal government. Membership in all government pension systems, whether federal, provincial, or municipal, and many large corporations, is almost always mandatory as a condition of employment.

It must be noted that the first major difference between the two forms of savings is that monies from all of the federal sources and many provincial sources above may be used to transfer to a life annuity, but once those monies are committed to a life annuity or pension, they may never again be transferred to other retirement vehicles such as RRSPs, RRIFs, LIFs, or TFSAs.

It must also be noted that the second major difference between the two forms of savings is that the legal title to the capital rests with the government or corporation who administers the pensions or life annuities. The legal title to the capital for RRSPs, RRIFs, TFSAs, rests with each individual person, and not with any government, corporation, or insurance company.

The majority of retired people do not live much beyond 15 - 20 years after retirement. The amount of income from pensions and life annuities during that time is little better than "bank rate" (low). Thus the payment of income to the individuals throughout their retirement is likely to preserve the original capital. It is also likely that the funds will grow in value during this time, to the benefit of the government, corporation, or insurance company.

On reflection then, one must realize that the governments and corporations have a vested interest in retaining the capital which is contributed to the pensions and life annuities. One must also realize that the governments and corporations are in a conflict of interest situation. For it is those very same governments and corporation who pass the laws and write the rules to ensure that the legal title to all these monies remains with them. Thus, the laws concerning pensions and life annuities are nothing more than legislative grand theft under the guise of benevolent paternalism. What should be done to right this inequity? We may once again turn to Cicero; . . . "The peoples' good is the highest law".

The solution to this is simply stated: all pensions and life annuities must be optional, commutable, and transferrable at any time at the direction of the individual to RRSPs and RRIFs. This is a democratic country with free choice, isn't it?

Consolidation of Retirement Savings Plans

Currently, there is a plethora of retirement savings and income vehicles. For legal and taxation reasons, a married couple may be obliged to manage five, ten, or more accounts. The new Tax Free Savings Accounts (TFSAs) which commenced in 2009 add another two accounts for a married couple. The TFSA is the ultimate and ideal investment vehicle, as the legal title to the monies belongs to the individual, and there are few restrictions on the application of the monies held in such vehicles. Consideration should therefore be given to the following two suggestions.

1. At some age, (eg over 50), where both spouses are mutually agreeable and of similar age (eg within 10 years), allow married

couples to consolidate their accounts for easier management by themselves, and simpler administration by the banks, insurers, and brokerages.

2. Over a period of years, allow previous generations to gradually transfer funds (eg 10% per year for 10 years, then all) from old RRSPs, RRIFs, LIFs, etc to TFSAs.

Simplification of the Taxation System
(Bibliography: The Economy - Flat Rate Taxes and VATs)

Taxation, in Canada and almost all countries of the developed world, is currently burdened with tax codes which, in the case of the USA, are over 9 million words long. They contain many loopholes, deductions, and exemptions. Advocates of flat taxes claim that all these exemptions render the collection of taxes and the enforcement of tax law complicated and inefficient. There are currently 22 countries in eastern Europe that have flat tax systems already in place, such as Russia since 2001. Countries in western Europe such as Britain, Germany, France, Spain, Poland, Hungary, and Greece are now considering such systems to remain competitive. Both business and government now function inefficiently with needlessly wasted time, money, and effort.

In 2008, Canada had 69 companies in the Forbes Global 2000, ranking 5th next to France, and Canada's total government debt burden was the lowest in the G8. The OECD had forecast that Canada's debt to GDP ratio would decline to 19.5% in 2009, about half the projected average of 51.9% for all G8 countries. Canada's debt burden would have fallen over 50 percent from the peak in 1995, when it was the second highest in the G8.

Pensions & Insurance in Canada & USA

Employment Insurance must offer fairness of access, but recent proposals to offer EI benefits to the self employed are a concern. The EI program is seemingly boundless already owing to its benefit coverage for sickness, maternity leave, parental leave, adoption leave, and disability. It would face nearly insurmountable issues, and function even more poorly than it now does, if these benefits were extended to the self employed.

Over the last 28 years the number of self employed has expanded by a surprising 33 per cent. The debate over the inclusion of self employed workers cuts right to the issue of fairness in EI access. Only self employed fishermen (who do not pay into the program) currently receive EI benefits. Why should self employed fishermen qualify for EI benefits, yet the self employed in the service sector cannot? Is employment insurance the right program for the task at hand? No, employment insurance is not the right program.

There are many potential problems. One problem is the moral hazard of insuring activities that are certain to encourage the workers to draw on the insurance. That in turn creates conditions that increase the likelihood of collecting benefits. So if the self employed were to be covered by EI, they would engage in excessively riskier behaviour and be less likely to pursue self sufficiency. Who would decide that a self employed person's termination is a legitimate outcome and not the consequence of misconduct? How can the records of employment properly verify the hours worked and the wages paid? Further, many of the self employed are family members, which poses the conflicts of nepotism.

A first option might be to allow self employed individuals to contribute a larger percentage of annual earned income to RRSPs, instead of the current 18 per cent. Currently, the self employed individuals may count only on social assistance or welfare as a safety net.

A second option might be to establish an individual savings account for the self employed which could function separately and in addition to the EI program. That would relieve the government of the decision as to what is best and fair, and leave the individual responsible for managing his own affairs and his own self insurance. The government should offer some tax shelter, increasing the appeal to contribute and to function much like an RRSP. Thus, if self employed workers faced only minimal job loss over their working careers, they could withdraw more generous retirement income later from the accumulated savings. The choice between current EI and health benefits versus future retirement benefits would be placed in the hands of each individual worker. Fraudulent claims and corruption would be far less likely to occur. The workers would become self reliant, independent, and responsible. They would likely enjoy a much better retirement in the bargain. And best of all, the intrusion and cost of government in the affairs of the people would be reduced.

In the United States, a Value Added Tax (VAT) has been suggested to pay for social security and medicare programs. Professor Ezekiel Emanuel, (brother of White House Chief of Staff Rahm Emanuel and author of "Health Care, Guaranteed"), argues that a 10% VAT would pay for every American not entitled to Medicare to enroll in a health plan with no deductibles and minimal co-payments. Yale law professor Michael Graetz, author of "100 Million Unnecessary *(Tax)* Returns", estimates that a VAT of 10% to 14% would raise enough money to exempt families earning less than $100,000 (about 90% of households) from income tax. "People are beginning to recognize that the mathematics of the current system are just unsustainable." Leonard Burman suggests in the Virginia Tax Review that a 25% VAT could do it all: pay for health care reform, balance the federal budget and exempt millions of families from the income tax while slashing the top rate to 25%.

The VAT is one of the world's most popular taxes, used in more than 130 countries. Among industrialized nations, rates range from 5% in Japan to 25% in Hungary and in parts of Scandinavia. A 21% VAT permitted Ireland to attract investment by lowering its corporate tax rate. The VAT has several important advantages. The tax is hard to avoid as producers, wholesalers, and retailers are required to record their transactions and pay a portion of the VAT. VATs punish spending rather than savings, which the administration should encourage.

Chile's Privatized Social Security
(Bibliography: The Economy - Chile's Privatized Social Security)

José Piñera, who as Chile's minister of labour privatized the state pension system, is president of the International Center for Pension Reform and co-chairman of the Cato Institute's Project on Social Security Privatization.

It's an honour for me to share with you some of the experiences we have had in Chile with our new private pension system. I would like to comment on how the new system works, how we were able to make the transition from the old system to the new one, and what have been the main economic, social, and political consequences of the new system. I will not explain the shortcomings of the old pay as you go system in Chile. Those shortcomings are well known because that is the system that is failing all over the world.

In Chile we accomplished a revolutionary reform. We knew that cosmetic changes, increasing the retirement age or taxes, would not be enough. We understood that the pay as you go system had a fundamental flaw, one rooted in a false conception of how human beings behave. That flaw was the lack of a link between what people put into their pension program and what they take out. In a government system, contributions and benefits are unrelated because they are defined politically, by the power of pressure groups.

So we decided to go in the other direction, to link benefits to contributions. The money that a worker pays into the system goes into an account that is owned by the worker. We called the idea a "capitalization scheme." *(Author's note: The idea ought to have been called an "allocation scheme", as the person had the benefit of the income only while he lived in retirement. The person had no right to invest the capital himself, no legal title to the capital, and the capital was not part of his estate.)*

We decided that the minimum contribution should be 10 percent of wages. But workers may contribute up to 20 percent. The money contributed is deducted from the worker's taxable income. The money

63

is invested by a private institution, and the returns are untaxed. By the time a worker reaches retirement age, 65 for men, 60 for women, a sizable sum of capital has accumulated in the account. At retirement the worker transforms that lump sum into an annuity with an insurance company. He can shop among different insurance companies to find the plan that best suits his personal and family situation. (He pays taxes when the money is withdrawn but usually at a lower rate than he would have paid when he was working.)

As I said, a worker can contribute more than 10 percent if he wants a higher pension or if he wants to retire early. Individuals have different preferences: some want to work until they are 85; others want to go fishing at 55, or 45, if they can. The uniform pay as you go social security system does not recognize differences in individual preferences. In my country, those differences had led to pressure on the congress to legislate different retirement ages for different groups. As a result, we had a discriminatory retirement age system. Blue collar workers could retire at 65; white collar workers could retire at 55; bank employees could retire after 25 years of work; and the most powerful group of all, the congressmen who make the laws, were able to retire after 15 years of work.

Under our new system, you don't have to pressure anyone. If you want to retire at 55, you go to one of the pension fund companies and sit in front of a user friendly computer. It asks you at what age you want to retire. You answer 55. The computer then does some calculations and says that you must contribute 12.1 percent of your income to carry out your plan. You then go back to your employer and instruct him to deduct the appropriate amount. Workers thus translate their personal preferences into tailored pension plans. If a worker's pension savings are not enough at the legal retirement age, the government makes up the difference from general tax revenue.

The system is managed by competitive private companies called AFPs (from the Spanish for pension fund administrators). Each AFP operates the equivalent of a mutual fund that invests in stocks, bonds, and government debt. The AFP is separate from the mutual fund; so if the AFP goes bankrupt, the assets of the mutual fund, the workers' investments, are not affected. The regulatory board takes over the fund and asks the workers to change to another AFP. Not a dime of the workers' money is touched in the process. Workers are free to change from one AFP to another. That creates competition among the companies to provide a higher return on investment and better customer service, or to charge lower commissions.

The AFP market opened on May 1, 1981, which is Labour Day in Chile and most of the world. It was supposed to open May 4, but I made a last minute change to May 1. When my colleagues asked why, I explained that May 1 had always been celebrated all over the world as a day of class confrontation, when workers fight employers as if their interests were completely divergent. But in a free market economy, their interests are convergent. "Let's begin this system on May 1," I said, "so that in the future, Labour Day can be celebrated as a day when workers freed themselves from the state and moved to a privately managed capitalization system." That's what we did.

Today we have 20 AFPs. In 14 years no AFP has gone bankrupt. Workers have not lost a dime. Of course, we created a regulatory body that, along with the central bank, set some investment diversification rules. Funds cannot invest more than x percent in government bonds, y percent in private companies' debentures, or z percent in common stocks. Nor can more than a specified amount be in the stock of any given company, and all companies in which funds are invested must have credit ratings above a given level.

We set up such transitional rules with a bias for safety because our plan was to be radical (even revolutionary) in approach, but conservative and prudent in execution. We trust the private sector, but we are not naive. We knew that there were companies that might invest in derivatives and lose a lot of money. We didn't want the pension funds investing workers' money in derivatives in Singapore. If the system had failed in the first years, we would never have been able to try it again. So we set strict rules 14 years ago, but we are relaxing those rules. For example, only three years ago we began to allow the funds to invest abroad, which they weren't allowed to do initially, because Chilean institutions had no experience in investing abroad. The day will come when the rules will be more flexible.

Let me say something about the transition to the new system. We began by assuring every retired worker that the state would guarantee his pension; he had absolutely nothing to fear from the change. Pension reform should not damage those who have contributed all their lives. If that takes a constitutional amendment, so be it.

Second, the workers already in the workforce, who had contributed to the state system, were given the option of staying in the system even though we thought its future was problematic. Those who moved to the new system received what we call a "recognition bond," which acknowledges their contributions to the old system. When those workers retire, the government will cash the bonds.

New workers have to go into the new private system because the old system is bankrupt. Thus, the old system will inevitably die on the day that the last person who entered that system passes away. On that day the government will have no pension system whatsoever. The private system is not a complementary system; it is a replacement that we believe is more efficient.

The real transition cost of the system is the money the government ceases to obtain from the workers who moved to the new system, because the government is committed to pay the pensions of the people already retired and of those who will retire in the future. That transition cost can be calculated. In Chile it was around 3 percent of gross national product. How we financed it is another story. It will be done differently in each country.

Suffice it to say that even though governments have enormous pension liabilities, they also have enormous assets. In Chile we had state owned enterprises. In America I understand that the federal government owns a third of the land. I don't know why the government owns land, and I don't know the value. Nor am I saying that you should sell the land tomorrow. What I am saying is that when you consider privatizing

Social Security, you must look at assets as well as liabilities. I am sure that the U.S. government has gigantic assets. Are they more or less than the liabilities of the Social Security system? I don't know, but the Cato project on privatizing Social Security will study that. In Chile we calculated the real balance sheet and financed the transition without raising tax rates, generating inflation, or pressuring interest rates upward. In the last several years we have had a fiscal surplus of 1 to 2 percent of GNP.

The main goal and consequence of the pension reform is to improve the lot of workers during their old age. As I will explain, the reform has a lot of side effects: savings, growth, capital markets. But we should never forget that the reform was enacted to assure workers decent pensions so that they can enjoy their old age in tranquillity. That goal has been met already. After 14 years and because of compound interest, the system is paying old age pensions that are 40 to 50 percent higher than those paid under the old system. (In the case of disability and survivor pensions, another privatized insurance, pensions are 70 to 100 percent higher than under the old system.) We are extremely happy.

But there have been other enormous effects. A second and extremely important one is that the new system reduces what can be called the payroll tax on labour. The social security contribution was seen by workers and employers as basically a tax on the use of labour; and a tax on the use of labour reduces employment. But a contribution to an individual's pension account is not seen as a tax on the use of labour. Unemployment in Chile is less than 5 percent. And that is without disguised unemployment in the federal government. We are approaching what could be called full employment in Chile. That's very different from a country like Spain, with a socialist government for the last 12 years, that has an unemployment rate of 24 percent and a youth unemployment rate of 40 percent.

Chile's private pension system has been the main factor in increasing the savings rate to the level of an Asian tiger. Our rate is 26 percent of GNP, compared to about 15 percent in Latin America. The Asian tigers are at 30 percent. The dramatic increase in the savings rate is the main reason that Chile is not suffering from the so called tequila effect that plagues Mexico. We do not depend on short run capital flows because we have an enormous pool of internal savings to finance our investment strategies. Chile will grow by about 6 percent of GNP this year. The stock exchange has gone down by only 1 or 2 percent and will be higher at the end of the year. Chile has been isolated from short run capital movement because its development is basically rooted in a high savings rate.

Pension reform has contributed to an increase in the rate of economic growth. Before the 1970s Chile had a real growth rate of 3.5 percent. For the last 10 years we have been growing at the rate of 7 percent, double our historic rate. That is the most powerful means of eliminating poverty because growth increases employment and wages. Several experts have attributed the doubling of the growth rate to the private pension system.

Finally, the private pension system has had a very important political and cultural consequence. Ninety percent of Chile's workers chose to move into the new system. They moved faster than Germans going from East to West after the fall of the Berlin Wall. Those workers freely decided to abandon the state system, even though some of the trade union leaders and the old political class advised against it. But workers can make wise decisions on matters close to their lives, such as pensions, education, and health. That's why I believe so much in their freedom to choose.

Every Chilean worker knows that he is the owner of an individual pension account. We have calculated that the typical Chilean worker's main asset is not his small house or his used car but the capital in his pension account. The Chilean worker is an owner, a capitalist. There is no more powerful way to stabilize a free market economy and to get the support of the workers than to link them directly to the benefits of the market economy. When Chile grows at 7 percent or when the stock market doubles, as it has done in the last three years, Chilean workers benefit directly, not only through higher wages or more employment, but through additional capital in their individual pension accounts.

Private pensions are undoubtedly creating cultural change. When workers feel that they own a fraction of a country, not through the party bosses, not through a politburo (like the Russians thought), but through ownership of part of the financial assets of the country, they are much more attached to the free market, a free society, and democracy.

By taking politicians out of the social security business we have done them a great favour because they can now focus on what they should do: stop crime, run a good justice system, manage foreign affairs, the real duties of a government. By removing the government from social security, we have accomplished the biggest privatization in Chilean history, someone even called it, paraphrasing Saddam Hussein, "the mother of all privatizations", because it has allowed us to go on to privatize the energy and telecommunications companies.

That has been our experience. Of course there have been some mistakes. There are some things that should be improved. There is no perfect reform. With time and experience, I know I would do some things differently. But on the whole, I can tell you that it has been a success beyond all our dreams.

Author's Note: The paragraphs above state the Chilean government's political position, but the author begs to differ *(as in the bracketted italics)* on legal and financial grounds. Every Chilean worker knows that he is the owner *(beneficiary, but not owner)* of an individual pension account. The government has calculated that the typical Chilean worker's main *(beneficial)* asset is not his small house or his used car but the capital in his pension account. The Chilean worker is an owner *(beneficiary)*, a capitalist *(worker)*. There is no more powerful way to stabilize a free market economy and to get the support of the workers than to link them directly to the benefits of the market economy. When Chile grows at 5 percent or when the stock market doubles, Chilean workers benefit directly, not only through higher wages or more employment, but through additional capital in their individual pension accounts *(for the future beneficial income)*.

Best Options for Pensions & Insurance

While the entire book "Canada in Crisis (1) - An Agenda to Unify a Nation" has dealt with matters pertinent to the federal government, the following concepts and proposals are also relevant as well to corporations, to provincial and municipal governments, and to all employees. The wisest approach is to adopt the best features of government programs and proposals in Canada, Chile, and the USA, over as broad a scope as possible. Thus the following concepts will encompass the best employment and health insurance, pensions, and other retirement savings programs from those countries. The major concepts derived from these reviews are;

- the Chilean government wisely decided to link the benefits derived from these programs to the contributions made by the worker,

- the Chilean government wisely sought to remove itself from direct involvement in the daily administration of their program,

- the Chilean government required a sensible annual contribution of 10% of earned income for its program, but also permitted an additional 10% at the worker's discretion,

- the Chilean government wrongly claimed to have converted their program from a socialist to a capitalist structure. *Author's Note: From the viewpoint of Canadians, this is an exaggeration as the workers and employees are only beneficiaries of the program. They have no legal title to the monies, they do not direct the investments themselves, and ultimately the monies do not devolve to their estate on their demise. The Chilean program still follows feudal or socialist concepts, either for self interest or the interests of third parties.*

- the Canadian government provides programs for employment insurance (EI), employee pensions (PSPP), pensions for all Canadians (CPP), and employee health insurance (PSHCP).

Author's Note: The Canadian programs are also still based on feudal or socialist concepts of self interest or the interests of third parties. Government workers and employees in Canada do not have legal title to the monies that are part of their employment benefits.

- the Canadian government recently introduced the Tax Free Savings Account (TFSA), the ultimate savings and retirement income system yet conceived. The TFSA is an enlightened and excellent example of retirement savings legislation enacted for the benefit of the people of Canada.   *(Cicero would approve)*

- the Tax Free Savings Account (TFSA) provides no tax discount for its contributions, but does provide tax free growth within the account, and tax free disbursements at any time, both before and after retirement. Most importantly, monies may be disbursed to the owner at any time for any purpose such as unemployment income, health expenses, education expenses, vacations, mortgages, retirement income, etc; followed by the optional replacement of any and all monies previously disbursed from the account (but no sooner than one year after the disbursement).

- A Value Added Tax (VAT), or a flat tax in place of Income Tax might be adopted to provide governments with general revenue and relieve Canadians from their heavy tax burden, to complement the introduction of private accounts for retirement savings and income, health insurance, unemployment insurance, and any other discretionary disbursements.

Greater Wealth and Health for Canadians

From these concepts, one must determine a structure that is in the best interests of the people of Canada, (again quoting Cicero, "*The peoples' good is the highest law*"). In these proposals, the paramount assumption is that the legal title to the capital rests with the individual, and subsequently to his family and estate. The attainment of the legal title to the capital is the first step on the path to greater benefits. The second step is the management and administration of that capital. There are two choices for the employee.

First, he may choose to leave the management and administration of his monies to competent companies in the private sector, such as the major banks and brokerages. This would likely be the wisest and most prudent course of action. Only top tier companies should be chosen for this task, such as the largest of the banks and brokerages in Canada. Other companies may be competent also, but great care should be exercised to avoid Ponzi schemes and scams by unscrupulous persons.

Second, the individual may choose to manage and direct the investment of the capital himself, provided that he has the time and competence to do so. While this is possible in this day and age, one would need to be well read and up to date, to be computer literate with programs such as Metastock, StockWatch or others, and to have the time and disposition to manage one's investments. He may also choose to manage and direct only a small portion of the monies himself, leaving the bulk of the money to the professionals. The daily administration of the monies and investments is best left to the banks and brokerages due to the complexities of government regulations and reporting.

No family became wealthy through membership in pensions or life annuities. It's better to keep the legal title and management of your retirement savings for yourself and your family than to leave the monies with government. It's better to keep the farm yourself, than to give the farm to government and become a sharecropper on your own farm.

Neither the Chilean model, nor the proposals from the many distinguished Americans, would be appropriate or acceptable for Canada and its peoples, who are quite different from the Chileans and the Americans.

- The Chilean model fails for its refusal to grant legal title of the private accounts to the workers contrary to its hollow claim to be a capitalist model. Their legislation requires the funds in the private accounts to be managed by third party pension administrators (AFPs), and ultimately to be used to purchase a life annuity from other third parties.

• The current Canadian model and the American proposals fail for their perpetuation of government involvement in the management and retention of the monies, and needlessly complicate the pension and insurance matters by linking those issues to taxation (which itself is a Pandora's box of plagues).

• The people of Canada are fortunate to be well educated and capable of managing their own investments. Canadians are also fortunate to have Tax Free Savings Accounts (TFSAs) which are the optimum vehicle for the investment and retention of pension and insurance contributions, with full legal title to those monies for individuals and their estates.

A Twin TFSA Model for Pensions & Insurance

The ultimate structure for the provision of pensions, health insurance, and unemployment insurance should require that all monies currently provided by governments, employers, and employees be placed in a TFSA for the individual employee. This first TFSA should be restricted in its use to income withdrawals for unemployment and health reasons as provided under current legislation, and for future income at full or even partial retirement.

The vehicle for additional private savings should be an unrestricted TFSA for each and every adult Canadian. The second TFSA should permit withdrawals for any purpose at any time as provided by current legislation. These additional savings are needed to encourage greater financial prudence and self reliance by individual Canadians, which in turn will enhance the rate of national savings and the overall economic prosperity of the nation.

The TFSA for pensions and insurance purposes should be restricted to those purposes only. In addition, the monies in that account would be more prudently invested if there were a Savings Exchange. On previous pages, a proposal had been made to establish a Savings Exchange restricted to certain companies, securities, and patterns of trading. The purpose was to provide a secure and stable market for the long term growth of retirement savings plans, with listings on that exchange at the option of the companies which would be sheltered from unwanted volatility of their shares by those restrictions.

The advantages of the proposed two TFSAs are significant compared to the current pension plans, unemployment and health insurance programs imposed as mandatory conditions of employment and administered by governments and large companies.

- First and most important with a TFSA is the connection between the contributions and the benefits of the private accounts when both are placed in the hands of the employees. The prudent and restrained use by the employee of the self insurance provisions of the TFSAs during his working career leads to his ultimate benefit in the form of much greater individual wealth and a much better retirement.

- Second, any monies withdrawn for reasons of unemployment or ill health may be restored to the TFSA accounts with new monies at a later time, although the loss of potential earnings on the capital withdrawn for the period of incapacity cannot be restored. And in addition, this new-found wealth constitutes part of the individual's estate and will accrue to his family and beneficiaries.

- Third, the unemployment and insurance programs administered by governments are prone to politically expedient but ill advised revisions or diversions to other purposes, and to abuse and fraud by the recipients of the programs in particular.

- Fourth, the government programs add to the further bloating of government for services more efficiently operated by banks and brokerages in the private sector.

- Fifth, the greater savings rate and wealth of individual Canadians will be reflected in a stronger currency and healthier economy for the entire country.

- It should also be noted that governments and companies will be loathe to transfer so much wealth to individuals, as it is a key element in obtaining low interest rates on monies the government and the companies must borrow, as well as the salaries, perquisites, and benefits of senior executives of the government and companies.

- Twin TFSAs provide a natural incentive to be more self-reliant, and it follows that there is less likely to be improper use of one's own savings for sickness or unemployment.

As suggested by the Chilean model, each Canadian should be allowed to contribute up to 20% of earned income to the combined two private TFSA accounts which he holds. To demonstrate that these two accounts would encompass all the needs of an individual Canadian, consider the results for a hypothetical Canadian by the name of John Galt on his retirement in 2009. John is a well educated professional graduated with BASc and MBA degrees, from excellent Canadian universities. Following graduation in 1978, John joined the federal government to make a contribution to the better management of the government and the nation of Canada.

The charts on the following two pages demonstrate the hypothetical financial results accruing to John Galt from the application of the Twin TFSA Model if it had been adopted at the time of his graduation. John was fortunate to be continuously employed and in good health during his entire career, and had no need of monies withdrawn from the TFSA accounts *(to simplify the model)*. The financial performance and resulting wealth of the twin TFSAs may be assessed in terms of current dollars in 2009.

Chart: Private TFSAs for Pensions & Insurance
continued next page

Year	Annual Salary @5%	PSPP	CPP	PSHCP	EI	Annual Contribution
Totals Finals	na	200,328	121,763	35,514	40,097	397,701
1980	25,000	2,600	2,475	1,184	865	7,124
1981	26,250	2,730	2,599	1,184	908	7,421
1982	27,563	2,867	2,729	1,184	954	7,733
1983	28,941	3,010	2,855	1,184	1,001	8,060
1984	30,388	3,160	3,008	1,184	1,051	8,404
1985	31,907	3,318	3,159	1,184	1,104	8,765
1986	33,502	3,484	3,317	1,184	1,159	9,144
1987	35,178	3,658	3,483	1,184	1,217	9,542
1988	36,936	3,841	3,657	1,184	1,278	9,960
1989	38,783	4,033	3,840	1,184	1,342	10,399
1990	40,722	4,235	4,032	1,184	1,409	10,859
1991	42,758	4,447	4,233	1,184	1,464	11,327
1992	44,896	4,669	4,445	1,184	1,464	11,761
1993	47,141	4,957	4,584	1,184	1,464	12,188
1994	49,498	5,353	4,584	1,184	1,464	12,584
1995	51,973	5,768	4,445	1,184	1,464	12,999
1996	54,872	6,205	4,584	1,184	1,464	13,436
1997	57,300	6,663	4,584	1,184	1,464	13,894
1998	60,165	7,145	4,445	1,184	1,464	14,376
1999	63,174	7,650	4,584	1,184	1,464	14,881
2000	66,332	8,181	4,584	1,184	1,464	15,412
2001	69,649	8,738	4,445	1,184	1,464	15,969
2002	73,132	9,323	4,584	1,184	1,464	16,554
2003	76,788	9,937	4,584	1,184	1,464	17,168
2004	80,627	10,582	4,445	1,184	1,464	17,813
2005	84,659	11,259	4,584	1,184	1,464	18,491
2006	88,892	11,971	4,584	1,184	1,464	19,202
2007	93,336	12,717	4,445	1,184	1,464	19,948
2008	98,003	13,501	4,584	1,184	1,464	20,732
2009	102,903	14,325	4,584	1,184	1,464	21,556

Chart, Private TFSAs for Pensions & Insurance
(see previous page)

Cumulative Contribution	Average Total % of Salary	Average Worker % of Salary 11.3%	Investment Gain on Wealth (@ 7.5%)	Total Retirement Wealth	Age	Year
397,701	25%	44,885	729,155	1,126,856	55	na
7,124	28	12		7,124	26	1980
14,545	28	12	534	15,079	27	1981
22,277	28	12	1,131	23,942	28	1982
30,337	28	12	1,796	33,798	29	1983
38,741	28	12	2,535	44,737	30	1984
47,506	27	12	3,355	56,857	31	1985
56,650	27	12	4,264	70,265	32	1986
66,192	27	12	5,270	85,077	33	1987
76,152	27	12	6,381	101,418	34	1988
86,551	27	12	7,606	119,423	35	1989
97,410	27	12	8,957	139,239	36	1990
108,737	26	12	10,443	161,010	37	1991
120,499	26	12	12,076	184,847	38	1992
132,686	26	12	13,863	210,898	39	1993
145,270	25	12	15,817	239,299	40	1994
158,269	25	11	17,947	270,245	41	1995
171,705	25	11	20,268	303,950	42	1996
185,600	24	11	22,796	340,640	43	1997
199,975	24	11	25,548	380,564	44	1998
214,856	24	11	28,542	423,987	45	1999
230,268	23	11	31,799	471,198	46	2000
246,237	23	11	35,340	522,507	47	2001
262,791	23	11	39,188	578,249	48	2002
279,959	22	10	43,369	638,786	49	2003
297,773	22	10	47,909	704,508	50	2004
316,263	22	10	52,838	775,837	51	2005
335,465	22	10	58,188	835,226	52	2006
355,413	21	10	63,992	937,167	53	2007
376,146	21	10	70,288	1,028,187	54	2008
397,701	21	10	77,114	1,126,856	55	2009

Chart: Private TFSA for Any Purpose: Mortgage, Vacation

Year Totals	Annual Salary (5% Growth) 1,660,971	Average 8.7% of Annual Salary Invested 144,504	Annual Gain on Salary Invested (@ 7.5%) 241,168	Grand Total of Wealth 385,672
1980	25,000	2,175		2,175
1981	26,250	2,284	163	4,622
1982	27,563	2,398	347	7,366
1983	28,941	2,518	552	10,437
1984	30,388	2,644	783	13,863
1985	31,907	2,776	1,040	17,679
1986	33,502	2,915	1,326	21,920
1987	35,178	3,060	1,644	26,624
1988	36,936	3,213	1,997	31,834
1989	38,783	3,374	2,388	37,561
1990	40,722	3,543	2,820	43,958
1991	42,758	3,720	3,297	50,975
1992	44,896	3,906	3,823	58,704
1993	47,141	4,101	4,403	67,209
1994	49,498	4,306	5,041	76,556
1995	51,973	4,522	5,742	86,819
1996	54,572	4,748	6,511	98,078
1997	57,300	4,985	7,356	110,419
1998	60,165	5,234	8,281	123,935
1999	63,174	5,496	9,295	138,726
2000	66,332	5,771	10,404	154,902
2001	69,649	6,059	11,618	172,579
2002	73,132	6,362	12,943	191,884
2003	76,788	6,681	14,391	212,956
2004	80,627	7,015	15,927	235,943
2005	84,659	7,365	17,696	261,004
2006	88,892	7,734	19,575	288,313
2007	93,336	8,120	21,623	318,056
2008	98,003	8,526	23,854	350,437
2009	102,903	8,953	26,283	385,672

Comparative Summary of the Two Systems (after retirement)

To compare the two systems, Pensions & RRSPs with Twin TFSAs, the following is a simple model with simple assumptions. Real life would be more complicated. Note: contributions and gains of an RRSP are assumed to be the same as a TFSA.

AT - After Tax   BT - Before Tax   NT - No Tax

Restricted (limited) TFSA (joint contributions)
(for retirement, health & employment insurance only - 11.3% employee salary)

Unrestricted (any use) TFSA (employee contributions only)
(for any purpose; eg mortgage, vacation, education - 8.7% employee salary)

* Assumes John died shortly after he retired (to make model simpler), and left his estate to his wife by tax free RRSP / TFSA rollover.

** Assumes his wife died shortly after John died (to make model simpler), and left her inherited & personal estates to their children after tax at 40%.

Comparative Summary of the Two Systems (after retirement)

Summary of Pensions & RRSP System (earning 7.5% at retirement)	Pensions & CPP	RRSP (@7.5%)	Totals
John's assets	0	385,672	385,672
John's total contributions	44,885	144,504	189,389
John's income (BT)	65,048	28,925	93,973
John's net income (AT @33%)	43,322	19,264	62,586
John's estate (on his death)	0	385,672	385,672
Wife' inheritance on John's death	0	385,672	385,672
Wife's income on his death (BT) (50% of John's pension)	21,661	28,925	50,586
Wife's income on his death (AT@25%)	16,246	21,694	37,940
Wife's estate on her death (AT@40%)	0	231,403	231,403

Summary of Twin TFSAs System (earning 7.5% at retirement)	TFSA (limited)	TFSA (any use)	Totals
John's assets	1,126,856	385,672	1,512,528
John's total contributions	44,885	144,504	189,389
John's net income (NT on TFSA)	84,514	28,925	113,440
John's estate (on his death)	1,126,856	385,672	1,512,528
Wife' inheritance on John's death	1,126,856	385,672	1,512,528
Wife's net income (NT on TFSA)	84,514	28,925	113,440
Wife's estate on her death (AT@40%)	676,114	231,403	907,517

Major Attributes of Pension & Insurance (after retirement)

Under the proposed private Twin TFSAs shown in the charts above, what were the advantages and benefits; firstly to John Galt himself, and secondly to his family?

1) John would have contributed $44,885 to his employer pension & CPP, and $144,504 into his RRSP account (income from both are taxable).

2) In his first year of retirement (2010), John would be the beneficiary (not owner) of his employer pension & CPP starting at $43,322, ($65,048 AT@33%), indexed.

3) He would also be the owner with legal title to $385,672 in his RRSP, which at 7.5% would earn $19,264, ($28,925 AT@33%).

4) John's total wealth from the pension is zero, and $385,672 (BT) from his RRSP.

5) His total net income after taxes from his pensions and the RRSP in that first year of retirement would be $62,586, ($93,973 AT@33%).

6) John and family would be beneficiaries of the health insurance during his retirement. On his death, John's wife would receive half his pension, and would transfer his RRSP of $385,672 to her RRSP in a tax free rollover. If John were to die in the first year, her income would be $37,940, ($50,586 AT@25%).

7) On the death of John's wife, their children would receive nothing from the pension plan. From her RRSP, the children would inherit $231,403, ($385,672 AT@40%).

Major Attributes of Private Twin TFSAs (after retirement)

1) John would have contributed $44,885 to his restricted TFSA account, and $144,504 to his unrestricted TFSA account, both of which are non-taxable (NT).

2) John would be the owner with legal title to the $1,126,856 in his restricted TFSA earning 7.5%, and may now draw retirement income at $84,514 (NT).

3) John would also be the owner with legal title to $385,672 in his unrestricted TFSA earning 7.5% would add more income of $28,925 (NT).

4) John's total wealth from both TFSAs would be $1,512,528 (NT).

5) His total net income (NT) in that first year of retirement would be $113,440, or ~81% more than the $62,586 under the pension and insurance system.

6) John would pay for private health insurance at a cost of ~$3,000. On his death, John's wife would transfer both of John's TFSAs to her own (unrestricted) TFSA, (restrictions on John's old TFSA cannot obligate his beneficiary). If John died in the first year of retirement, his widow's inheritance by tax free rollover into her TFSA would be the same $1,512,628, earning $113,440 (NT), (or ~3 times as much as the $37,940 (AT) under the pension system).

7) If John's wife died, the children would inherit $907,517 ($1,512,528 AT@40%) from her combined TFSA, compared to $231,403 in the pension and insurance system.

Feasibility of Twin TFSAs

There has been continuous discussion of methods of improving pensions plans in Canada, particularly with respect to the inclusion of persons not currently in receipt of an employer pension. The discussion is led by life insurance companies, pension planners, and organizations in the private sector who administer many of the pension plans. Not surprisingly, their recommendations do not extend very far beyond MOTS, (More Of The Same). None of their proposals attempts to place greater onus and incentive for savings on the individual in such retirement schemes as pension plans. There are at least four reasons for this; one is the lack of legal title to the capital and its future bequest to family members, a second is the high taxes payable on monthly receipts, a third is the recent dismal investment performance on the capital of the plan or the complete bankruptcy of the employer, and fourth is the declining ratio of working contributors to retired beneficiaries (currently about 1.5 to 1) of pension plans.

The Twin TFSA model has none of these failings, and has additional economic benefits. One is that the restricted TFSA combines the employer pension, the CPP and OAS, and the employment and health insurance plans within one system. Governments and private sector employers would both follow this model. That then obligates the individual to determine for himself the trade off between two choices: any dubious abuse of the restricted TFSA for employment or health income during his employment years; and his prospects for a far better income in retirement. Given that health costs are rising almost exponentially, such trade offs by the individual are the best way to restrain health costs; greater prudence on the part of the employee. The same holds true for employment insurance claims (and parental leave for fathers etc). The final and winning reason is the end of the government pension and insurance programs, and the minimal involvement of government in future, ie the simple transfer of monthly payments to employees' restricted Twin TFSAs. MOTS is not the answer.

The privatization of pensions (including CPP), and employment and health insurance plans to a restricted TFSA, as well as personal savings for any purpose in an unrestricted TFSA, when incorporated in a Twin TFSA system, would transfer enormous sums of money into the hands of virtually all Canadians, those still working and those who are retired. These monies, when invested in a secure and stable environment, could be available for corporate financing needs. If placed in a new Saving Exchange, these monies representing a large portion of the wealth of virtually all Canadians, would ensure that there would be satisfactory levels of liquidity for the corporations listed there. Companies listed on such an exchange should be restricted by such attributes as size; for example, over $5 billion in assets, low debt, stability, history, etc. In addition to those qualifications for listing, the trading should be restricted to reduce volatility by limiting trading; for example, one trade weekly per stock, no derivatives, no shorts, no options, common or preferred stock only, and similar basic criteria for retirement planning.

In his illuminating new book, economist Brian Lee Crowley anticipates an historic restoration of the principles by which the country governed itself in the past . . . among them, the classical principles of less government and more personal responsibility. In his book, "Fearful Symmetry". Mr. Crowley explains why he holds this contrarian assessment, demographic step by demographic step. Essentially, he believes that the fading of Quebec nationalism will combine with an eroding population to reverse the dysfunctional trends of the past 50 years. Simply put, Canada will soon lack the workers necessary to fund Big Government. The only alternative will be less government and more personal responsibility.

Comparisons of the Canadian banking system and the Canadian investment system show some startling differences. First, the banking system is controlled solely by the federal government, while the investment system is controlled by 13 different provincial and territorial bodies with great variations in management capacity. The banking system withstood the challenges of the recent recession, perhaps the worst in history, better than any other country in the world. In the banking system, peoples monies were secure and stable. In the investment system, the peoples' retirement savings were ruthlessly ravaged; either by the recession, or by Ponzi schemes, and scam artists. The damage has been so severe that it has reached the point where many Canadians can foresee little hope for the future they had once carefully planned. Why is Canada's investment system, its stock exchanges, its professional money managers, and the peoples' future now in such dismal and heart-breaking disarray? Why should Canada's investment system and stock exchanges not be as secure and stable as the Canadian banking system? Clearly, a more secure and stable Savings Exchange under federal control would be a major improvement to protect the retirement savings and the futures of the Canadian people.

Suggestions and Proposals

There should be only one National Stock Exchange (with regional and type branches) and one National Securities Commission for the entire country of Canada.

There should be a Savings Exchange established, with restrictions on certain forms of securities and trading, with the sole purpose of providing a secure and stable market with minimal volatility for the long term growth of the retirement savings plans of Canadians, with listings at the option of the companies subject to the restrictions of that exchange.

All pensions and life annuities must be optional, commutable, and transferrable to other investment vehicles, RRSPs, RRIFs, LIFs, etc, at any time at the direction of the individual, except as subject to taxation rules.

Retired couples should be permitted to consolidate their registered retirement savings and income plans under certain conditions, such as being over some age such as 50, being of similar age to each other, and having a desire to simplify the management of their wealth.

The government should give serious consideration to replacement of the current but archaic taxation system with a VAT or simple flat tax system.

The government should consider consolidation and privatization of the employer pensions, CPP, and the health and employment insurance to individual employees with private twin TFSAs.

The government should attempt to reduce its portion of the Gross Domestic Product to half the current levels, and should encourage the provinces to take similar measures.

The government should abolish the formation of unions in the federal civil service, as all of its services should be deemed to be essential to the economy of the nation.

The government should apply both quantitative and qualitative measures of performance, based on cost and benefit analysis at the highest levels, to ensure that the programs and conduct of its departments and Crown corporations are in the best interests of Canadians.

The federal and provincial governments, by the passage of new legislation, should ensure the commercial mobility of products, services, professionals, and tradesmen within the Canadian borders.

The federal government should pass legislation to authorize its management of the inter-provincial and international transmission of electrical power over the electrical grid system of the nation.

The federal government should encourage the rapid conversion of oil and coal fired electrical generating stations to gas fired or processes based on water, solar, or nuclear energy sources.

Chapter 7 - One Religion (Official)

(Bibliography: One Religion - Religions in Canada)

One Religion: *"conduct indicating a belief in, reverence for, and desire to please a divine ruling power; a particular system of faith and worship"*

Christian: official acceptance of Christianity; tolerance of other peaceful religions.

The Canadian Government and Religion

Canada today has no official church, and the government is officially committed to religious pluralism. Of the total population in 2001, Christians constituted 77% (Catholics 43.6%, Protestants 29.2%, Others 5.2%), Muslims 2%, Jews 1.1%, Buddhists 1%, Hindus 1%, Sikhs 0.9%, no religion 16%.

Canada is a Commonwealth in which the head of state is shared with 15 other countries, including the United Kingdom. The UK's succession laws forbid Roman Catholics and their spouses from occupying the throne, and the reigning monarch is also ex officio Supreme Governor of the Church of England, but Canada is not bound by these laws. Within Canada, the Queen's title includes the phrases "By the Grace of God" and "Defender of the Faith." While the Canadian government's official ties to Christianity are few, it overtly recognizes the existence of God and even the supremacy of God. Both the Canadian Charter of Rights and Freedoms and the national anthem in both languages refer to God.

Christmas and Easter are national holidays, and while Jews, Muslims, and other groups may take their own holy days off work, they do not share the same official recognition. In some parts of the country Sunday shopping is still banned, but this is becoming less common. There was an ongoing battle in the late 20th century to have religious garb accepted throughout Canadian society, mostly focussed on Sikh turbans. Eventually the Royal Canadian Mounted Police, the Royal Canadian Legion, and other groups accepted members wearing turbans. Some religious schools are government funded. In 1957, Parliament declared Thanksgiving, "A day of general thanksgiving to almighty God for the bountiful harvest with which Canada has been blessed", stating that God is almighty and that Canada is blessed.

Christianity in Canada

The majority of Canadian Christians attend church infrequently. Cross national surveys of religious observance such as the Pew Global Attitudes Project indicate that Canadian Christians are less observant than those of the United States but still more overtly religious than their counterparts in Britain or in western Europe. In 2002, 30% of Canadians reported that religion was very important to them. This figure was similar to that in the United Kingdom (33%) and Italy (27%). In the United States, the equivalent figure was 59%, in France, a mere 11%.

Regional differences within Canada exist, with British Columbia and Quebec reporting low measures of religious observance, while Alberta and rural Ontario saw high rates of religious attendance. The rates for weekly church attendance in Canada are estimated to be 11% to 25%. The U.S. has reported weekly church attendance at about 40% since the Second World War, while weekly church attendance rates are higher than those in Northern Europe, for example, Austria 9%, Germany 6%, France 8%, Netherlands 6 % and UK 10%.

The large churches, Roman Catholic, United, and Anglican, account for more than half of the Canadian population as adherents. The Egyptian population in Ontario and Quebec has seen a large influx of the Coptic

Orthodox population in just a few decades. There is a relatively large Ukrainian population in Manitoba and Saskatchewan, while southern Manitoba has been settled largely by Mennonites. Baptists are especially numerous in the Maritimes. Both the Maritimes and prairie provinces have significant numbers of Lutherans. Southwest Ontario has seen large numbers of German and Russian immigrants, including many Mennonites and Hutterites, as well as many Dutch Reformed. Alberta has a significant Mormon minority in that province. In 2001, the Jehovah Witness claimed 111,963 active members in Canada.

Non-Christians in Canada

Non-Christian religions in Canada are overwhelmingly concentrated in metropolitan cites such as Montreal, Toronto and Vancouver, and to a much smaller extent in mid-sized cities such as Ottawa, Quebec, Calgary, Edmonton, Winnipeg and Halifax. A possible exception is Judaism, which has long been a notable minority even in smaller centres. Much of the increase in non-Christian religions is attributed to changing immigration trends in the last fifty years. Increased immigration from Asia, the Middle East and Africa has created growing Muslim, Buddhist, Sikh, and Hindu communities. Canada is also home to smaller communities of the Baháí Faith, Unitarian Universalists, Pagans, and subscribers to First Nations religions.

Islam in Canada

The Muslim community in Canada is almost as old as the nation itself. Four years after Canada's founding, the 1871 Canadian Census found 13 Muslims among the population. The first Canadian mosque was constructed in Edmonton in 1938, when there were some 700 Muslims in the country. This building is now part of the museum at Fort Edmonton Park. The years after World War II saw a small increase in the Muslim population. However, Muslims were still a distinct minority. It was only with the removal of European immigration preferences in the 1960s that Muslims began to arrive in significant numbers. According to 2001 census, there were 579,640 Muslims in Canada, just under 2% of the population. In 2006, Muslim population is estimated to be 783,700 or about 2.5%.

Sikhism in Canada

Sikhs have been in Canada since 1897. One of the first Sikh soldiers arrived in Canada in 1897 following Queen Victoria's Diamond Jubilee. Sikhs were one of the few Asian immigrant communities who were loyal members of the British Empire. The irony was that greater entry restrictions were placed on prospective Sikh immigrants as compared to the Japanese and Chinese. While Canadian politicians, missionaries, unions and the press did not want Asian labour, British Columbia industrialists were short of labour and thus Sikhs were able to get an early foothold at the turn of the century in British Columbia. Of the nearly 5,000 East Indians in Canada by 1907, over 98% were Sikhs, mostly retired British army veterans. Sikh immigration to Canada was banned in 1908, and the population began to shrink.

With the advent of World War II and the internment of Japanese Canadians, Sikhs were able to prosper. Before going to the internment camps Japanese preferred to sell their homes and properties to their Sikh neighbours whom they had known for so long. As the war economy picked up speed and moved into high gear, Sikhs were given positions of greater responsibility on the factory floors across the country as well as sharpening their skills as successful businessmen. Just as the war helped to emancipate North American women, showing that they were capable of doing a man's job, Sikhs were showing that they were just as talented as their European counterparts. One of the last major roadblocks remained the right to vote. The year was 1947, fifty years since the first Sikh immigrants had arrived, yet they were still denied this fundamental right. A right that was long overdue and Sikhs rallied to the cause, holding town hall meetings and lobbying local politicians and the government in Ottawa to change the law.

After the 1960s Canada's immigration laws were liberalized and racial quotas were removed, allowing far more Sikhs to immigrate to Canada. The Sikh population has rapidly increased in the decades since. Major Sikh communities exist in most of the major cities of British Columbia and Ontario. Sikhs have become an integral part of Canada's economy and culture.

Commentary

The Canadian People and Religion

As noted in the review of religions in Canada, 77% of the total population in 2001 belonged to the Christian faith. Since that time, there have been changes due to pressure to be "politically correct" and remove or ignore the observance of religion or any religious symbols in Canada. For example, the wearing of a "kirpan", a small ornamental dagger worn by male Sikhs, came into dispute in schools, as did the wearing of turbans by Sikh members of the RCMP. That has also been the case in other Christian countries in Europe, where head scarves worn by girls have been banned in schools in France, and burqas are unwelcome. In Holland, new laws have been passed that immigrants must dress like the Dutch, must speak Dutch in a reasonable time, and must conduct themselves as do the Dutch. Belgium has banned the burka.

The issue is the observance of religious affiliations within the immigrants' new country. Canada, as with most other Christian countries in Europe and other parts of the world, is quite tolerant of the private religious observances and practices of other peoples. This may well be due to the relatively long standing separation between church and state found in most Christian countries. The separation of church, state, and the people themselves is not as common for other cultures, where religious activity may play a large part of the daily life of the people. That religious activity is the definition and the identity of people who adhere to religious beliefs quite different from Christianity. An example would be the very public practice and observance by devout Muslims of praying five times every day to Mecca while facing in that direction. To most Canadians, such public religious practice would be considered immoderate and improper in Canada where there is such a respected separation of church and state.

That does not mean that Canadians and Christians never permit themselves the pleasure of public displays. However, when they do so, it is more along the lines of rejoicing as a congregation of people, rather than an individual and personal custom. There are events that are highly symbolic to Christians, such as the birth of Christ, the resurrection of Christ, and many other lesser occasions that give cause for joint celebration. A few of these historic events are traditionally celebrated in Canada as national holidays for people of all faiths, and in some Christian countries even more religious holidays may be celebrated. In addition to such celebrations by Christians, other faiths are welcome to celebrate their traditional events as well. Christians in today's world are tolerant of other peaceful faiths and are quite prepared to allow their peaceful celebrations. The issue is one of assimilation of the faiths of other religions into the mosaic of Canadian traditions and customs.

Canadians value their institutions and traditions from their early pioneering days to the current modern lifestyle. They have strong feelings for those religious values and traditions, and expect the government to publicly safeguard and preserve those values and traditions. While still maintaining the separation of church and state, Canadians do not want the governments to cast aside those traditions or their nomenclature in the interests of placating other minority faiths. Canadians want governments to accept that the country is Christian, and to proudly celebrate that with Christmas holidays, Christmas trees, Easter Sundays, and other traditions. The rights of society of the nation must have precedence over the rights of any individual or minority group of individuals, who may prefer or even demand that these references be abandoned.

Suggestions and Proposals

The federal government must recognize and legislate Christianity as the only official religion, but exercise tolerance of other peaceful, private, and law abiding religions.

Chapter 8 - One Language (Official)

(Bibliography: One Language - Languages of Canada)

One Language: *"the whole body of words and methods of combining them used by a people, nation, or race"*

    English: the education and usage of proper English in all affairs of the nation, with tolerance toward the private use of other languages.

The Canadian Government and Language

A multitude of languages is spoken in Canada. According to the 2006 census, English and French are the preferred language (language spoken at home) of 67.1% and 21.5%, respectively. English and French are recognized by the Constitution of Canada as official languages. This means that all laws of the federal government are enacted in both English and French and that federal government services are available in both languages where numbers warrant.

Many Canadians believe that the relationship between the English and French languages is the central or defining aspect of the Canadian experience. Canada's Official Languages Commissioner has stated, "In the same way that race is at the core of an American experience and class is at the core of British experience, I think that language is at the core of Canadian experience".

However, the official point of view gives only a partial perspective of Canada's linguistic diversity. About 20% of Canadians (roughly 6.1 million people, most of whom are first generation immigrants) have a language other than English or French as their first language or mother tongue. Many immigrants and aboriginal Canadians use English or French more often than their native language, but nearly 3.5 million of them continue to use a non-official language most often, when in home or social settings. The five most widely spoken non-official languages are Chinese (2.6% of Canadians), Punjabi (0.9%), Spanish (0.7%), Italian (0.6%), and Dutch (0.6%). Aboriginal languages, many of which are unique to Canada, are spoken by fewer than one percent of the population, and are mostly in decline.

Although 85% of French speaking Canadians live in Quebec, there are Francophone populations found in Ontario, Alberta, Manitoba, Nova Scotia, Cape Breton Island, Prince Edward Island, and New Brunswick. Ontario has the largest French speaking population outside Quebec. The Charter of the French Language makes Quebec unilingual, and makes French the only official language in Quebec. New Brunswick is the only province to be officially bilingual under its constitution. Other provinces have no official languages, but French is used in courts, and for other government services in addition to English. Manitoba, Ontario and Quebec allow both English and French to be spoken in the provincial legislatures, and laws are enacted in both languages. In Ontario, French has some legal status but is not fully official.

Inuktitut is the majority language in Nunavut, and one of three official languages in the territory. Several aboriginal languages have official status in the Northwest Territories. Other recognised regional languages are Inuinnaqtun, Cree, Dëne, Sutiné, Gwich'in, Inuvialuktun, Slavey, Dogrib, Yatii. Non-official languages are important in Canada, with over five million people listing one as a first language. Some significant mother tongues include Chinese (853,745), Italian (469,485), German (438,080), and Punjabi (271,220).

Until 1969, Quebec was the only officially bilingual province in Canada and most public institutions functioned in both languages. English was also used in the legislature, government commissions and courts. With the adoption of the Charter of the French Language by Quebec's National Assembly in August 1977, however, French became the sole official language of the government of Quebec. However, the French Language Charter also provides certain rights for speakers of English and aboriginal languages and most government services are available in both French and English. Regional institutions in the Nunavik region of northern Quebec offer services in Inuktitut and Cree.

Commentary

The Canadian People and Language

In the public service of the federal government, the advent of official bilingualism in 1967 required a gradual introduction of French language capability where demand warranted. To that purpose initially, certain positions were designated as bilingual. Where the incumbent was not bilingual, training in either French or English was provided to bring the individual up to satisfactory levels in both languages. By the year 2000, virtually all senior positions in the federal government were designated as bilingual. The primary qualification for employment and staffing in the majority of positions in the federal civil service is currently thought to be the highest degree of fluency in French, above all other criteria such as professional qualification, proven competence, past experience, or passable fluency in English for the position.

As for the politicians who govern the nation of Canada, advancement for any elected Member of Parliament to a responsible position in cabinet or caucus is largely dependent on a high fluency in the French language, there being an implicit assumption that only passable fluency in English will be sufficient. Even many politicians serving as Cabinet Ministers of the Crown might not be acceptable candidates for positions such as their own subordinate Deputy Ministers, or even lower level staff in the public service of Canada.

Despite the billions of dollars spent over 40 years since the adoption of the Official Languages Act in 1969, the rates of bilingualism are falling in English Canada. Parents may pine for French immersion classes, but mostly for reasons that have nothing to do with bridging the solitudes. There is no substantive evidence of any improvement in management commensurate with the effort, time, and cost spent on bilingual programs. English speaking employees regularly spend more time in language training than doing their jobs. They go for months or even years to get the highest attainable bilingual status, only to return as functionally unilingual as before.

It should be noted in passing, that old style English as taught to our forefathers 50 years ago (grammar, literature, writing, spelling, sentence structure) is no longer taught in schools in such provinces as Ontario. The emphasis is more on letting the children be creative and express themselves; *"like man you now wot I meen"*. It's makes it much easier for the teachers, but terrible to hear from the television media, or worse, to see in print in the nation's newspapers, which no longer seem to have editors who know English grammar themselves.

Since 2000, the paramount criterion for staffing in the federal civil service has been fluency in French, which criterion has surpassed and overridden managerial, professional, or technical competence, past performance and experience. It is rare that any person from outside Quebec can achieve the necessary competence in the French language to prevail over candidates from Quebec. Hence virtually all levels now in the federal civil service, especially the highest levels, are staffed by francophones, and virtually all are from the province of Quebec. Many careers of competent anglophones have been dashed by the strict enforcement of the bilingual policy.

Even the private sector is adversely affected by the bilingual policy of the federal government. Top level executives in corporations across Canada must also have staff who are fluent in French to advance their concerns or business with the government. Even some children in schools are adversely affected by bilingualism. French immersion is the equivalent to an elitist private school outside the public system of the provinces. Only the highest achieving children are chosen. Class sizes are generally smaller. Parents of talented children are pleased that their children are being "filtered away from the dregs", as some have stated.

The benefits to the francophone people, primarily the people of Quebec, are obvious. Language teachers and translators are in constant demand for employment at high wage levels in the federal civil service, with full health and pension benefits. Other professionals with mediocre competence in their chosen fields may now expect to surpass their betters for employment with the government, again with high wages and pensions. At the highest levels of the bureaucracy, it is the civil servants from Quebec who recommend the policies and implement programs for the francophone elite in the realm of the Canadian government.

The benefits to francophone politicians are substantial as well. All politicians with federal aspirations realize that to advance their careers, they too must be fluent in French, and in particular, the French that is spoken in Quebec *(c'est à dire, le français tel qu'on parle dans la belle Province)*. As for the Members of Parliament who govern Canada, they too are affected by the bilingual policy they have forced upon the bureaucracy beneath them. After the end of World War I, and the election of Louis St Laurent in 1948, six of the Prime Ministers of Canada have been from the province of Quebec, and have ruled as head of the Canadian government for all but 12 of those 60 years.

One must note the relative influence and population of Quebec within Canada. The total population of Canada in 2008 was 33.3 million. Ontario had 12.9 million, the Prairies and BC 10.3 million, the Atlantic provinces 2.3 million, and Quebec 7.7 million. The French speaking population of Quebec constitutes 82% of the Quebec total for 6.4 million, of which one may estimate only some 3.2 million are adults, and a third of those may be separatists. Thus, the political and bureaucratic elite of the Canadian federal government is essentially derived from this small pool of people, less than ten percent of Canada's population. The Quebeçois expression for these elite people might well be "pure laine" (literally pure wool, or loosely translated as "blue bloods" . . . or should that be "pull the wool over their eyes" ?).

No country rigidly ruled by a mere ten percent of its population may credibly claim to be a true democracy. The bilingual policy must be rescinded as being incompatible with Canada's claim to be a democracy, and English must be the only official language of the federal government and the nation of Canada. The English may have won the battle on the Plains of Abraham in Quebec city in 1759, but the French have won the war on Parliament Hill in Ottawa in 2010. The adult Quebecois now rule the nation, despite constituting only ~10% of the population.

Suggestions and Proposals

The bilingual policy of the federal government must be rescinded as being incompatible with true democracy in Canada, and English must be legislated as the only official and working language of Parliament and the federal government.

In both the Parliament of Canada and the federal public service, professional and managerial competence, past performance and experience, and fluency in the English language must be the major criteria for office, rather than fluency in the French language.

Federal and provincial governments (except unilingually French Quebec) should initiate programs to encourage much higher standards of spoken and written English in all educational institutions, all levels of government, businesses, the media, and the public at large.

Chapter 9 - One Culture

(Bibliography: One Culture - The Culture of Canada)

One Culture: *"worship; the training and refinement of mind, tastes and manners; the intellectual side of civilization"*

    Canadian: educated, self reliant, industrious, ethical, honest, tolerant.

The Canadian Government and Culture

Canadian culture is a term that encompasses the artistic, musical, literary, culinary, political and social elements that are representative of Canada, not only to its own population, but people all over the world. Canada's culture has historically been influenced by European culture and traditions, especially British and French. Over time, elements of the cultures of Canada's Aboriginal peoples and immigrant populations have become incorporated into mainstream Canadian culture. It has also been strongly influenced by that of its linguistic, economic, and cultural neighbour, the United States.

Canada's culture, like that of most any country in the world, is a product of its history, geography, and political system. Being a pioneering nation, Canada has been shaped by waves of migration that have combined to form a unique blend of customs, cuisine, and traditions that have marked the cultural development of the nation.

Most of Canada's territory was inhabited and developed later than other European colonies in the Americas, with the result that themes and symbols of pioneers, trappers, and traders were important in the early development of Canadian culture. The British conquest of Canada in 1759 brought a large Francophone population under British rule, creating the need for compromise and accommodation. The migration of United Empire Loyalists from the Thirteen Colonies brought in strong British and American influences.

Although not without conflict, Canada's early interactions with populations of First Nations and Inuit were relatively peaceful compared to the experience of native peoples in the United States. Combined with relatively late economic development in many regions, this peaceful history has allowed Canadian native peoples to have a relatively strong influence on the national culture while preserving their own identity.

Commentary

The Canadian People and Culture

The great majority of American immigrants to Canada between 1755-1815 were drawn there by promises of land for their loyalty to Britain during the American War for Independence. At the same time, peoples from western Europe were attracted to Canada for promises of land, and freedom from wars among feudal monarchies.

Most of these peoples came with few possessions and settled in various locations across the country. They were basically self reliant, and fiercely independent (there was often little if any government). Of necessity, they usually formed bonds with their new Canadian neighbours, who were often of different origin or language, for mutual cooperation in clearing land and homesteading. Their survival depended on their resilience and their determination to make a success of their new freedoms, lands, and country. These people retained the best parts of their old music, songs, and language in private gatherings, but publicly were bound together by their determination to make a success of their new life, lands, and freedoms in Canada.

During the period 1700 to 1900, the commonality found among these new Canadians lay in their origin from western industrialized countries, their predominantly Christian religion, their education, their worldly knowledge from explorations, and most importantly their dreams for their new country. During the period from 1900 to 1950, these new Canadians had fought in minor wars in South Africa and Spain, and in two major world wars in Europe. All of these hard- ships had brought a great sense of identity and pride to the peoples who had come from such disparate lands and languages, and had now been united as Canadians. The period just after the end of World War II was an intensely proud moment for Canada, and perhaps its finest hour in its brief history. The culture of the country and its citizens was now well defined.

The Canadian people at the end of World War II were self reliant, and industrious, well educated in business, science, history, music and the arts, and knowledgeable of worldly events. They were moderate followers of the Christian religion, ethical and respectful of the rights of all persons equally, and fiercely democratic, with a government quite independent and separate from religion.

During the most recent 50 years, liberal governments introduced several major social changes . . . legislation in support of multiculturism, bilingualism, and immigration policies expanded to include non-Christian peoples and their family members not previously eligible. These changes marked an abrupt departure from the previous limitations on immigration which had been essentially those from Christian countries of western Europe. The following years brought a great influx of people from the Mid-east, Asia, and Africa, almost all of whom were from cultures and religions quite markedly different from western Christianity.

These more recent immigrants were preponderantly from other religions such as Sikhs, Hindus, Muslims, Buddhists, Taoists, and others. Virtually none of these was from a democracy such as Canada. They were governed by tribal or clan traditions, theocracies, dictatorships, caliphates, or absolute monarchies. Their languages, alphabets, dress and deportment, their foods, their respect for life, their customs, and the equality of women, were markedly different. Many of their ancient and medieval customs were seen as barbaric to 20th century Canadians.

Canadians, as well as the people of many western European countries, have become deeply troubled by the failure of these peoples from other cultures to assimilate with Canadian culture. The concern is whether Canadians should be more accommodating of the recent but quite different immigrant culture, or whether the newer immigrants should more readily adopt and accommodate themselves to established Canadian culture and customs.

Many of these newer immigrants entered Canada with the belief that the Canadian government would and should respond to their demands for care and protection. They believed that a country so blessed as Canada could afford to maintain them under a generous welfare regime. They looked to the government for all their needs and shortfalls. Such attitudes were in stark contrast to older generations of Canadians, those who had been crucial to the development of Canada throughout its difficult pioneering days. Such attitudes by immigrants were not welcomed by the older Canadians, who were rightfully disappointed and concerned.

Some of the western European nations have also suffered disappointment with newer arrivals. Germany has had difficulties with *Gastarbeiter* (guest workers) from Turkey and their high birth rates which threatened German culture and language. France has had trouble with its colonial immigrants from Algeria with similar birth rates and attitudes to the Turks. The French government has been outraged, but politically challenged by the wearing of burqas by Muslim women, which is contrary to French culture. President Nicholas Sarkozy has said that the burqa is not welcome in France, and is seeking a ban on the wearing of the burqa in public. But the French government fears reprisals from the five million Muslims now living in France.

The Dutch, normally a very hospitable and open minded people, have been enraged at the murders of parliamentarian Pim Fortuyn, and filmmaker Theo van Gogh. Both of these men were highly regarded citizens, who were murdered by recent immigrants who were simply offended by the public activities of these distinguished native Dutch citizens. Geert Wilders, a Dutch Member of Parliament has suggested that no further immigration of Muslims into the Netherlands be permitted. The English have been astonished and angered to discover that there are already 85 sharia courts established in their country, long famous world wide for their English common law. The Swiss have done the sensible thing in allowing the people to decide by a binding referendum to prohibit the construction of minarets on Muslim mosques as being incompatible with the Swiss landscape and culture. The religion belongs to the Muslims: the landscape and culture belong to the Swiss. Apparently the Swiss peoples did not trust the dithering politicians and their parties to make such difficult decisions.

The Dutch parliament recently passed legislation requiring all applicants for citizenship to pass an extensive language test at a personal cost of 350 euros prior to their immigration to the Netherlands. The Dutch government has considered a proposal to place unemployed immigrant youth in empty military barracks under military discipline as an introduction to job training programs and the realities of the working world in the Netherlands. Both the French and the Dutch have restricted the public dress and deportment of immigrants to encourage greater assimilation with the national values, traditions and customs.

The traditions and customs of the Muslim people mentioned above have nothing to do with religion. The traditions and customs are attributes of the Muslim culture dating back to tribal days from the 7th century, not the religion of Islam. The rights to freedom of religion provide no logical support or rationale for their customs and culture. Consider for a moment the different cultures of Muslims, the high birth rates of Muslin, the absolute integration of church and state demanded by most Muslims, and the fervour of most Muslims to spread their religion. Clearly, it would be better for western democracies to endure the displeasure of Muslims now, rather than subjugation to their laws and customs in ten or fifteen years time.

The introduction of any of those customs and traditions, such as the wearing of niqabs and burqas, the adoption of sharia law, or acceptance of Islamic banking are the means of continuing the 7th century tribal traditions and customs which permit the church to control the people. If given control of the dress and behaviour, the law and the money, and further empowered by the insistence that any deviation from the faith is a sin . . . the clerical and political elite would control the very lives of the people, and especially their votes even if the state were a democracy initially. That latter condition could soon be altered.

The people of Canada and those of western European countries have the paramount right to preserve their values, customs, and traditions. Citizenship in Canada must represent both privileges and obligations under which all immigrants must be prepared to accept and adopt Canadian values. Immigrants should not bring old customs, traditions, wounds, complaints, quarrels, wars and other baggage from their former lands into Canada, where that baggage does not accord with Canadian customs and culture. Traditions from the 7th century are not compatible with the 21st century, as confirmed by the European Court of Human Rights,

Suggestions and Proposals

The federal and provincial governments of Canada must preserve and protect the long established and paramount Canadian values and customs of being self reliant, industrious, educated, ethical, respectful of the rights of society over the rights of individuals, moderately religious and maintaining the separation of church and state, strongly democratic, and especially concerned that the status of women as the equals of men be respected absolutely.

All feudal customs and traditions of non-Christian peoples in Canada such as dress and deportment, sharia law and Islamic banking, and political direction from a clerical elite, must be prohibited from their introduction in any guise to the public life of the nation. Christian and western values, democracy, and cultures must be maintained and preserved in Canada.

Chapter 10 - One People

(Bibliography: One People - The People of Canada)

One People: *"the persons belonging to a place, constituting a particular*
               concourse, congregation, company, or class; the whole body of
               enfranchised or qualified citizens considered as the source of
               power especially in a democratic state"
Canadian: those devoted to, defending, and swearing
               allegiance to the entire country.

The Canadian Government and People

Canada, which occupies almost the entire northern part of the North American continent, is the second largest country in the world, after Russia. Despite its vast expanses, extending over 4 million square miles, Canada has a relatively small population of some 34 million people. The majority of Canadians are concentrated in the southern part of the country, near the border with the United States. Most of the good agricultural land is found in the more densely populated southern areas, while the rest of Canada is dominated by enormous wilderness regions that are inhospitable for farming, but rich in natural resources. Although a century ago, the majority of Canadians lived in rural areas, today over 80% of the country's population lives in urban centres of 10,000 or more.

The country is made up of five distinctive regions, including ten different provinces and three territories: British Columbia with its stunning mountains and Pacific coastline, the prairie provinces of Alberta, Saskatchewan, and Manitoba, the central heartland areas of

English Ontario and French Québec, the Atlantic provinces of New Brunswick, Nova Scotia, Prince Edward Island, and Newfoundland, and the Arctic territories of Nunavut, the Northwest Territories, and the Yukon. Culturally and physically, Canada is a very diverse and complex country.

The first inhabitants of Canada arrived via the Bering Strait, at least 20,000 B.C., and reached the eastern areas of the country by about 10,000 B.C. As the ice of the glaciers melted, other waves of migrants entered the regions of the high Arctic about 4,000 years B.C. At the time of the arrival of the Europeans, it has been estimated that the native population of Canada was about 250,000 people. Most of these native groups were semi nomadic Algonquian speaking peoples, with large pockets of Iroqoian speaking peoples located in the East, the highly sophisticated Northwest Coast tribes, with their own complex linguistic patterns, and the Inuit in the Arctic areas.

While the first permanent European occupation started with the French and the founding of Québec City in 1608, Basque fishermen and whalers had plied Canada's eastern shorelines long before this period. The French created a colony of farmers and fur traders in the St. Lawrence River Valley, which by the time of the English Conquest in 1759, had reached a population of 60,000 people. During the English colonial period, 1759 - 1867, large numbers of immigrants came to Canada from the British Isles and settled in the areas of the Canadian Maritimes and what is now Ontario. Still today, these two eastern regions have strong Scottish, English, and Irish traditions among their populations.

In 1867, Canada became a semi-independent nation and set about the populating of its western regions. In 1885, Canadian Pacific Railway completed the country's first transcontinental railway, and by 1914, over 2 million settlers had poured into the prairies and the western coastal areas. Almost half of these settlers came via the United States, while many of the others came from the United Kingdom, or Eastern Europe.

There began a great influx of peoples from many countries of western Europe; Portugal, Spain, Iceland, Germany, Poland, Russia, Czechoslovakia, Hungary, Italy, Holland, Belgium, the Scandinavian countries, Switzerland, the Balkans, and other European countries. The vast majority of these early settlers were Christians. There were much smaller numbers of people from China, Japan and other Asia nations. In most cases, the new people arrived with little wealth and learned to clear and settle the lands under severe deprivations and struggles with the environment.

By the beginning of the 20th century, the population had grown to some five million people. By the beginning of World War I in 1914, the population had grown to almost eight million. When the war broke out, Canada proudly joined the battle under British command in the defence of France and the rest of Europe. When World War II broke out in 1939, Canada fought under Canadian command with the Allies against the Axis of Germany, Italy, and Japan.

By the end of World War II, Canada had achieved international recognition as a major power. To quote Mark Steyn, "If you go back to 1945, the Royal Canadian Navy had the world's third largest surface fleet, the Royal Canadian Air Force was one of the world's most effective air forces, and Canadian Army troops were assigned to the toughest beach on D-Day". In the last 100 years, the people had defined themselves through hard work, education, determination, and courage in warfare to become a great people in a great nation. It was their finest time.

World War I and World War II were both major turning points for Canada as a nation. Closely linked with the United Kingdom, Canada made tremendous contributions to the Allied war effort. These sacrifices helped mature the young nation and prepared it for a gradual transition to full sovereignty. Canada had obtained control of its foreign policy in 1931, and then in 1982 brought home its constitution (which had originally been an Act of the British Parliament). Today, Canada is a vibrant and sophisticated country, with one of the highest living standards in the world. Its riches include a highly educated population, vast natural resources, and the extraordinary beauty of its wilderness areas. During the last thirty years, Canada has opened its doors to immigrants from around the world, and by 2005, it is calculated that 12% of our population will be made up of visible minorities. The future looks bright for Canada.

Commentary

The Canadian People and the Nation

Following World War II, immigration began again, with people clamouring to go to Canada. There were many war brides brought home by returning soldiers from Britain and other European countries. Liberal governments changed the Immigration Act in 1967 to encourage peoples from all over the world, not only western Europeans, to settle in Canada. People arrived in droves from India, Pakistan, the Mid-east, the Far-east, and South America. To make all these disparate peoples feel that they would be welcome, the policies of successive Liberal governments led to the emergence of a new Canadian identity, marked by the implementation of official bilingualism in 1969, followed by multiculturalism in 1971. The new Canadians maintained their languages and traditions privately in various arts, social, and sport clubs.

Thirty years later at the beginning of the 21st century, questions were being raised about the behaviour and assimilation of all these new peoples. Aboriginal bands demanded to be known as "First Nation", and the Quebecois demanded recognition as a distinct society with a national legislature and greater autonomy. The demands of workers' unions made Canadian businesses less competitive, sometimes attributed to the "British Disease" of lax, lolly gagging workers. Sixty percent of new immigrants were now from Asia and many have brought old baggage, cultures and conflicts with them to Canada, where these have continued to fester. As well, the rising tide of terrorists from many parts of the world was finding both moral and financial support from recent immigrants with dual citizenships in Canada. Some of these have spent some of their time returning to their homelands and acquiring the pejorative nickname of "Canadians of Convenience".

The definition and perception of a Canadian was now less certain and more contentious.

There are basically three groups of people of interest pertinent to a discussion of culture. Those who lived in Canada before the past 50 years, those who immigrated during the past 50 years, and those who may immigrate in the future. One may reasonably assume that those from the first group of people already possess the desired attributes of the previous Chapters on the language, religion, and culture of Canadians, and are of little or no concern.

As for the second group of immigrants, the great majority have provided a useful enrichment and broadening of our culture. A small minority have been less positive in their contribution to Canada's reputation as a leading country of the western world. There are reputedly some 40,000 or more recent immigrants against whom deportation warrants are outstanding. Of even greater concern is that the federal government cannot locate many of these people to execute those warrants. This demonstrates a laxity in management by the Department of Immigration and Citizenship that is intolerable and must be accorded the highest priority by the government under the justice system. Such cavalier treatment regarding these recent immigrants by the Department and by national police forces must be changed. In future, the federal government must ensure that persons subject to deportation orders are properly detained until the execution of those orders is complete. A careful review of other members of this second group may be warranted as well to ensure compliance with government goals.

As for the third group of future immigrants, they should be prepared to conform to government goals. Those goals should establish suitable attributes to be applied to potential immigrants. Those attributes may then be used to determine which immigrants have the potential to make positive and demonstrable contributions to Canada's future growth and development, and which are compatible with its officially recognized culture.

Suitable attributes for future immigration should include fluency in

English, no serious criminal convictions abroad or in Canada, proven respect for the equality of women with men, and a sworn oath of loyalty to Canada. The government should consider an interim state of citizenship "on good behaviour" for a period of time up to ten years, with quick deportation accorded those who contravene the interim conditions. The latest identification technology should be used with all applicants to confirm their identity and previous history, and should be retained by the government throughout the immigrants' life as citizens.

The acquisition of Canadian citizenship by immigrants must be a privilege, not a right. The current legislated process granting any landed person the full rights of a citizen before any review by the government is untenable and must be rescinded. Bogus refugee claims should also be dealt with by the prompt return to the countries from which they came, or to other countries who are willing to accept them. The current legislation permitting an endless chain of appeals against deportation must also be discontinued. There is no arguable need for more than one appeal to ensure propriety in the process of the original entry to Canada. No subsequent application on different grounds for entry should be tolerated. No further appeals should be tolerated to prolong temporary residence in Canada. Revocation of Canadian citizenship for those having dual citizenship might also be considered for those who are mere "Canadians of convenience", or those who have failed to meet the standards for citizenship.

It may be that the European Commission for Human Rights (ECHR) was correct in 2003, when the court held "that sharia is incompatible with the fundamental principles of democracy". Of the 48 countries with more than 50% of the population classed as Muslim in Wikipedia, only five including Iraq, are listed as being parliamentary democracies.

Perhaps the Dutch MP Geert Wilders is more perceptive and practical than other politicians and is correct in suggesting that there be a ban on all Muslim immigrants from non-Western countries. "What is the alternative to restricting Muslim immigration to Western countries?" added Frank Hilliard. "If we don't do something while we still can, the growing Muslim minority will demand shariah law first for itself and then for everyone." With increased immigration, proselytization of the Muslim religion, death threats against apostasy from Islamic beliefs, and the high birth rates of Muslims, there may well be an irreversible loss of democracy in the not too distant future. Certainly, the citizens of the United Kingdom, France, Germany, Holland, Belgium, Switzerland, and Denmark are becoming more concerned.

Suggestions and Proposals

The government must preserve and protect the current citizens of Canada. There must be a major restructuring of the legislation concerning immigration and citizenship, and a major restructuring of the departments of the federal government given those responsibilities.

The government should create a modern and efficient system of personal identification for the greater security and protection of all of its citizens, and all persons who enter the country temporarily. Such a system might be based on finger prints, iris (eye) scanning, and DNA structure, encoded on a credit card sized passport, in addition to the standard passport. Such a card should contain a radiofrequency identification (RFID) chip. The Department should work closely with all law enforcement agencies on this issue.

The acquisition of Canadian citizenship by immigrants must be a legislated privilege, and not a right. Granting the full rights of a Canadian citizen to recent arrivals prior to a thorough review by the government is an untenable policy denigrating the value of that citizenship and must be rescinded. Eligibility to immigrate must be based on the ability of a candidate to speak fluent English, to contribute to the Canadian way of life, to respect the equality of women with men, and to obtain gainful employment in the economy. Current legislation permitting an endless chain of appeals must also be rescinded.

No other government than the federal government should have ultimate responsibilities for immigration policy, although the federal government should consult with the provinces who are responsible for the welfare of immigrants after their acceptance into Canada.

The federal government should revise the immigration criteria for admission to Canada. The granting of full citizenship must ensure that the culture and democratic governance of the nation will not be endangered by those who seek other forms of governance and justice.

Chapter 11 - Summary of Proposals

Canada: One Country (Nation)

The Constitution should guarantee and protect the rights of its peoples to the peaceful enjoyment of their property and business affairs.

The Constitution should ensure that the rights of society prevail over the rights of the individual where the culture and security of the peoples and the nation are concerned.

The Constitution should provide clear distinctions between the rights and privileges of its peoples, and the duties, obligations, and loyalties of those peoples.

The Charter of Rights and Freedoms should be amended to subordinate the right to freedom of religion to all other rights under the Charter, to ensure that the transgressions of any other rights are not permitted, excused, or condoned by pretentious claims of freedom of religion.

Canada should revise the Constitution to benefit the peoples rather than the government. The issue is one of propriety at the highest level: whether the Constitution should protect the rights of the government . . . or the rights of the people.

To quote Cicero, (106– 43 BC), a Roman statesman, lawyer, political theorist, and constitutional expert . . . *"The peoples' good is the highest law"*. Until the political situation permits the Constitution and the Charter to be amended, Canada shall remain a lesser country than its potential warrants.

Canada: One Nation (Country)

All legislation and official sanctions by government which recognize any group of people, or any organization, or any territory, as a nation within Canada should be rescinded.

Canada: One Governance

The British North America Act and the Constitution should be amended (or rescinded and a new Constitution established) with the division of responsibilities between federal and provincial levels of government revised to better accord with the 21 st century political climate and the people's wishes.

The structures of politics, parliament, and legislatures should be reviewed to determine whether they are relevant and the best suited for modern management of a country such as Canada.

The Constitution should be amended to deny eligibility for election to Parliament to any person who has a criminal record in Canada or abroad, or advocates the dissolution of Canada or the separation or secession of any part of Canada.

The Constitution should be amended to abolish the Senate and create a unicameral Parliament.

The Constitution should be amended to abolish political parties at the federal level to permit the formation of a consensual federal parliament.

The Constitution should be amended to require referenda on issues of national importance in the interests of true democracy to protect the rights of the people of Canada.

Canada: One Justice

There is a justice system for the vast majority of Canadians, and a different justice system and special restrictions for Indians. If action is not taken, the Indian Act and the English common law of treaties and trusts will persist into the future in the maintenance of Apartheid in Canada.

The government should rescind the Indian Act to abolish Indian status and the Indian reserves, and should abrogate the Indian treaties, the trusts, and fiduciary duties, and the discrimination that those entail. Better abrogation once . . . than discrimination forever!

The government should provide compensation to each individual Indian at the time of abolition. First, the lands and trust funds could be disbursed (or compensation given) or returned to all status Indians on a per capita basis. To provide time for reasonable assimilation into the mainstream of society in Canada, the federal government should provide some form of annual income for some length of time, even as long as a generation. Assuming the annual administration budget remains at $8,000,000,000 and there are about 400,000 status Indians on reserves, the annual tax free direct income payments should amount to some $20,000 per person. The monies due to minors should be held, with interest, by the government until the age of their majority. Assistance with education including Bachelor level at university should be considered, but subject to academic qualification and financial need and not as a right. And, finally, the existing land claims must also be resolved in addition to these changes.

After the assimilation period, there should be a complete termination of the assimilation payments. Of greatest importance, should be a complete termination of the treatment of Indians as second class citizens under the system of Apartheid. The aboriginal peoples of Canada may then be able to hold their heads high as distinguished Canadians, much as do the Maori people of New Zealand, and the Sami people of Finland, Sweden, and Norway.

Canada: One Economy

There should be only one National Stock Exchange (with regional and type branches) and one National Securities Commission for the entire country of Canada.

There should be a savings exchange established, with restrictions on certain forms of securities and trading, with the sole purpose of providing a secure and stable market with minimal volatility for the long term growth of the retirement savings plans of Canadians, with listings at the option of the companies subject to the restrictions of that exchange.

All pensions and life annuities must be optional, commutable, and transferrable to other investment vehicles, RRSPs, RRIFs, LIFs, etc, at any time at the direction of the individual, except as subject to taxation rules.

Retired couples should be permitted to consolidate their registered retirement savings and income plans under certain conditions, such as being over some age such as 50, being of similar age to each other, and having a desire to simplify the management of their wealth.

The government should give serious consideration to replacement of the current but archaic taxation system with a VAT or simple flat tax system.

The government should consider the consolidation and privatization of employer pensions, CPP, and health and employment insurance to individual employees with private Twin TFSAs.

The government should attempt to reduce its portion of the Gross Domestic Product to half current levels, and should encourage the provinces to take similar measures.

The government should abolish the formation of unions in the federal civil service, as all of its services should be deemed to be essential to the economy of the nation.

The government should apply both quantitative and qualitative measures of performance, based on cost and benefit analysis at the highest levels, to ensure that the programs and conduct of its departments and Crown corporations are in the best interests of Canadians.

The federal and provincial governments, by the passage of new legislation, should ensure the commercial mobility of products, services, professionals, and tradesmen within Canadian borders.

The federal government should pass legislation to permit its management of the inter-provincial and international transmission of electrical power over the electrical grid system of the nation.

The federal government should encourage the rapid conversion of oil and gas fired electrical generating stations to gas fired or other generating processes based on water, solar, or nuclear energy sources.

Canada: One Religion (Official)

The federal government must recognize and legislate Christianity as the only official religion, but exercise tolerance of other peaceful, private, and law abiding religions.

Canada: One Language (Official)

The bilingual policy of the federal government must be rescinded as being incompatible with true democracy in Canada, and English must be legislated as the only official and working language of Parliament and the federal government.

In both the Parliament of Canada and the federal public service, professional and managerial competence, past performance and experience, and fluency in the English language must be the major criteria for office, rather than fluency in the French language.

Federal and provincial governments (except unilingually French Quebec) should initiate programs to encourage much higher standards of spoken and written English in all educational institutions, all levels of government, businesses, the media, and the public at large.

Canada: One Culture

The federal and provincial governments of Canada must preserve and protect the long established and paramount Canadian values and customs of being self reliant, industrious, educated, ethical, respectful of the rights of society over the rights of individuals, moderately religious and maintaining the separation of church and state, strongly democratic, and especially concerned that the status of women as the equals of men be respected absolutely.

All feudal customs and traditions of non-Christian peoples in Canada such as dress and deportment, sharia law and Islamic banking, and political direction from a clerical elite, must be prohibited from their introduction in any guise to the public life of the nation. Christian and western values, democracy, and cultures must be maintained and preserved in Canada.

Canada: One People

The government must preserve and protect the current citizens of Canada. There must be a major restructuring of the legislation concerning immigration and citizenship, and a major restructuring of the departments of the federal government given those responsibilities.

The government should create a modern and efficient system of personal identification for the greater security and protection of all of its citizens, and all persons who enter the country temporarily. Such a system might be based on finger prints, iris (eye) scanning, and DNA structure, encoded on a credit card sized passport, in addition to the standard passport. Such a card should contain a radiofrequency identification (RFID) chip. The Department should work closely with all law enforcement agencies on this issue.

The acquisition of Canadian citizenship by immigrants must be a legislated privilege, and not a right. Granting the full rights of a Canadian citizen to recent arrivals prior to a thorough review by the government is an untenable policy denigrating the value of that citizenship and must be rescinded. Eligibility to immigrate must be based on the ability of a candidate to speak fluent English, to contribute to the Canadian way of life, to respect the equality of women with men, and to obtain gainful employment in the economy. Current legislation permitting an endless chain of appeals must also be rescinded.

No other government than the federal government should have ultimate responsibilities for immigration policy, although the federal government should consult with the provinces who are responsible for the welfare of immigrants after their acceptance into Canada.

The federal government should revise the immigration criteria for admission to Canada. The granting of full citizenship must ensure that the culture and democratic governance of the nation will not be endangered by those who seek other forms of governance and justice.

Chapter 12 - A Generation Later: 2008 - 2030

In 2008, Canada was suffering from the collapse of the American and world financial systems, as were all countries. Many Canadians had suffered losses to their investments and retirement savings, as well as losses to pensions from some troubled companies. But Canada was more fortunate than most countries in having a conservative and prudent banking system. The International Monetary Fund had recently praised the Canadian banks as the best of the G8 group of developed countries. The minority government was determined to pursue its plans to strengthen and unify the country further, and to ensure that such catastrophes as the current crisis did not threaten its people and the nation in future.

The Period 2008 - 2012

The federal government chose to implement changes in the financial system, in particular the stock exchanges, to bring those entities within the same unified structure as the Canadian banks. Even from its minority position, the government was able to introduce and secure passage of several changes, as these were clearly moving to a simpler and more effective structure. First was the introduction of one National Exchange Commission, and one National Stock Exchange, supported by various divisions representing sub-exchanges for Commodities, Venture Capital, Savings, and Bonds etc. Each of these in turn had regional offices in the five major regions of Canada, the Western provinces, the Northern Provinces and Territories, Ontario, Quebec, and the Atlantic Provinces.

In 2011, the Savings Exchange had been established for the investment of retirement savings and income securities, with restrictions to reduce volatility and trading, to ensure steady and reliable growth. Older married couples had been encouraged to voluntarily consolidate their accounts for simpler and more efficient administration by themselves and by the insurance companies, brokerages, and banks. Former savings and income vehicles such as RRSPs and RRIFs were permitted to enjoy gradual tax free rollovers to Tax Free Savings Accounts (TFSAs) which had been introduced in 2009, and which were the best retirement savings vehicles.

Best of all, the government passed legislation to ensure that all federal pensions were optional, commutable, and portable to RRSPs and RRIFs, at any time at the direction of the individual employee or former employee. The provinces, municipalities, and corporations quickly followed these initiatives. So many Members of Parliament and federal civil servants immediately chose to transfer their pension plans to their private TFSAs, that considerable cost savings were achieved in the administration of the few remaining pension plans until they too expired. All new members of the federal civil service (and the provinces, municipalities, and corporations) were automatically enrolled in the Twin TFSA system, and eventually all of the pension and insurance plans administered by the government would cease to exist. The onus for the use of the Twin TFSAs, for either health and employment insurance or for future retirement savings, would now rest upon the self reliance of individual Canadians. It's their choice now.

All of these changes had been supported by the opposition parties as proper and sensible. The effect of these changes was to reduce the overhead costs and to remove restrictions to freedom of choice that had previously been imposed by excessive regulation of monies that were morally the property of each individual Canadian. Most people were now protected with health and employment insurance throughout their working careers with the Twin TFSAs. They alone were responsible for their own insurance versus retirement trade offs and choices during their working careers. This produced a considerable reduction in lost time at work and a noticeable increase in productivity. Needless to say, the people of Canada were very pleased with these changes, as were all political parties who gave their non-partisan support.

In a similar vein, the federal government, with the consent of the opposition, passed legislation to permit the filing of income taxes on a flat rate basis. There are currently 22 countries in eastern Europe that have a flat tax system already in place, even Russia since 2001, and Britain, Germany, France, Spain, Poland, Hungary, and Greece are contemplating its adoption. Businesses and individuals were immensely relieved that the non-partisan cooperation in Parliament facilitated passage of the new legislation. The effectiveness of both government and business will be enhanced by the reduction of previously wasted money, time, and effort.

In a welcome display of cooperation, the provinces agreed with the government's proposed legislation to remove virtually all remaining impediments to the free and open mobility of products, services, professionals, and tradesmen within Canada. All of the Premiers have enacted similar provincial legislation to accord with the federal initiative. These new and cooperative initiatives have reduced unemployment rates in virtually all provinces and territories, and as well as the costs of the federal employment insurance program.

The government continued to review both quantitative and qualitative measures of management performance in its operations based on economic cost and benefit analysis at the highest levels, to ensure that the conduct of those departments was in the best interests of Canadians.

In late 2010 the federal government, with the consent of the opposition, passed legislation to recognize Christianity as the official religion of Canada. The government was careful to stress that all peaceful religions in Canada would be welcome to practise in their traditional manner and customs as they had in the past. The legislation was intended merely to clarify that Christmas, Easter and other national holidays were to be accorded their traditional terminology.

In a rare occurrence in 2011, the federal government rescinded its official recognition of Quebec and Indian bands as nations within Canada, and passed legislation that no group of people or territory would be recognized as a nation within Canada. The term was simply misleading and causing confusion. The government also passed legislation to rescind the power of unions within the federal civil service to strike or withhold services, on grounds that all of the government's services were essential to the economy of Canada. If new contracts were not in place before the termination of a current contract, then increases in salaries and wages equal to the cost of living would be automatically and immediately imposed upon the government.

Albeit with some lively dissension, the government finally succeeded in securing an amendment to the Constitution to deny eligibility for election to the federal Parliament of any person who advocates the dissolution of Canada or the secession of any part of Canada. Persons previously denied the privilege of eligibility for election were those in some government appointed positions, and those who had criminal records in Canada or abroad.

By the end of 2012, the goals for one nation, one official religion, and a major portion of one economy had been achieved. The changes to the financial and investment environment alone had greatly improved the lifestyle and retirement security for all Canadians. People were more confident and content about their futures, that of their families, and that of the nation.

The Period 2012 - 2016

In the previous four years the federal government, with the provinces collaborating on occasion, introduced major changes to legislation to improve the operations of their many departments and Crown corporations. Many agencies, boards, and Crown corporations had been privatized or simply abolished. The voting public was impressed, and the government received a comfortable majority in the election of 2012. Canadians in general had had their faith restored, as well as their financial fortunes, as unemployment shrank and the stock markets swelled with activity.

The recent creation of tax free savings plans (TFSAs) had caused a quantum increase in the savings rate of Canadians, and the gradual transfer of monies form old RRSPs and RRIFs had begun. The consolidation and privatization of employer pensions, CPP, and health and employment insurance to individual employees with private Twin TFSAs was warmly received by the employees, banks and other financial corporations. Business had become less burdened with taxes and had come to live in comfort with the higher dollar, albeit with the usual concerns from exporters. The Canadian dollar had risen to parity with most other major currencies, and governments now played a much smaller role in the economy.

On the basis of the recent success at the polls, the federal government introduced legislation to rescind the Official Languages (Bilingual) Act of 1969, as amended in 1988. There were strong objections from some quarters, but as the Bloc Quebecois party no longer existed in Parliament, the resistance was far more muted than it would have been when the Bloc constituted one sixth of the Members of Parliament. As the French language had steadily fallen from its former position among the many languages spoken by Canadians, and as the Province of Quebec persisted in being unilingually French, the federal government could no longer justify any moral or official obligation to operate under the tardy and costly administrative burden of more than one language.

As the issue of bilingualism was so divisive and of national importance, the government decided to hold a referendum. It used the newer, faster, and far less expensive means of internet voting (with ample security measures) to sanction abolition of the country's bilingualism policy. The result was participation by 76% of the population, agreement by 67% of Canadians and even 21% of francophones. The legislation was then introduced and passed in the summer of 2012 to amend the Official Languages Act and to declare English to be the only official language of the federal government, to the relief of the overwhelming majority of Canadians.

During the next winter, the government introduced new legislation to rescind the Indian Act, and to abrogate all treaties and trusts with the Indian bands of Canada. This had been proposed some 40 years ago by Jean Chrétien as Minister of Indian Affairs. The Indian Act was an anachronism, and a form of "Apartheid" that was no longer tolerable in Canadian society. Again, because of its importance, the government held a referendum by internet voting. The results were positive, with approval by 83% of adult Canadians, and even 63% of Indians.

The "Notwithstanding" clause of the Constitution was invoked to abrogate restrictions imposed under the Constitution on the government's treatment of Indians. The process of assimilation was to be gradual, with the return of all lands and trust monies to individual Indians on a per capita basis. In addition, program monies were to be provided over one generation for the education and interim income assistance of Indians until full assimilation was achieved. Canadians were pleased that the aboriginal people were finally to be treated as equals with all other Canadians.

Although financial support for the aboriginal people was to endure for another 20 years, Canadians appreciated that the government program with annual expenditures of $8 -10 billion for the Indian people would finally end. Such costs were bearable until that time as a result of foreseeable longer term savings by the eventual cancellation of the Indian programs.

Without passage of official legislation, the government gave tacit recognition to the evolving culture of Canadians. In public announcements, various publications, and political events, the government stressed the country's traditions and pioneering qualities of self reliance, hard work, independence, ethical behaviour, and respect for the equality of women with men.

Changes had been made as well in the immigration process. New candidates for Canadian residence and citizenship were cautioned that such status was a privilege to be earned by proper behaviour. Citizenship was not a right acquired simply by arriving on the shores of the country. Eligibility to immigrate was based on the ability of a candidate to speak fluent English, to contribute to the Canadian way of life, to respect the equality of women and men, and to find gainful employment in the economy.

The former practice of permitting related family members to follow in the footsteps of the youngest and brightest was quietly abandoned in favour of requiring positive contributions to the economy and social fabric of the country from virtually all immigrants. Citizenship was granted on a probationary level for ten years, and immigrants were expected to quickly assimilate themselves to the English language, culture, dress and behaviour of the Canadian population. They were also assured of tolerance of their private and peaceful religious activities, customs, and traditions in Canada, provided that these were not in conflict with Canadian culture and customs. Following the rescission of the rights of dual citizenship, some recent immigrants had left Canada to return to their native lands and customs. The introduction of high technology identification cards to all Canadians had facilitated the location of 87% of the 40,000 recent immigrants under deportation orders, and the subsequent swift execution of those orders.

In 2015, the government passed legislation to assume total management control over the transmission of electrical power over the nation's power grid system. This was done in the interests of national security in the event of natural or man-made disasters. By that date, almost 70% of the older oil fired electric generating stations had been converted to gas fired stations. Many of the coal fired stations had been refurbished as well.

By the end of 2015, the goals of one official language, one culture, and essentially one people were well underway or had already been achieved. Canadians from all regions and walks of life were becoming more confident in their government and its achievements, more comfortable with the majority government, and much prouder of their newly renovated country. Other countries had begun to take note of Canada's achievements, and visitors to the country, both tourists, business people, and other government officials spoke highly of the changes.

The Period 2016 - 2030

Based on its performance over the previous eight years, the people gave the government an overwhelming majority in the election of early 2016. Over those years, a much greater rapport had been developed between the federal, provincial, and major municipal levels of government. Following on those achievements, the government bent itself to the task of reforming the Constitution and the governance of the country.

As the government had done before, it now held meetings with the provincial premiers, other political parties, businesses, major cities, and the people, to set the stage for wide-ranging amendments to the Constitution. For the most part, the proposed amendments were not contentious, especially with regard to the first three of the five major constitutional issues.

- First, to enshrine the distinctions between rights, privileges, duties, and obligations.

- Second, to enshrine the rights of society over the rights of individuals, particularly in matters of culture, national security, and preservation of democracy in the nation.

- Third, to enshrine the peoples' rights to the peaceful enjoyment of their individual and business properties in accordance to recent Supreme Court rulings.

The fourth major issue was the abolition of the Senate, about which there was much *"Sturm und Drang"*, or more heat than light. Following the previous successes with internet referenda, the government proposed the abolition of the Senate to the people. The response was again a resounding success, with 83% in favour of abolition of the Senate, and a response by 79% of the voting population. Referenda for major issues were proving popular.

- The government prepared to abolish the Senate among proposed amendments to the Constitution.

The remaining fifth major issue to be amended in the Constitution was the sharing of the control and revenues from Canada's abundant natural resources. What was needed was a simple and common solution applicable to all regions of the country. Past experience on this issue by various Prime Ministers since 2000 was key to the successful resolution of this. Almost every conceivable formula had been tried before, but not always consistently in every region, which had created considerable discord. Eventually, mutual agreement on the sharing of these resources was established, with a simple and common formula acceptable to both levels of government.

- The federal and provincial governments reached an accord on sharing the control and revenue of natural resources by a single, simple formula for all regions of Canada.

In April of 2016, federal and provincial agreement was achieved for the introduction and passage of amendments to the Constitution of Canada, containing clauses for all of the above, and the amended Constitution was officially ratified in June of 2016. The government of Canada then reverted to a unicameral structure consisting solely of the House of Commons.

A Consensual Parliament

In 2017, the federal government sought to change the very structure of the House of Commons, which was now synonymous with Parliament, by conversion from a confrontational party structure to a consensual non-party Parliament. In 2008, Ontario had flirted with discussions of a consensual legislature with greater cooperation among the political parties. Well argued support had been offered for such a change by Vaughan Lyon, Professor of political studies at Trent University in

Peterborough. But the government wished to go further, to remove the last vestiges of adversarial confrontation from the federal Parliament by the abolition of all federal political parties. Such a consensual Parliament would then be modelled not on the English Parliament, but rather on the legislature of Nunavut. In April 1999, legislation had been passed by the federal government to establish the Canadian Territory of Nunavut.

The first election in Nunavut was held in 1999, and 19 members were elected to the Nunavut Legislative Assembly. Nunavut comprised one fifth of the area of Canada, and had a population of fewer than 30,000 persons in 2006. Unlike provincial legislatures, the Nunavut Legislative Assembly did not operate on the basis of political parties, but instead operated on a consensual basis. With a party system, the leader of the party which won the most seats in an election became premier. In Nunavut, the elected members chose the premier and cabinet ministers. The premier then assigned portfolios to the ministers most suitable for those duties.

On reflection, one must realize that political parties are a redundant intercession between the citizens and their government. They are an artifice for control designed by members of the parties themselves for financing and winning elections, based on the axiom "united we stand, divided we fall". Unfortunately, the goals and political ambitions of the parties may often supercede the best interests of the people and the nation. For example, there is a compulsion based on sheer ego for any political party to be continually in power, regardless of its lack of competence or loss of confidence of the House of Commons. Under a consensual parliament, there would be no "trained seals" clapping in the back rows and forced to follow party lines, even though those party lines were against the principles and beliefs of their constituents.

There have been many egregious activities by political parties or politicians, such as the sponsorship scandal (1993 to 2006) involving the Liberal party, or the strange consulting fees of a former Conservative Prime Minister. Another shameful party activity was the cancellation of the Sea King helicopter contract. On his first day in office in 1993 with a liberal majority, Jean Chrétien cancelled a signed contract to purchase 28 navy helicopters and 15 search and rescue versions. Chrétien said the country could not afford "Cadillac" helicopters when the national deficit was so high. The cancellation of the project triggered more than $1 billion in penalties, write offs, and extra maintenance costs for the existing fleet of Sea King helicopters.

In 1959 in a similarly repugnant activity, Prime Minister John Diefenbaker ordered the destruction by cutting torches of five prototype Avro Arrow CF-105 fighter aircraft. The result was the virtual dismemberment and diaspora of Canada's highly respected and innovative aerospace industry, which sadly left for better employment opportunities in the United States. During the liberal reign of the 1990s, the government oversaw the inexcusable obsolescence and decay of Canada's military equipment in its army, navy and air force. At the same time, dangerous military commitments had been and continued to be made to position Canadian forces in harm's way in the former Yugoslavia, Afghanistan and other conflicts. And finally in the midst of these egregious activities, were the continued but unwarranted entitlements to excessive pensions for Members of Parliament.

Such activities as these would have been inconceivable without the power and protection of "the party". Such activities as these would have been equally inconceivable under a consensual government. A political party is an anachronism from the past which no longer serves a useful purpose in a western democracy such as Canada in the 21st century.

There was strong opposition by the politicians and initially by some of the public to the government's proposal to abolish all federal political parties. The Bill to enact the required legislation failed to pass in the existing Parliament in 2017. Following the defeat of the bill to abolish all federal political parties, the government launched an information campaign to bolster its proposal for a consensual parliament over the following years. In 2019, and still with a strong majority, the government held another referendum on the proposed abolition of federal political parties to create a consensual parliament. The referendum succeeded

129

this time, with a vote of 84% in favour of the change and a voter participation rate of 73%. The requisite legislation was passed officially in 2020. There were then no concerns or fears of dictatorial governments, or weak minority governments, or unstable coalitions.

After ten years of working within a consensual parliament, the improvement in decorum and effectiveness was astounding. The principal reason was the absence of delays and filibustering (and plain blustering) by an opposition party or a recalcitrant Senate. In addition to those factors, all 185 members (a reduction from the former 305) were now working to a common purpose. Draft bills prepared by sub-committees were more quickly and effectively reviewed, and subsequently placed before the full parliament for debate and passage. All appointments to federal government office were based on competence, rather than on party patronage.

The success of the change to a consensual parliament by the federal government was noticed by the Atlantic provinces, who were burdened historically with excessive bureaucracies and were badly in need of reform themselves. After much negotiation, the four provinces agreed to amalgamate into a single entity called the Atlantic Province, with a consensual legislature having one third the number of members as the total of the four previous legislatures. Amendments to the Constitution and to federal and provincial legislation to achieve this were passed in 2023.

With another election coming within a year, the government decided to provide an overview of its achievements over the past years in office. In addition to simplifications and qualitative improvements, there were substantial financial savings from reductions in program costs or outright cancellation of some programs, as follows:

- greatly reduced costs by conversion from income tax to a value added tax (VAT)
- reduced costs by conversion of pensions to TFSAs for Members of Parliament.

- greatly reduced costs by conversion of pensions & employment insurance to TFSAs.
- greatly reduced costs by cancellation of the bilingual program.
- reduced costs by abolition of strikes by employee unions in the federal service.
- reduced costs by privatization or abolition of some agencies, boards, corporations.
- greatly reduced costs (and imminent cancellation) of the Indian program.
- reduced costs under more selective and restrictive immigration policies.
- reduced costs in immigration and law enforcement by use of biometric ID cards.
- reduced costs and time delays by exclusion of separatist MPs (Bloc Quebecois).
- reduced costs and time delays by abolition of the Senate.
- greatly reduced costs by conversion from confrontational to consensual parliament.
- government appointments were based on competence, (no parties, no patronage).
- reduced federal government portion of GDP from 43% in 2007 to 27% in 2028.

The public was so pleased with the new structures of parliament that the election of 2024 was held without any negative campaigning, and at greatly reduced cost. The candidates who were standing for office did so based on their professional competence and proven experience to represent their ridings. The professional competence of the successful candidates also provided greater choice from a larger field of elected members for the prime minister to form a strong cabinet.

Canada in 2030 - a Nation Unified

By 2030, all of the goals for Canada to become a unified country had finally been accomplished; One Country, One Nation, One Governance, One Justice, One Economy, One Religion, One Language, One Culture, and One People. Both Canada the nation, and the Canadian people had regained their identity.

By the year 2030, Canada was a stronger and prouder nation than it had ever been before.

Epilogue

Throughout the history of the world, the single most dominant constant has been change. There are those who favoured and welcomed change . . . and there are those who have fought and disavowed change. As one considers the various peoples who comprise the population of the world today, the disparity among those peoples is enormous.

Those peoples of the world who disdained and disavowed change continue to live in difficult situations under restrictive governance. They lack good health, education, longevity, freedom, and creature comforts which others take for granted. Many continue to live under tribal, feudal, or religious leadership, and will likely remain uneducated and unable to change their situations. The leadership in such countries will continue to deny any changes to improve their lot, and to restrict their peoples to customs and traditions that have endured for centuries or millennia.

Those peoples who have favoured and welcomed change have done so in difficult circumstances and often at great danger to their lives, families, and careers. They have fought both physically and intellectually for education, equality, and freedom, to improve their situations. There are many examples in the developed nations of the world of the difficulties that individuals have overcome to effect changes in science, commerce, engineering, architecture, governance, law, medicine, music, and many other fields.

The greatest adversaries of change are ignorance, a lack of courage, a lack of vision, and an unyielding adherence to past experience, customs, and traditions. Professional associations, self governing societies, political parties, unions, commercial monopolies, religions, centres of academic learning, and similar organizations must shoulder most of the blame for their obstruction of change within nations. The habitual challenge from such organizations is "Why change? *(i.e. a standard practice or tradition)*".

Western European countries struggled for centuries under feudalism, but changes to more democratic or enlightened governance eventually arrived, and those nations flourished. In 1811 in England, the Luddites attempted to impede the industrial revolution but eventually failed, the change became a reality, and Britain prospered.

The scientific elite initially denied funding to Madame Marie Kowalski Curie for her research into radioactivity. Following her amazing discovery of radium, she was eventually rewarded with generous grants, and finally with a Nobel prize in chemistry. Change came to the scientific community, science survived, and the world benefitted.

Slavery had been practised by aboriginal bands in Canada for centuries, and remained legal under English and French law for years. Changes were successfully resisted by slave owners on grounds that slaves were essential to commerce. Slavery existed in Upper and Lower Canada until 1834, when the British Slavery Abolition Act abolished slavery in all parts of the British Empire. Finally, abolitionists had won their argument: "Why not abolish slavery?" Change came to Canada, the economy survived, and Canada prospered.

Under English common law, women were regarded for years as chattels, yet eventually changes were made to recognize women as persons. In 1929, the Lord Chancellor of the British Privy Council announced the decision that: "Yes, women are persons . . . and eligible to be summoned and may become Members of the Senate of Canada." The Privy Council decision also said; *"that the exclusion of women from all public offices is a relic of days more barbarous than ours. And to those who would ask why the word 'persons' should include females, the obvious answer is, why should it not?"* Change came, and Canada prospered.

Most, and perhaps all of the proposals of this document to unify Canada are sensible, feasible, and beneficial to the people and the nation: "Why NOT change?"

For those who have no vision of Canada's future, no explanation is possible.

For those who do have a vision of Canada's future, no explanation is needed.

The Bibliography for Canada in Crisis (1)

An Agenda to Unify the Nation

Preface

The author's goal is to create a book that every Canadian may read and appreciate the process of governance in our nation. Part of that goal was to make such reading easy, without recourse to a computer or a library to learn more about a subject. Traditionally, many books provide their research material only by a numerically annotated reference and attribution of the source. People today generally do not have the time, interest, energy, or facilities to locate the reference and conduct such research themselves. Hence the author's attempt to provide full-text information, either in the beginning of each chapter for the proper background and context, or in the Bibliography for more additional and extensive reading on a subject. Thus the book may be easily read in the shade or in the sun, on the patio or on the dock at a cottage or resort.

The backgrounds for historic events in each chapter provide extensive information on complex matters which would generally be unfamiliar to most people. Those backgrounds are meant to provide reasonably reliable information of historic events. The backgrounds are attributed to such sources as Wikipedia which in turn were often from academic sources, the Canadian federal Department of Finance, and other government organizations.

The backgrounds for current events in each chapter express the concerns of the Canadian people in their daily lives. These backgrounds are usually attributed to newspaper articles or opinions written by well known journalists. The references show that the readers may not be alone in forming similar opinions on the subject matter. These current event citations should also assure the governments at federal, provincial, and municipal levels as to which issues concern the people of Canada, as well as the opinions of the people on those issues.

The governance of our nation is forever changing, hopefully for the better, but not always. Where the change is neither understood, nor found acceptable, the governments should be aware of the sentiments of the people, especially before the election of new governments.

And lastly, the author trusts that his suggestions and proposals have been made on the basis of reliable information, observation, simple truths and common sense. Given proper knowledge of history and events, one might say, "Don't let the obvious (solutions) elude you."

One Country

Canada's Lands and People

From Wikipedia; lightly edited and formatted:
http://en.wikipedia.org/wiki/Canada

Canada is a country, mostly north of the 49th parallel and the Great Lakes of North America, extending from the Atlantic in the east, to the Pacific in the west, and to the Arctic in the north. It is the world's second largest country with a total area of 9,984,670 km² of which almost 9% is water, and shares land borders with the United States to the south and northwest.

The land occupied by Canada was inhabited for millennia by various aboriginal peoples. Beginning in the late 15th century, British and French expeditions explored and later settled the Atlantic coast. In 1763 after the Seven Years' War, France ceded all of its colonies in North America, except the two small islands of St Pierre and Miquelon off Newfoundland. In 1867, with the union of three British North American colonies through Confederation, Canada was formed as a federal dominion of four provinces. The addition of more provinces and territories led to increasing autonomy from the United Kingdom, culminating in the Canada Act in 1982 which severed the last vestiges of legal dependence upon the British parliament.

A federation now comprising ten provinces and three territories, Canada is a parliamentary democracy and a constitutional monarchy. It is a multicultural country, with both English and French as official languages at the federal level. Technologically advanced and

139

industrialized, Canada maintains a diversified economy that is heavily reliant on its abundant natural mineral and water resources, gold, silver, iron, copper, zinc, molybdenum, diamonds, potash, and especially the oil, gas, and tar sands. It is a member of the G8, NATO, and the Commonwealth of Nations. Canada fought valiantly in World War I (1914-1918), World War II (1939-1945), finished that war with one of the largest armed forces in the world, and was one of the first countries to join the UN. Canada fought in Korea 1950-1953, and is currently serving in many other countries under UN or NATO mandates.

The recent influx of people to Canada began with the French and English settlers in the 1700's. Others soon followed over the centuries, from Portugal, Spain, Iceland, Germany, Poland, Russia, Czechoslovakia, Hungary, Italy, Holland, Belgium, Scandinavia, the Balkans, and other western European countries. These settlers were entirely from Christian religions and European cultures. Following the new Immigration Acts introduced in 1967 and 1976, and official multiculturalism in 1971, waves of non-European immigration changed the face of the country. Peoples from the mid-East, Asia, Africa, and South America joined the previous settlers, primarily in urban centres of Vancouver, Toronto, and Montreal. The variety of religions and cultures, (Christianity, Islam, Hinduism, Buddhism, Judaism, Confucianism, Taoism, Shinto), and governments of the peoples from these countries expanded within a milieu charged with the responsibility of mutual respect and tolerance.

The Constitution of Canada

From Wikipedia; lightly edited and formatted:
http://en.wikipedia.org/wiki/Constitution_of_Canada

The Constitution of Canada (La Constitution du Canada in French) is the supreme law in Canada; the country's constitution is an amalgamation of codified acts and uncodified traditions and conventions. It outlines Canada's system of government, as well as the civil rights of all Canadian citizens.

The composition of the Constitution of Canada is defined in subsection 52(2) of the Constitution Act, 1982 as consisting of the Canada Act 1982 (including the Constitution Act, 1982), all acts and orders referred to in the schedule (including the Constitution Act, 1867, formerly the British North America Act), and any amendments to these documents. The Supreme Court of Canada held that the list is not exhaustive and includes unwritten doctrines as well.

Constitutional History of Canada

The first semblance of a Constitution for Canada was the Royal Proclamation of 1763. The Act renamed Canada "The Province of Quebec" and redefined its borders and established a British-appointed colonial government. The proclamation was considered the de facto constitution of Quebec until 1774 when the British government passed the Quebec Act of 1774 which set out many procedures of governance in the area of Quebec. It extended the boundaries of the colony and adopted the British criminal code among other things.

The colony of Canada received its first full constitution in the Constitutional Act of 1791 which established much of the composition of the government. This was later superseded by the British North America Act in 1867 which established the Dominion of Canada. This Act gave all dominion countries equal legislative authority with the United Kingdom. This was followed up in 1982, when the British Parliament passed the Canada Act, 1982 ((UK) 1982, c.11) giving up all remaining constitutional and legislative authority over Canada.

In 1931, the British Parliament passed the Statute of Westminster, 1931 (22 Geo. V, c.4 (UK)). This Act gave all dominion countries within the Empire legislative authority equal to and independent from the United Kingdom. From 1931, the British Government's only remaining role in Canadian affairs was to make amendments as requested to the Canadian Constitution, which was still an Act of the United Kingdom. In 1982, Canada agreed on an amendment formula and the British Parliament passed the Canada Act, 1982 ((UK) 1982, c.11) giving up all remaining constitutional and legislative authority over Canada. The enactment of the Canada Act is often referred to in Canada as the 'patriation' of the constitution and it was largely due to the work of Pierre Elliot Trudeau, the Prime Minister of Canada at the time. The Canada Act also entrenched the Canadian monarchy, and Queen Elizabeth II as Queen of Canada signed the Constitution proclamation in Ottawa in 1982.

With the introduction of the Canada Act and the accompanying Charter, much of Constitutional law in Canada has changed. The Canada Act has entrenched many constitutional conventions and has made amendments significantly more difficult (see amendment formula). The Charter has shifted the focus of the Constitution to individual and collective rights of the inhabitants of Canada. Before the enactment of the Canadian Charter of Rights and Freedoms in 1982, civil rights and liberties had no solid constitutional protection in Canada. Whenever one level of government passed a law that seemed oppressive to civil rights and liberties, Canadian constitutional lawyers had to argue creatively, such as by saying that the oppressive law violates division of federal and provincial powers or by citing some other technical flaw that had little to do with the concept of civil rights and liberties. Since 1982, however, the Charter has become the most often cited part of the Constitution and has thus far solidified the protection of rights for people in Canada.

Constitution Act, 1867

This was an Act of the British Parliament, originally called the British North America Act 1867, that created the Dominion of Canada out of three separate provinces in British North America (Province of Canada, New Brunswick, and Nova Scotia) and allowed for subsequent provinces and colonies to join this union in the future. It outlined Canada's system of government, which combines Britain's Westminster model of parliamentary government with division of sovereignty (federalism). Although it is one of many British North America Acts to come, it is still the most famous of these and is understood to be the document of Canadian Confederation (i.e. union of provinces and colonies in British North America). With the patriation of the

Constitution in 1982, this Act was renamed Constitution Act, 1867. In recent years, the Constitution Act, 1867 has mainly served as the basis on which the division of powers between the provinces and federal government have been analyzed.

Constitution Act, 1982

Endorsed by all the provincial governments except Quebec's, this was an Act by the Canadian Parliament requesting full political independence from Britain. Part V of this Act created a constitution-amending formula that did not require an Act by the British Parliament. Further, Part I of this Act is the Canadian Charter of Rights and Freedoms which outlines the civil rights and liberties of every citizen in Canada, such as freedom of expression, of religion, and of mobility. Part II deals with the rights of Canada's Aboriginal peoples.

Canadian Charter of Rights and Freedoms

As noted above, this is Part I of the Constitution Act, 1982. The Charter is the constitutional guarantee of collective and individual rights. It is a relatively short document and written in plain language in order to ensure accessibility to the average citizen. It is said that it is the part of the constitution that has the greatest impact on Canadians' daily lives, and has been the fastest developing area of constitutional law for many years.

Amending formula

With the Constitution Act, 1982, amendments to the constitution must be done in accordance with Part V of the Constitution Act, 1982 which provides for five different amending formulas. Amendments can be brought forward under section 46(1) by any province or either level of the federal government. The general formula is set out in section 38(1), known as the "7/50 formula", requires: (a) assent from both the House of Commons and the Senate; (b) the approval of two-thirds of the provincial legislatures (at least seven provinces), representing at least 50% of the population (effectively, this would include at least

Quebec or Ontario, as they are the most populous provinces). This formula specifically applies to amendments related to the proportionate representation in Parliament, powers, selection, and composition of the Senate, the Supreme Court and the addition of provinces or territories. The other amendment formulas are for exceptional cases as provided by the Act:

* In the case of an amendment related to the Office of the Queen, the number of senators, the use of either official language (subject to section 43), the amending formula, or the composition of the Supreme Court, the amendment must be adopted by unanimous consent of all the provinces in accordance with section 41.
* However, in the case of an amendment related to provincial boundaries or the use of an official language within a province alone, the amendment must be passed by the legislatures affected by the amendment (section 43).
* In the case of an amendment that affects the federal government alone, the amendment does not need approval of the provinces (section 44). The same applies to amendments affecting the provincial government alone (section 45).

Vandalism of the paper proclamation

In 1983, Toronto artist Peter Greyson entered Ottawa's National Archives (known today as Library and Archives Canada) and poured red paint over a copy of the proclamation of the 1982 constitutional amendment. He said he was displeased with the federal government's decision to allow US missile testing in Canada, and wanted to "graphically illustrate to Canadians" how wrong the government was. A grapefruit-sized stain still remains on the original document. Specialists opted to leave most of the paint intact fearing attempts at removing it would only do further damage.

Sources of the Constitution

There are three general methods of constitutional entrenchment:

1. Specific mention as a constitutional document in section 52(2) of the Constitution Act, 1982, such as the Constitution Act, 1867.

2. Constitutional entrenchment of an otherwise statutory English, British, or Canadian document because of subject matter provisions in the amending formula of the Constitution Act, 1982, such as provisions with regard to the monarchy in the English Bill of Rights 1689 or the Act of Settlement 1701. English and British statutes are part of Canadian law because of the Colonial Laws Validity Act, 1865, section 129 of the Constitution Act, 1867, and the Statute of Westminster 1931. Those laws then became entrenched when the amending formula was made part of the constitution.

3. Reference by an entrenched document, such as the Preamble of the Constitution Act, 1867's entrenchment of written and unwritten principles from the constitution of the United Kingdom or the Constitution Act, 1982's reference of the Proclamation of 1763.

Unwritten sources

The existence of an unwritten constitution was reaffirmed by the Supreme Court in Reference re Secession of Quebec.

The Constitution is more than a written text. It embraces the entire global system of rules and principles which govern the exercise of constitutional authority. A superficial reading of selected provisions of the written constitutional enactment, without more, may be misleading. In practice, there have been three sources of unwritten constitutional law:

Conventions: Constitutional conventions form part of the Constitution, but they are not legally enforceable. They include the existence of the Prime Minister and Parliamentary Cabinet, the fact that the Governor General is required to give assent to Bills, and the requirement that the Prime Minister call an election upon losing a vote of non-confidence.

Royal Prerogative: Reserve powers of the Canadian Crown; being remnants of the powers once held by the British Crown, reduced over time by the Parliamentary system. Primarily, these are the Orders-in-Council which give the Government the authority to declare war, conclude treaties, issue passports, make appointments, make regulations, incorporate, and receive lands that escheat to the Crown.

Unwritten Principles: Principles that are incorporated into the Canadian Constitution by reference from the preamble of the Constitution Act, 1867. Unlike conventions, they are legally binding. Amongst the recognized Constitutional principles are federalism, democracy, constitutionalism and the rule of law, and respect for minorities. Other principles include responsible government, judicial independence and an Implied Bill of Rights. In one case, the Provincial Judges Reference (1997), it was found a law can be held invalid for contradicting unwritten principles, in this case judicial independence.

One Nation

Canada Dream Series

From The National Post 2007/10/27 (p18)   Editorial

We nave a dream. Actually, we have 14 of them - spelled out in the 14 entries in the "Fixing Canada" series that appeared in the National Post comment pages these last two weeks. Each of our 13 authors - and one cartoonist - was asked to describe the single thing about Canada that he or she would change if magically empowered with the prerogatives of benign dictatorship (or, to borrow a less disquieting image from George Jonas' column, a genie's wish).

Some of the topics touch on pressing policy matters, and so their inclusion might have been predicted beforehand. Michael Coren, for instance, offered an impassioned and persuasive plea to remedy's Canada's lack of any sort of abortion law. Andrew Coyne argued for strengthening Canada's economic union by getting rid of internal trade barriers.

Father Raymond de Souza wrote that we should put meaning back into marriage. Both David Asper and Robert Fulford put forward sensible plans to reform our public schools. Mr. Fulford urged an end to the union imposed cult of mediocrity that pervades the education system, while Mr. Asper seeks to empower schools to teach students a "unified national identity."

But several of the entries surprised us. Conrad Black urged that Canadians adopt the confident, winning habits of mind that befit our expanded role and opportunities in a booming world. Colby Cosh noted that Canada would retain more of its fine minds if it were a little warmer - a controversial statement given what it implies about our interest (or lack thereof) in fighting global warming. And Mr. Jonas, who has witnessed his share of misguided government "fixes" on both sides of the Atlantic, suggested the best fix would be to make Canadians stop trying to fix things, since most social engineering plans that have come down the pipe in the last few decades have made things worse.

Indeed, the legacy of this very trend drew the focus of several of the contributors. Karen Selick, for instance, urged the destruction of Canada's Byzantine "human rights" apparatus, which purports to protect various politically fashionable minority groups, but does so at the expense of freedom of contract and private property rights. "These laws are not about banning bigotry," she wrote. "They're about transferring rights and power from the categories of people the legislators deemed over endowed to those the legislators deemed under endowed. They're really a form of wealth redistribution.

Echoing the same principles of classic liberalism, David Frum wrote that he would liberate the airwaves from busybody regulators who seek to squelch potentially offensive opinions. Free speech is the "great lever" that permits all other liberties and reforms to come forward.

Barbara Kay, too, attacked Canada's censorious cult of political correctness. Her focus was the nation's universities, which, she wrote, are run by "leftist ecclesiastics (who) rigorously monitor the four credos from which no dissent is permitted: relativism, feminism, postcolonialism and multiculturalism."

Jonathan Kay also focussed on the toxic notion of group rights. His target was Canada's native reserves, whose impoverished state he called Canada's "signature disgrace." His solution is to eliminate the reserve system as we know it entirely, and replace it with a policy by which natives are treated as individuals - not members of a tribal collective and integrated as such into the mainstream Canadian economy.

Though all of these essays covered disparate themes, they are bound together by a unifying vision: a confident nation where free speech, free trade and freedom of contract are guiding lights; a nation where people are treated as thick skinned individuals who are capable of making their own way in the world, and who must be held responsible for their own decisions, rather than children in need of heavy handed paternalist supervision by a union, band council or government.

The impediment to this vision of Canada is not so much our institutions, which could be changed if the political will existed, but our nation's statist mind set. To quote Lorne Gunter's essay, "We view governments as the guardians of our human rights, failing to appreciate that throughout history governments have been the greatest rights abusers . . . we cheerily pay high taxes in the belief the state can improve our quality of life better than we can ourselves. We accept government pensions that pay one-third the return of private alternatives for fear the market will cheat us, support making farmers sell their wheat to the government's grain department, for their own good, and let regulators choose what we may see on television and listen to on radio in the belief this will somehow make us more of a nation."

This is the attitude that our columnists, and the newspaper they write for, stand against. Notwithstanding the conceit of our Fixing Canada Series, we know that this country cannot be repaired all at one blow. But we also know that sustained pressure from an engaged citizenry and press can help roll back the damage done by decades of heavy handed government policies. Our cartoonist, Gary Clement, may think there are too many pundits in this country. But until Canada is fixed, we beg to differ.

Canada is the Nation

From Wikipedia; lightly edited and formatted:
http://en.wikipedia.org/wiki/Nation

One Nation

A nation is a territory or country as a political entity or a grouping of people who share real or imagined common history, culture, language or ethnic origin, often possessing or seeking its own government. The development and concept of a nation is closely related to the development of modern industrial states and nationalist movements in Europe in the eighteenth and nineteenth centuries, although nationalists would trace nations into the past along uninterrupted lines of historical narrative. Benedict Anderson argued that nations were "imagined communities" because "the members of even the smallest nation will never know most of their fellow members, meet them, or even hear of them, yet in the minds of each lives the image of their communion". Although "nation" is also commonly used in informal discourse as a synonym for state or country, a nation is not identical to a state. Countries where the social concept of "nation" coincides with the political concept of "state" are called nation states.

The concept of a national identity refers both to the distinguishing features of the group, and to the individual's sense of belonging to it. All of the characteristics may be disputed, and opposition to secessionist nationalism often includes the denial that a separate nation exists. Almost all nationalist movements make some claim to shared origins and descent, and it is a component of the national identity in most nations. The fact that the ancestry is shared among the members of the nation unites them, and sets them apart from other nations, which do not share that ancestry. A language is the primary ingredient in the making of a nation. Without a common language a nation cannot evolve. A common culture, a common history is dependent on language.

Also dealing with everyday affairs within a group of people living in a specified boundary needs a common mean of communication to trade and socialize. Many nations are constructed around the idea of a shared culture, the national culture. The national culture may be assumed to be shared with previous generations, and includes a cultural heritage from these generations. As with the common ancestry, this identification of past culture with present culture may be largely symbolic. A nation may be constructed around a common history or chronologically recorded events in the past, which their ancestors have endured. Religion is sometimes a defining factor for a nation, although some nationalist movements such as those in Ireland de-emphasize it as a divisive factor.

A state which identifies itself explicitly as the home of a cultural nation is a nation state. Many modern states try to legitimize their existence in this way, although there might be disputes as to the appropriateness of this. Because so many of the states are nation states, the words "nation", "country", and "state" are often used synonymously.

The First Nations & Sovereignty

Globe & Mail 2009/08/25   by Jeffery Simpson

First Nations aren't big enough for true sovereignty.

Pouce Coupe, British Columbia, has a population of about 700 people. Gravenhurst, Ontario, boasts about 11,000 people. Estevan, Saskatchewan, has a population of about 10,000.

Would we think it fair, plausible, desirable or doable to give Gravenhurst, let alone Pouce Coupe, the responsibilities that go with provincial sovereignty - justice, schooling, health, policing, roads, welfare? Of course we wouldn't, nor would the people of those communities expect it. Their numbers would be too small, their tax bases too constrained, their capacities too limited. We wouldn't do it and they wouldn't ask, not because there aren't good and capable people in those communities, but because the numbers would defeat their best efforts.

We have something like this dilemma in aboriginal policy, dealing with first nation demands for sovereignty, political status and other attributes that normally accompany "nationhood." The Indian Register, while not perfect, is arguably the best source available for registered Indian numbers. (The census is another source, but some reserves refuse to co-operate with it, and there have been scattered disputes about it.) While the Register's numbers might be off, it's usually by only a little. The Register does convey the general sense of where Indians live, on reserves and off, although many first nations people move on and off their own reserves. What does it show?

The average size of a band, or first nation, across Canada is 1,260 people, about twice the size of Pouce Coupe but just a little over 10 per cent the population of Estevan. Eighteen per cent of all bands have populations above 2,000. There are 19 bands, or nations, with populations above 5,000. The rest of the Register breakdown: 21 per cent between 1,000 and 1,999; 27 per cent between 500 and 999; 18 per cent between 250 and 499; 12 per cent between 100 and 249; 3 per cent with fewer than 100.

Be careful with nomenclature. An Indian nation, such as the Cree or Mohawk, can contain a number of communities, and therefore collectively be much larger than a division by reserve would indicate. Another warning: The population of a band should not be confused with how many people live on a reserve. For example, Shawn Atleo, the newly elected grand chief of the Assembly of First Nations, comes from the Ahousaht First Nation. The Register lists a population of 1,876, but only 676 people actually live on the reserve on the west coast of Vancouver Island.

For many decades now, aboriginal leaders have used the "nation" terminology to describe Indian groups, because they have the characteristics of a nation: language (in many cases now lost), cultural specificity, a historical sense of distinctiveness, defined territory (shrunken drastically from centuries ago). With that discourse have come demands for more land and funding, new treaties or respect for old ones, and the delivery by the "nation" of services to its members.

These are all understandable goals, but they crash repeatedly against the reality of numbers. Just as Pouce Coupe, no matter how much better funded, cannot deliver the same range of services a "sovereign nation" expects, neither can the 77 first nations listed in the Register with populations between 600 and 800. In some cases, the numbers also crash against the realities of geography, since many reserves are isolated from larger population centres, difficult to service and situated on land with limited economic potential.

We have been living a myth in aboriginal policy: that "nations," in the sociological sense of the word, can be effective "sovereign" entities, in the sense of doing what sovereign governments are expected to do. When the population of a "nation" is a few hundred people, or even a few thousand, we are kidding ourselves, whether aboriginal or non-aboriginal, if we think that sovereignty can be anything more than partial.

The Inuit of Nunavut and the Dene of the Northwest Territories have populations that make the claim of sovereignty a real one, although Nunavut's terrible disappointment is a lack of formally educated Inuit to run their own administration. Prime Minister Stephen Harper was right last week in saying that aboriginals should staff more of their own institutions. Alas, the small populations of most first nations will make that ambition difficult or impossible, declarations of sovereignty notwithstanding.

The Nation of Canada & First Nations

Excerpt from The National Post 2009/06/08
John Carpay and Jeffrey Rustand

A 'seismic shift'? Most certainly.

Shortly before his re-election, BC Premier Gordon Campbell backed away from his controversial plan to give aboriginal peoples de facto control over the province's land and resources. But a fresh mandate from voters will likely have the Premier trying to revive the plan, which was announced in the government's Throne Speech in February.

In February, the provincial government and the First Nations Leadership Council agreed in a joint discussion paper to support new legislation to recognize 30 "reconstituted" indigenous (aboriginal) nations, and divide BC into 30 aboriginal territories, each with its own aboriginal government and aboriginal laws. This "Recognition and Reconciliation Act" would also recognize that these indigenous nations have aboriginal title throughout British Columbia, including the power to make laws.

British Columbia lacks the constitutional jurisdiction to accomplish Mr. Campbell's proposals. His plans amount to a constitutional amendment creating a new order of government that is neither federal nor provincial nor municipal; the plans are directed at aboriginal matters, which are an exclusively federal area of jurisdiction.

The proposed act would extend aboriginal title over all or most of the province. Aboriginal title includes the right to exclusive occupation and land management, and entitlement to rents, such that 30 indigenous nations would have effective ownership over most of BC. This is fatally flawed because aboriginal title, as defined by the Supreme Court of Canada, gives aboriginal peoples only a fraction of the province's land base: those areas over which they can prove continuing and exclusive occupation. Aboriginal title does not include the power to make laws.

Every provincial government ministry and agency would be subject to the act, which will take priority over all provincial statutes concerning land and resources. In the result, the act would require British Columbia to treat aboriginal peoples as if they had ownership of the province and their own tier of government with law making powers.

Aboriginal peoples would be treated as if they had ownership of the province.

It is one thing for the provincial government to refer to aboriginal peoples as "nations" in the ethnic or cultural sense of that word. But it is another thing entirely for the provincial government to recognize the existence of aboriginal governments and aboriginal laws passed by those governments, and to establish "government-to-government" relations as called for in the Throne Speech and the discussion paper.

Gordon Campbell's proposed act would also give these new aboriginal governments shared decision making power with the provincial government regarding the economic development of lands and resources. This power would be very real, providing the new layer of aboriginal government with a potential veto over new economic activity anywhere in BC. The legislation would lay the foundation for a whole new set of compensation claims, and would create mechanisms for "revenue sharing" to divert revenues from taxes and royalties to the aboriginal governments.

Supporters of this new act may argue that this legislation is no more than a symbolic gesture of recognition that facilitates consultations. It is much more than that. The existing legal rights of British Columbians under current law, including property law, will inevitably be denied, infringed or diminished. And there will of course be massive confusion and uncertainty in business circles. It would indeed be the "seismic shift" promised by Michael de Jong, British Columbia's Minister for Aboriginal Affairs.

The act would create a system of dual competing governments. First, British Columbia's constitutionally valid government and law. Second, an extra-constitutional network of aboriginal government and its laws. The first would subject itself, and thereby all British Columbians, to the claims and powers of the second, thereby creating a real-life catch-22 situation for public officials, investors, industry leaders and citizens. Virtually all economic activities in British Columbia would be affected, because the land title and decision making powers given to the "reconstituted nations" and their governments would strike at the heart of property rights, the rule of law and other fundamental pillars of prosperity.

While the act will almost certainly be struck down by the courts for violating Canada's constitution, it would bring long-standing damage to British Columbia's reputation as a good place to invest and create new jobs. Citizens should equip themselves with knowledge of their Constitution in order to prevent governments from embarking on destructive adventures like this one.

National Post Lawyers John Carpay and Jeffrey Rustand are, respectively, Executive Director and in-house Counsel of the Canadian Constitution Foundation.

History of Rupert's Land

From The Olive Tree Genealogy; lightly edited and formatted:
http://www.olivetreegenealogy.com/can/ont/hist.shtml

The History of Ontario
Researched and written by Lorine McGinnis Schulze
Copyright © 1996

Understanding the geographical changes in Ontario's borders can assist anyone researching in Ontario. The following is a brief overview of the changes in boundaries and name changes for present day Ontario.

* In 1615 Champlain and Brule explored what is now southern Ontario.
* Present day northern Ontario was part of the territory given to the Hudson's Bay Company.
* In 1673 Frontenac founded Cataraqui (near present day Kingston)
* The British captured Fort Niagara in 1759
* Prior to December 26, 1791 Ontario was known as the Western part of the Montreal District of the Colony of Quebec.
* 1783 saw the arrival of the first United Empire Loyalists (UEL)
* In 1788 present day southern Ontario was divided into four districts: Hesse, Lunenburg, Mecklenburg and Nassau
* In 1791 the colony of Quebec was divided into the two provinces of Upper and Lower Canada. Upper Canada (now Ontario) was all that land lying west of the Ottawa River, while Lower Canada (now Quebec) was all the land lying east.
* In 1792 the first parliament began. The four original district names were changed. Hesse became the Western District; Lunenburg became the Eastern district; Mecklenburg became the Midland district and Nassau became the Home District.
* In 1800 the districts were divided into counties

* In 1812 war broke out with the United States (The War of 1812). At this time approximately 2/3 of the population of present day Ontario were non-loyalists who had been attracted by offers of free land
* In 1813 during The War of 1812, the town of York (present day Toronto) was burned. Newark (Niagara) was also burned. Many records were lost.
* 1815 saw large immigration from Scotland to Lanark County.
* 1820-1850 saw large numbers of immigrants from Great Britain
* 1833 saw over 66,000 British immigrants arrive, many via the Erie Canal from the port of New York
* In 1842 Upper and Lower Canada united to form the Province of Canada. Upper Canada (present-day Ontario) became known as Canada West while Lower Canada (present day Quebec) became known as Canada East. For complete details consult Districts of Canada West in 1846
* In 1843 fire destroyed government records at York
* In 1867 Upper Canada, or Canada West was given the name of the province of Ontario. It was one of four original provinces at the time of Canadian Confederation on July 1, 1867.
* 1868 The Rupert's Land Act admitted it to the Dominion of Canada. Rupert's Land was originally owned by Hudson's Bay Company and consisted of part of the present day provinces of Ontario and Quebec North of the Laurentians and West of Labrador; all of Manitoba; most of Saskatchewan; the southern half of Alberta; the eastern part of Nunavut Territory; and portions of Minnesota and North Dakota in the United States.
* In 1912 Ontario's boundaries moved northward to Hudson Bay
* In 1916 fire destroyed the Centre Block of the Parliament Buildings in Ottawa

Rupert's Land and Quebec

From Wikipedia: lightly edited and formatted:
http://en.wikipedia.org/wiki/Rupert%27s_Land

Rupert's Land, also sometimes called "Prince Rupert's Land", was a territory in British North America, consisting of the Hudson Bay drainage basin, that was nominally owned by the Hudson's Bay Company for 200 years from 1670 to 1870, although numerous aboriginal groups lived in the same territory and disputed the sovereignty of the area. The area once known as Rupert's Land is now mainly a part of Canada, but a small portion is now in the United States of America. It was named after Prince Rupert of the Rhine, a nephew of Charles I and the first Governor of the Hudson's Bay Company.

Areas once belonging to Rupert's Land include all of Manitoba, most of Saskatchewan, southern Alberta, southern Nunavut, northern parts of Ontario and Quebec, as well as parts of Minnesota and North Dakota and very small parts of Montana and South Dakota.

The Hudson's Bay Company and the Fur Trade

In 1670, the Hudson's Bay Company (HBC) was granted a charter by King Charles II, giving it a trading monopoly over the watershed of all rivers and streams flowing into Hudson Bay, thereby making the HBC owners of the whole of Rupert's Land (named in honour of Prince Rupert of the Rhine, the king's cousin and the company's first governor). This covered an area of 3.9 million square kilometres (1.5 million sq mi), over one-third the area of Canada today.

The Hudson's Bay Company dominated women in Rupert's Land during the 18th-19th centuries and drew on the local population for many of its employees. This necessarily meant the hiring of many indigenous and Métis workers. Fuchs (2002) discusses the activities of these workers and the changing attitudes that the company had toward them. George Simpson, one of the most noted company administrators, held a particularly dim view of mixed-blood workers and kept them from attaining positions in the company higher than postmaster. Later administrators, such as James Anderson and Donald Ross, sought avenues for the advancement of indigenous employees.

Morton (1962) reviews the pressures at work on that part of Rupert's Land where Winnipeg now stands, a decade before its incorporation into Canada. It was a region completely given over to the fur trade, divided between the Hudson's Bay Company and private traders. There was strong business and political agitation in Upper Canada for annexing the territory; in London the Company's trading license was due for review; in St. Paul there was a growing interest in the area as a field for U.S. expansion. The great commercial depression of 1857 dampened most of the outside interests in the territory, which itself remained comparatively prosperous.

Rupert's Land and The Law

Baker (1999) uses the Red River Settlement in the "District of Assiniboia" south of Lake Winnipeg, the only non-native settlement on the Canadian Prairies for most of the 19th century, as a site for critical exploration of the meaning of "law and order" on the Canadian frontier and for an investigation of the sources from which legal history might be rewritten as the history of legal culture. Previous historians have assumed that the Hudson's Bay Company's representatives designed and implemented a local legal system dedicated instrumentally to the protection of the company's fur trade monopoly and, more generally, to strict control of settlement life in the company's interests. But this view is not borne out by archival research. Examination of Assiniboia's juridical institutions in action reveals a history formed less through the imposition of authority from above than by obtaining support from below. Baker shows that the legal history of the Red River Settlement - and, by extension, of the Canadian West in general - is a story of local legal culture in formation, dependent for its viability on community notions of law, justice, and reason.

Following the forced merger of the North West Company with the HBC in 1821, British Parliament applied the laws of Upper Canada to Rupert's Land and the Columbia District and gave enforcement power to the HBC. The Hudson's Bay Company maintained peace in Rupert's Land for the benefit of the fur trade; the Plains Indians had achieved a rough balance of power between themselves; the organization of the Métis provided internal security and a degree of external protection. This stable order broke down in the 1860s with the decline of the Hudson's Bay Company, the arrival of smallpox and trade-whiskey, and the disappearance of the bison. Anarchy was prevented by the creation of the North-West Mounted Police. But the basic need was for capital to convert to a farming economy and this did not come until the railway opened the area to settlers.

Rupert's Land and Aboriginal People

In 1857, a British parliamentary select committee investigated the Hudson's Bay Company. In the course of its hearings, the committee often directed its attention to Rupert's Land's First Nations. Despite an obvious polarization between supporters and opponents of the company on many issues, a consensus emerged on the fate of Rupert's Land's indigenous citizens in what all presumed to be the inevitable European settlement of the Plains and adjacent woodlands. Hudson's Bay Company officials and their opponents shared the paternalistic assumption, based on 19th-century liberalism, that the Native peoples would be unable to cope with the onslaught of a supposedly superior, modern, and educated population. Without consulting the objects of their concerns, the participants at the committee's hearings agreed that it was the task of the state and church to protect the aboriginal nations and educate them into the new order. On this point, the committee's report was an important omen for the subsequent history of western Canada's Native inhabitants.

Although it is widely assumed that the royal charter that granted the land to the Hudson's Bay Company in 1670 encompassed the entire territory, international law supports the argument that the company only had sovereignty over the relatively small portion it actually possessed and controlled. Court cases in the following centuries involving continuing aboriginal claims to the land reflected the government's ethnocentric view that the Indians had no sovereignty rights. Latter 20th-century rulings, however, have held that the Hudson's Bay Company never had the rightful sovereignty to return the land to the British government, which in turn gave it to Canada. The key question is whether the Crown gained sovereignty of the land in 1670 or later in a series of treaties signed between Canada and the aboriginal nations from 1871 and 1921. The problem of aboriginal claims is further complicated by the fact that the aboriginal nations that occupied the land involved in the treaties were not the same ones that occupied it in 1670 when the British initially claimed sovereignty.

Quebec and Secession

Excerpt from the National Post 2010/02/19

by Lorne Gunter

My Canada can take or leave Quebec

I have long had a sort of hands off approach to Quebec sovereignty. Let them stay or let them go, it's their decision, just so long as they appreciate the consequences of either action. Last weekend, after it was reported that several Quebecers complained to the federal language commissioner about the perceived lack of French at the opening ceremonies of the Vancouver Olympics, there were scores of nasty posts made on major newspapers' websites by English Canadians wanting the ingrates tossed from Confederation. "Evict Quebec, then all of this crying, whining and nonsense will stop" was typical.

While I understand this sentiment, it is not mine.

While I, too, have experienced the frustration over the years of being held hostage by the shrew wife antics of successive Quebec premiers, "If you loved us, you'd know what we want", my bile has never risen to the level where I was prepared to call for a referendum in the rest of

Canada over whether to let Quebec stay. But neither am I of the "My Canada includes Quebec," crowd, the hand wringing, sentimental, two founding nations types who think it proves something about their own tolerance and sophistication if they accede to every one of the province's nationalist demands.

Rather, I look on Confederation as a more of family. Just as it would be unwise to try and force an independent minded young adult to keep living in the basement when what he wants is his own apartment, it would be corrosive to insist Quebec stay in Canada if at some point it wants to be its own state. However, just as the stay at home offspring may chafe at the optics of having to live just off the rumpus room at his age, I think that Quebecers have come to understand that for all the perceived indignities they must endure as a province, rather than an independent nation, their lives are pretty good. Their lives would be tougher on their own.

The family's a little dysfunctional, but it's not any worse than any other on the block and, besides, the life style is pretty good. Moving out would mean smaller accommodations, no access to family assets, the end of home cooking and free laundry, and no more money.

I think this understanding that Canada may not be perfect, but it's not that bad, has slowly crept into the Quebec subconscious, which is why sovereignty has ceased to be a hot topic in recent years. That understanding may also be behind Lucien Bouchard's assertion on the weekend that "sovereignty is not achievable," at least not in his lifetime.

The former leader of the Bloc Quebecois and the former Parti Quebecois premier of Quebec remains the only person capable of leading Quebec out of Confederation, as he almost did in 1995 during the last separatist referendum. Thankfully for Confederation, Bouchard seems to have come the realization during the past decade that Quebecois political culture, as it is now, is too narrow-minded to survive on its own. Before Quebec can leave and thrive, its economic nationalism and cultural nativism must be reformed.

It has to be remembered that Mr. Bouchard stepped down as premier in 2001 at least in part because he could no longer stomach the xenophobes and anti-Semites in his own party. While many Quebecers are among the most tolerant Canadians, there is still a large "pure laine" element within the sovereignist movement that wants an independent Quebec precisely so it can limit the influence of Jews, anglophones and immigrants.

Mr. Bouchard was not above a little nativism of his own, particularly on language laws. Nonetheless, his contention that an independent Quebec would be a bleak place if it were based primarily on the need to suppress all cultures except that of the Quebecois is a valid one. An inward looking country of Quebec would eventually choke on its own suspicions.

Mr. Bouchard's remarks this past weekend are also in keeping with the manifesto he signed in 2005 calling on Quebecers to work harder, trade more and seek higher education as a way to create the economic conditions that would sustain Quebec, whether or not it eventually chose its own path or stayed in Canada. I hope Quebec never leaves Confederation. I hope it adopts Mr. Bouchard's recommendations for an open culture and a free trade economy and remains a vital part of Canada. Still, if it eventually does go, Quebecers must know that leaving to become an socialist, nationalist museum exhibit is a recipe for decay.

Quebec Sovereignty Movement

From Wikipedia; lightly edited and formatted:
http://en.wikipedia.org/wiki/Quebec_sovereignty_movement

Introduction

The Quebec sovereignty movement or Quebec rebellion (French: Mouvement souverainiste du Québec) refers to the history and present status of multiple, multi-lateral political movements aimed at attaining statehood for the Canadian province of Quebec. Supporters of the movement advocate a variety of proposals. While some sovereignists do advocate full independence, others have advocated sovereignty association or sovereignty partnership, under which Quebec, while becoming a country of its own, would still continue to maintain an economic and political relationship with Canada. The association or partnership with Canada does not mean that Quebec would still be a part of Canada; it would create a new relationship between two sovereign states.

In practice, "separatist" and "sovereignist" are terms used to describe individuals wanting the province of Quebec to separate from Canada to become a country of its own. However, the former term is perceived as pejorative for people related with the movement.

The most apparent justification for Quebec's sovereignty is its unique culture and its French speaking majority (80%) in contrast to the rest of Canada, which consists of eight overwhelmingly (greater than 90%) English speaking provinces. New Brunswick is officially bilingual and about one-third Francophone. The territory of Nunavut primarily speaks Inuktitut, a central justification for that territory's creation, splitting from the Northwest Territories (which is far more multi-lingual). With regards to the creation of the sovereignist movement, language issues were but a sub-stratum of larger cultural, social and political differences. Many scholars point to historical events as framing the cause for ongoing support for sovereignty in Quebec, while more contemporary pundits and politicians may point to the aftermath of more recent developments like the Canada Act of 1982, the Meech Lake Accord or the Charlottetown Accord.

Overview

Supporters of sovereignty for Quebec believe that the current relationship between the province of Quebec and Canada doesn't reflect Quebec's social, political and economic development. Moreover, many ascribe to the notion that without appropriately recognizing that the people of Quebec are culturally distinct, Quebec will remain chronically disadvantaged in favour of the English Canadian majority. There is also the question of whether the French language can survive within the geographic boundaries of Quebec and where French Canadian society and culture impact what is an inherently multi-cultural country. Further, given Canada's modern founding as a French colony and the constant and consistent influence of French Canadian culture and society on Canada's historical development, it becomes increasingly difficult to determine whether Canada could exist at all without Quebec.

Separatists and Independentists are generally opposed to the present federal system in Canada and do not believe it can be reformed in a way that could satisfy the needs of Quebec's French speaking majority. A key component in the argument in favour of overt political independence is that new legislation and a new system of governance could best secure the future development of modern Québécois culture. Additionally, there is wide ranging debate as to defence, monetary policy, currency, international trade and relations and whether renewed federalism - a process which would give political recognition to the Quebec nation (in as much as other 'founding' nations, such as Canadian Natives and Inuit in addition to British Islanders) could satisfy the historic disparities between these cultural nations and create a more cohesive and egalitarian Canada.

Several attempts at reforming the federal system of Canada have thus far failed because of the conflicting interests between the sovereignists' representatives and the other provincial governments' representatives (see Constitutional debate of Canada). There is also a degree of resistance throughout Quebec and the rest of Canada to re-open constitutional debate for a number of reasons, in part, because of the nature of these failures, not all of which were the result simply of sovereignists and federalists not getting along.

To cite one case, in a recent round of constitutional reform (see the Meech Lake Accord), Elijah Harper, an aboriginal leader from Manitoba, was able to prevent ratification of the agreement in the provincial legislature, arguing that the accord did not address the interests of Canada's aboriginal population. This was a move to recognize that other provinces represent distinct cultural entities, such as the aboriginal population in Canada's Prairies or the people of Newfoundland (which contains significant and culturally distinct French Canadian, English Canadian, Irish Canadian and Aboriginal cultures).

The Absurdity of the Bloc

From the National Post, 2010/04/09

by Rex Murphy

The following is a transcript of Rex Murphy's Point of View commentary from the April 8 broadcast of The National on CBC Television.

It's a little puzzling that Giles Duceppe, the leader of the separatist Bloc Quebecois, is on a tour of the alien nation of Canada. He was in Newfoundland a few nights ago telling my crowd that we were once a nation, too. That's not news: It's a lonely Newfoundlander who doesn't already know Newfoundland went from nation to Commission to province a little over half a century ago. I don't suppose Mr. Duceppe found it agreeable to give equal prominence to the fact that we chose the' Canadian route.

It's natural for Mr. Duceppe to tell us we can separate, but awkward I suppose that Newfoundlanders actually made the choice to join Canada. Just as it as awkward that our federal system is so flexible that it incorporates within its federal parliament as federal politicians, a movement, a Bloc, of 50 members of parliament, whose function in that parliament is essentially to bring it, and the federalism it represents, to an end.

Those who recall Lincoln's prophetic words House divided against itself cannot stand - must sometimes wonder how federal Canada can be so "broad" about its own interests. The existence of the Bloc in the federal parliament, apart from being, in my view, a constitutional oxymoron, is now sanctioned by time and usage. We've grown accustomed to their place. We wear the oxymoron - federal parliamentary separatists - as one of those badges of extended tolerance that Canadians strangely cherish.

I doubt, however, that Mr. Duceppe's tour will deal with how a band of separatists in a federal Parliament works inescapable injury to our federal system; how the existence of a "sovereignist" movement in federal elections almost necessarily impedes the formation of real national governments - certainly of representative majorities. How our federal parliament has to "work around" a concentrated grouping of declared separatists (whom Duceppe absurdly likened to the "French resistance" of the Second World War) in forging genuine national policies. This is one of the epic curiosities of that broad tolerance: We actively subsidize the weakening of our own federal system. We pay federal salaries and offer federal pensions to activist anti-federalists.

The "sovereignitst" presence in federal elections impedes the formation of real national governments.

There's something of a game about all this. Separatist politicians get a couple of decades as Canadian federal politicians; the Quebec "fact" gets more political leverage than other regions of the country; we, Canadians in general, get to look ever so tolerant. But the cost is a system that is structurally impaired. A lack of coherence in our federal Parliament, and a succession of minority governments unable to forge a real national agenda. These would be nice items for Mr. Duceppe to address on his farewell tour of the disappointing country he is so anxious to leave - as they certainly haven't been in any real sense for the majority of his term as a "resister" in the federal House of Commons over the last 20 years.

Rex Murphy offers commentary weekly on CBC TV's The National, and is host of CBC Radio's Cross Country Checkup.

The Coalition & Quebec

From Galganov.com by Howard Galganov; lightly edited and formatted:
http://www.galganov.com/editorials.asp?id=1073

I received an interview request from a reporter with the Journal de Montreal Newspaper (December 3, 2008) the day before Harper's meeting with the Governor General. She wanted to know my reaction to the proposed Coalition between the NDP, Liberals and the Bloc Quebecois. For those of you who don't know much or anything about the Journal de Montreal, it is a French language daily that is the closest thing Quebec has to a 'national newspaper'. It is also a very racist Quebecois nationalist rag, to the point of being Quebec's Separatist cheerleader.

During my QPAC days in Quebec, the Journal de Montreal liked to refer to me in their headlines as l'Anglohone Juif Galganov. In translation: Anglo Jew Galganov. Where was the Human Rights Commission then? The Journal de Montreal can best be described as a sensationalist tabloid that mixes gossip, sports and news. It should also be noted that more than a million French Quebecers read the Journal de Montreal every day.

The reporter expected me to answer her question with a degree of outrage towards this coalition, so imagine her surprise when I told her that I was all for it? She asked if I was kidding? How could I possibly be for a federal political union that includes the Bloc Quebecois? She was more surprised with my answer when I told her that this coalition between Socialists and Separatists will not last beyond a month or so, and will guarantee two unexpected and unintended consequences.

The first consequence will be the end of any hopes for Leftist electoral victories for either the Liberals or the Socialist NDP for a generation or more to come, freeing Canada from the type of freebie leftist policies that are destroying the fabric of our country.

The next consequence really shook her when I explained that a coalition with the Quebec Separatist Bloc would hasten the departure of Quebec from Confederation, allowing Canada to finally grow without the Quebec anchor around our neck. The interview became more of a discussion as she asked me if I thought the rest of Canada would throw Quebec out. And if they did, why would they do that now and not before?

My answer stunned her even more. And from the sound of her voice, she was more than somewhat depressed when I explained to her that Canada does not need Quebec. More to the point, Canada will be far better off without Quebec. It is Quebec that needs Canada, since Quebec brings nothing to the table other than threats, costs and complications that hinder the growth of our country.

I also explained that the rest of Canada didn't need our domestic and foreign policies decided upon by a beggar province. Not to mention that Canada's official bilingualism policies are discriminating against more than 97% of the Canadian population (English speaking) living outside of Quebec. With this proposed coalition, the Bloc will win several big concessions that will include: more money from the rest of Canada, but the rest of Canada is broke. Ontario is a have-not province. And if it isn't yet, it certainly will be soon.

At less than $50 per barrel, and still falling like a lead balloon, Alberta is dying with the lack of demand for its petroleum products, and will not earn enough money to sustain its budgetary goals without cutting programs, raising taxes, or dipping into its Heritage Fund. All of which are akin to cancer for Albertans.

Where else will Quebec expect to get the billions of dollars their deal with the two idiots, Stephane Dion and Taliban Jack have promised? Just imagine the outrage from the West, when Alberta has to write a check to a Separatist province that helped wipeout a government Albertans voted for near unanimously? Just imagine the added outrage from the West when six Quebec Separatists are named to Canada's Senate as part of the deal? Just imagine the boiling over outrage from the West when Quebec Separatists must first vet all of Parliaments business before it can be brought to the floor, much less implemented?

I CAN'T WAIT I TOLD HER!

Then I reminded her that certain inalienable decisions would be made the moment Quebec and Canada part company. By federal law, Canadian Banks and Insurance companies must be headquartered within Canada. There go the banks. By law, airlines cannot pick up and deliver passengers from one national location to another national location unless that airline is headquartered in that nation. Goodbye Air Canada.

Then there's the Canada Export and Development Corporation that underwrites just about all of Bombardier's sales abroad. Goodbye Bombardier along with other federally financed corporations in Quebec. Goodbye all the federal government jobs that disproportionately employ French Quebecers. Especially those who can speak some English.

And Goodbye official bilingualism.

At this point in our conversation, her voice was quite subdued when she asked if I think Canada will push Quebec out the door? No was my response. I think Quebec and Canada will separate from each other much like Czechoslovakia did, when the Czechs and Slovaks both decided to go their separate ways without any fanfare, great debates, referendums or anything else. It just happened, much the way I see it just happening between Canada and Quebec where there will be no reason for Quebec to stay within Canada once the financial tap is closed.

And there will be no reason for Canada to want Quebec within Confederation when the rest of Canada finally learns that we will be far better off without Quebec dragging us down. Even though Harper bought himself and the Conservatives six weeks of political peace by suspending Parliament to the end of January, much of the damage has already been done to the long-term future between Quebec and Canada by this attempted Putsch by the Coalition of Idiots.

The rest of Canada really doesn't care much for what Quebec wants anymore, since the rest of Canada is more concerned with what it needs to stay afloat. I explained to her that I am just one political Blogger out of thousands who are spreading a similar message by asking pertinent questions while bringing demographic facts to the table. And in spite of what the out of touch conventional media seems to think, Quebec's future within Canada is not looking all that good. And that looks pretty good for the rest of Canada. We owe Duceppe, Dion and Taliban Jack our gratitude for finally pushing the envelope too far.

Best Regards . . . Howard Galganov

One Governance

Canada's Governance

From Wikipedia; lightly edited and formatted:
http://en.wikipedia.org/wiki/Government_of_Canada

The Crown of Canada

As per the Constitution Act, 1867, Canada is a constitutional monarchy, wherein the role of the reigning sovereign is both legal and practical. The Crown is regarded as a corporation, with the monarch, vested as she is with all powers of state. The Crown has thus been described as the underlying principle of Canada's institutional unity.

The Canadian monarchy is a federal one in which the Crown is unitary throughout all jurisdictions in the country, with the head of state being a part of all equally. As such, the sovereignty of the federal and provincial regions is passed on not by the Governor General or the federal parliament, but through the overreaching Crown itself. Though singular, the Crown is thus "divided" into eleven legal jurisdictions, or eleven "Crowns"; one federal and ten provincial. A Lieutenant Governor serves as the Queen's representative in each province, carrying out all the monarch's constitutional and ceremonial duties of state on her behalf, not the federal government's or the Governor General's.

Executive Powers

The government is defined by the constitution as the Queen acting on the advice of her Privy Council. However, the Privy Council, comprised mostly of former members of parliament, Chief Justices of the Supreme Court, and other elder statesmen, rarely meets in full. Responsible government requires that those who directly advise the Monarch and Governor General how to exercise the Royal Prerogative be accountable to the elected House of Commons. The day to day operation of government is guided only by a sub-group of the Privy Council made up of individuals who hold seats in parliament. This body of Ministers of the Crown is known as the Cabinet.

One of the main duties of the Crown is to "ensure that a democratically elected government is always in place," which means appointing a prime minister, presently Stephen Harper, to head the Cabinet. By convention, the Governor General must appoint as Prime Minister the person who holds the confidence of the House of Commons. In practice, this is typically the leader of the political party that holds more seats than any other party in that chamber, currently the Conservative Party. Should no party hold a majority in the Commons, the leader of one party, either the one with the most seats or one supported by other parties, will be called by the Governor General to form a minority government. Once sworn in by the viceroy, the Prime Minister holds office until he resigns or is removed by the Governor General, either after a motion of no confidence or after his party's defeat in a general election.

The Parliament of Canada

Canada's bicameral legislature, located on Parliament Hill in the national capital of Ottawa, consists of the sovereign, the House of Commons, and the appointed Senate. The Governor General summons and appoints each of the 105 members of the upper house on the advice of his or her Prime Minister, while the 308 members of the lower house are directly elected by eligible voters in the Canadian populace, with each Member of Parliament representing a single electoral district for a period of not more than four years. By democratic tradition, the House of Commons is the dominant branch of parliament, the Senate and Crown rarely opposing its will. The Senate, thus, reviews legislation from a less partisan standpoint, and the monarch and viceroy provide the necessary Royal Assent to make bills into law and summon, prorogue, and dissolve parliament to call an election, and read the Throne Speech.

The Constitution Act 1867, directs that the Governor General alone is responsible for summoning parliament. A parliamentary session lasts until a prorogation, after which both chambers of the legislature cease all legislative business until the Governor General issues another royal proclamation to open a new session. After a number of such sessions, each parliament comes to an end via dissolution. As a general election typically follows, the timing of a dissolution is usually politically motivated with the Prime Minister selecting a moment most advantageous to his or her political party. The end of a parliament may also be necessary if the majority of Members of Parliament revoke their confidence in the Prime Minister's ability to govern, or the legally mandated four year maximum is reached; no parliament has been allowed to expire in such a fashion.

Qualifications of Members of Parliament

From Wikipedia; lightly edited and formatted:
    http://en.wikipedia.org/wiki/House_of_Commons_of_Canada

Under the Constitution Act, 1867, Parliament is empowered to determine the qualifications of members of the House of Commons. The present qualifications are outlined in the Canada Elections Act, which was passed in 2000. Under the act, an individual must be an eligible voter, as of the day on which he or she is nominated, in order to stand as a candidate. Thus, minors and individuals who are not citizens of Canada are not allowed to become candidates. The Canada Elections Act also bars prisoners from standing for election (although they may vote). Moreover, individuals found guilty of election related crimes are prohibited from becoming members for five years (in some cases, seven years) after conviction.

The act also prohibits certain officials from standing for the House of

Commons. These officers include members of provincial and territorial legislatures (although this was not always the case), sheriffs, crown attorneys, most judges, and election officers. The Chief Electoral Officer and Assistant Chief Electoral Officer (the heads of Elections Canada, the federal agency responsible for conducting elections) are prohibited not only from standing as candidates, but also from voting. Finally, under the Constitution Act, 1867, a member of the Senate may not also become a member of the House of Commons and MPs must give up their seats when appointed to the Senate or the bench.

The Canada Elections Act

From the Department of Justice; lightly edited and formatted:
http://laws.justice.gc.ca/eng/E-2.01/page-4.html

PART 6 - CANDIDATES

Qualifications

Ineligible candidates

65. The following persons are not eligible to be a candidate:
    (a) a person who is not qualified as an elector on the date on which his or her nomination paper is filed;
    (b) a person who is disentitled under paragraph 502(3)(a) while they are so disentitled;
    (c) a member of the legislature of a province, the Council of the Northwest Territories or the Legislative Assembly of Yukon or Nunavut;
    (d) a sheriff, clerk of the peace or county Crown Attorney in any of the provinces;
    (e) a person who is not entitled under section 4 to vote;
    (f) a judge appointed by the Governor in Council, other than a citizenship judge appointed under the Citizenship Act;
    (g) a person who is imprisoned in a correctional institution;
    (h) an election officer; and

(i) a person who was a candidate in a previous election and for whom a return, report, document or declaration has not been provided under subsection 451(1), if the time and any extension for providing it have expired.

2000, c. 9, s. 65; 2002, c. 7, s. 92.

Consensus Democracy

From Wikipedia; lightly edited and formatted:
http://en.wikipedia.org/wiki/Consensus_democracy

Consensus democracy is the application of consensus decision making to the process of legislation in a democracy. It is characterised by a decision making structure which involves and takes into account as broad a range of opinions as possible, as opposed to systems where minority opinions can potentially be ignored by vote winning majorities.

Consensus democracy also features increased citizen participation both in determining the political agenda and in the decision making process itself. Developments in information and communication technology may be seen as potential facilitators of such systems.

Consensus democracy is most closely embodied in certain countries such as Switzerland, Lebanon, Sweden and Belgium, where consensus is an important feature of political culture, particularly with a view to preventing the domination of one linguistic or cultural group in the political process. The term consociational state is used in political science to describe countries with such consensus based political systems. An example of such a system could be the Dutch Polder model.

In Canada, the territorial governments of the Northwest Territories and Nunavut also operate on a non-partisan consensus government model, unlike the oppositional political party structure that prevails elsewhere in Canada.

Consensus (non-party) government also operates in Guernsey in the Channel Islands, part of the British United Kingdom. Guernsey also operates a non-ministerial system of government in which government departments are headed not by ministers with executive authority, but by boards or committees of five members. A proposition to introduce executive/cabinet style government was heavily defeated in the States of Deliberation (Guernsey's Parliament) when the matter was last debated in 2002.

Ontario & Consensual Legislature 2008

From Canadian Parliamentary Review; lightly edited and formatted: http://www2.parl.gc.ca/Sites/LOP/Infoparl/english/issue. asp?param=103&art=509

For a Consensual Style of Parliamentary Government
by Vaughan Lyon

At the time this article was written Vaughan Lyon was professor of political studies at Trent University in Peterborough. The following is a précis.

The House of Commons is governed by unwritten conventions and traditions and by its 'statute law' the standing orders. This special statute has a constitutional aspect. It sets out some of the rights of the minority parties in the House of Commons vs the majority party, and the rights of all backbenchers vs the executive. The standing orders may be amended by a simple majority (unlike most constitutional documents), but are regarded as a matter for the whole House to determine.

Objectives of Reform

First, changes in the rules might expedite the adoption of the government's program. While increased efficiency is desirable but not uppermost for reform of Parliament.

Second, procedural reform might reduce excessive power of the executive

/ bureaucratic hierarchy, especially that of the Prime Minister's Office, and strengthen accountability.

Third, rule changes might allow a wider range of elected representatives to contribute to the government program, add authority to programs, add credibility to the House of Commons, and increase public confidence in the representative system.

Each crisis of public authority has been followed by expansion of government, followed by demands for expansion of representation. While not a crisis of democratic legitimacy, public support for the system has been eroded.

First, an MP will have little impact on policy development, and the public is confirmed in its dim view of Parliament by parliamentarians.

Second, regional alienation from Parliament has seldom been as marked, caused by cabinet domination of the Commons.

Obstacles to Reform

Efforts to reform legislatures have been disappointing for three major reasons. First, reformers have not faced the power of the prime minister. Second, reformers neglect a consensual parliament for the adversarial version. Third, reformers have been handicapped by a colonial mental set.

Executive Dominance

The executive will resist most change as inconsistent with its interests. The control of the executive is formidable, and that is the target of most significant reforms.

The pattern of executive dominance has extra-parliamentary and parliamentary dimensions. The prime minister is chosen by the party and beyond the control of the public. For a member to challenge the power of the executive is damaging to his personal and party interests.

The conventions of parliamentary government and the partisan nature of Canadian politics allow the prime minister to demand voting support. The prime minister makes a mockery of representative democracy. It is difficult to reform House rules dominated by the government party. The beneficiary of such efforts is often the executive. The problem of getting reform of executive power past the executive seems intractable.

The Adversarial Model

There is general support for rules to allow MPs to control the executive more effectively. Nor does it seem right that any elected representative be relegated strictly to narrowly defined roles when his reason and the interest of his constituents demand that he shift from one position to another. There is a pervasive but inconsistent idea that one party should be solely responsible for the legislative and administrative record of the government.

A one-party monopoly on policy making is rationalized as being in the public interest. To share that confuse the public about where to place responsibility for political developments. Citizens trying to assess political performance would have to consider; the mess left by predecessors in office, world economic conditions, attitudes of provinces, constitutional restrictions, actions of multinationals, or a disloyal bureaucracy as being responsible for social and economic problems rather than the current government.

After six years of minority government in Ontario (1975 - 81), where opposition and government backbenchers had more direct impact on legislation than ever before, the voters had no difficulty in assessing government performance and assigning responsibility. The electorate would lose little or nothing by wider Commons participation in developing programs, and a great deal could be gained. Broader sharing of responsibility for program development would allow regions better representation in the policy process.

Our exaggeratedly adversarial style of parliamentary government should be firmly rejected in favour of a more open, less partisan model.

The election would indicate the general policy thrust preferred by the public, and would be respected by all parties, but opposition Mps who represent over half the voting population would have more opportunity than now.

The recent minority government in Ontario provides an example of the pattern of government that reforms should seek to institutionalize. The opposition parties insisted that their views on a wide range of issued be reflected in legislation. There was an unprecedented amount of government and opposition consultation on legislation. In moving toward a consensual model, the Ontario legislature gave us a glimpse of a better style of parliamentary government.

We are now engaged in debate about drastically changing the Senate and our electoral system to counter the failure of the House of Commons to represent regional interests.

Colonial Mental Set

All too often proposals for change have been rejected because they represent either creeping Americanism, or departure from tried and true principles of British parliamentary government, instead of being discussed on their merits. The proper goal is an executive more responsive to the legislature.

What Ought to be Done?

The current dominance of the executive must be reduced both by revising existing rules and by altering the 'statute law' of the Commons to include existing conventions.

Confidence and Calling Elections

The cabinet should be prepared to accept defeat of any proposal including financial measures at the hands of the Commons. Revised rules should ensure that the government will lose the confidence of the House only on a specific want-of-confidence motion. Only the passage of such a motion should empower the prime minister to seek dissolution of the House before its term.

Control of the Agenda

It is not appropriate that the government party exercise complete control over the agenda of the Commons. The Speaker should be charged with the responsibility to ensure that bills originating with the opposition or government backbenchers be brought to a vote in the Commons. Where the House leaders are unable to agree on a division of House time between government and opposition, the Speaker should have the casting vote.

Conclusion

The domination of the executive has become overbearing and seriously interferes with the ability of members to represent their constituents and their regions. Reform is long overdue.

Nunavut & Consensual Legislature

From: Canadaonline.about.com; lightly edited and formatted:
        http://canadaonline.about.com/cs/nunavut/a/nunavut.htm

Nunavut - A Canadian Arctic Territory

In 1993, two significant pieces of Canadian legislation were passed leading to the creation of Nunavut, a new Canadian territory in the Arctic. One piece of legislation ratified a land claims agreement with the Inuit of Nunavut and the other set the legal framework for the establishment of the government of the Canadian territory of Nunavut by April 1, 1999.

Nunavut Geography

The word "Nunavut" means "our land" in Inuktitut, the Inuit language. To put the geography of this vast Canadian territory in perspective,

Nunavut covers more than 2 million sq. km, (over 800,000 sq. miles) or approximately one-fifth the total area of Canada. The total population of Nunavut is approximately 29,000, about 80 percent of whom are Inuit. Canada has a total population of around 30 million, and a total Inuit population of about 25,000.

Government of Nunavut

The steps leading to establishment of Nunavut are found in Road to Nunavut, a short history.

The first Nunavut election was held in 1999, and 19 members were elected to the Nunavut Legislative Assembly. Unlike provincial legislatures in Canada, the Nunavut Legislative Assembly does not operate on the basis of political parties, but operates on a consensus basis. With the party system, the leader of the party which wins the most seats in an election becomes premier. In Nunavut, the elected members choose the premier and cabinet ministers. The premier then assigns portfolios to the ministers. The first Premier of Nunavut was Paul Okalik, Canada's first Inuit lawyer who had been called to the bar just the month before. Since the new Nunavut government was established on April 1, 1999, it has been undergoing rapid changes. You can track many of those changes at the Nunavut government Web site.

Nunavut & Consensual Legislature 1999

From Wikipedia; lightly edited and formatted:
http://en.wikipedia.org/wiki/Nunavut

Nunavut is the largest and newest federal territory of Canada; it was separated officially from the Northwest Territories on April 1, 1999 via the Nunavut Act and the Nunavut Land Claims Agreement Act, though the actual boundaries had been established in 1993. The creation of Nunavut – meaning "our land" in Inuktitut – resulted in the first major change to Canada's map since the incorporation of the new province of Newfoundland in 1949.

Nunavut comprises a major portion of Northern Canada, and most of the Canadian Arctic Archipelago, making it the fifth largest country subdivision in the world. The capital Iqaluit (formerly "Frobisher Bay") on Baffin Island, in the east, was chosen by the 1995 capital plebiscite. Other major communities include the regional centres of Rankin Inlet and Cambridge Bay. Nunavut also includes Ellesmere Island to the north, as well as the eastern and southern portions of Victoria Island in the west and Akimiski Island in James Bay to the far south. Nunavut is both the least populated and the geographically largest of the provinces and territories of Canada. It has a population of 29,474, mostly Inuit, spread over an area the size of Western Europe. Nunavut is also home to the most northern permanently inhabited place in the world, Alert.

Geography of Nunavut

Nunavut covers 1,932,255 km2 (746,048 sq mi) of land and 160,935 km2 (62,137 sq mi) of water in Northern Canada including part of the mainland, most of the Arctic Archipelago, and all of the islands in Hudson Bay, James Bay, and Ungava Bay (including the Belcher Islands) which belonged to the Northwest Territories. This makes it the fifth largest national administrative division in the world. If Nunavut were a country, it would rank 15th in area. Nunavut has land borders with the Northwest Territories on several islands as well as the mainland, Manitoba to the south of the Nunavut mainland, Saskatchewan to the southwest, and a tiny land border with Newfoundland and Labrador on Killiniq Island. It also shares maritime borders with the provinces of Quebec, Ontario, and Manitoba and with Greenland.

Nunavut's highest point is Barbeau Peak (2,616 m (8,583 ft) on Ellesmere Island. The population density is 0.015 persons per square kilometre, one of the lowest in the world. By comparison, Greenland, to the east, has approximately the same area and nearly twice the population.

History of Nunavut

The region now known as Nunavut has supported a continuous indigenous population for approximately 4,000 years. Most historians also identify the coast of Baffin Island with the Helluland described in Norse sagas, so it is possible that the inhabitants of the region had occasional contact with Norse sailors.

The written history of Nunavut begins in 1576. Martin Frobisher, while leading an expedition to find the Northwest Passage, thought he had discovered gold ore around the body of water now known as Frobisher Bay on the coast of Baffin Island. The ore turned out to be worthless, but Frobisher made the first recorded European contact with the Inuit. The contact was hostile, with both sides taking prisoners, who subsequently perished. Other explorers in search of the elusive Northwest Passage followed in the 17th century, including Henry Hudson, William Baffin and Robert Bylot.

Cornwallis and Ellesmere Islands feature in the history of the Cold War in the 1950s. Concerned about the area's strategic geopolitical position, the federal government relocated Inuit from the High Arctic of northern Quebec to Resolute and Grise Fiord. In the unfamiliar and hostile conditions, they faced starvation (11) but were forced to stay. Forty years later, the Royal Commission on Aboriginal Peoples issued a report titled The High Arctic Relocation: A Report on 1953-55 Relocation. The government paid compensation to those affected and their descendants, but it did not apologize. The story is told in Melanie McGrath's The Long Exile: A Tale of Inuit Betrayal and Survival in the High Arctic.

In 1976 as part of the land claims negotiations between the Inuit Tapiriit Kanatami (then called the Inuit Tapirisat of Canada) and the federal government, the division of the Northwest Territories was discussed. On April 14, 1982, a plebiscite on division was held throughout the Northwest Territories. A majority of the residents voted in favour and the federal government gave a conditional agreement seven months later. The land claims agreement was decided in September 1992 and ratified by nearly 85% of the voters in Nunavut. On July 9, 1993, the Nunavut Land Claims Agreement Act and the Nunavut Act were passed by the Canadian Parliament. The transition to establish Nunavut Territory was completed on April 1, 1999.

In September 2008, researchers reported the evaluation of existing and newly excavated archaeological remains, including yarn spun from a hare, rats, tally sticks, a carved wooden face mask depicting Caucasian features, and possible architectural material. The materials were collected in five seasons of excavation at Cape Banfield. Scholars have determined these are evidence of European traders and possibly settlers on Baffin Island not later than 1000 CE. They seem to indicate prolonged contact, possibly up to 1450 CE. The origin of the Old World contact is unclear as the article states: "Dating of some yarn and other artifacts, presumed to have been left by Vikings on Baffin Island, have produced an age that predates the Vikings by several hundred years. So (...) you have to consider the possibility that as remote as it may seem, these finds may represent evidence of contact with Europeans prior to the Vikings' arrival in Greenland."

Ten largest communities

Municipality	2006	2001	growth
Iqaluit	6,184	5,236	18.1%
Rankin Inlet	2,358	2,177	8.3%
Arviat	2,060	1,899	8.5%
Baker Lake	1,728	1,507	14.7%
Igloolik	1,538	1,286	19.6%
Cambridge Bay	1,477	1,309	12.8%
Pangnirtung	1,325	1,276	3.8%
Pond Inlet	1,315	1,220	7.8%
Kugluktuk	1,302	1,212	7.4%
Cape Dorset	1,236	1,148	7.7%

Demographics of Nunavut

As of the 2006 Census the population of Nunavut was 29,474, with 24,640 people identifying themselves as Inuit (83.6% of the total population), 100 as First Nations (0.34%), 130 Métis (0.44%) and 4,410 as non-aboriginal (14.96%).

The population growth rate of Nunavut has been well above the Canadian average for several decades, mostly due to birth rates which are significantly higher than the Canadian average. This is a trend that continues to this day. Between April and July of 2009, Nunavut saw the highest population growth rate of any other Canadian province or territory, at a rate of 0.68%. The second highest was Alberta, with a growth rate of 0.59%. However, Nunavut has a large net loss from migration, due to many native Inuit leaving the territory for better economic opportunity elsewhere.

Consensual Governments & Cooperation

From Capitalnewsonline; lightly edited and formatted:
http://carleton.ca/Capital_News/03112006/n6.shtml

Consensus governments stress co-operation over conflict
By Steve Rennie
Producer: Lesli Strang

OTTAWA Nov. 3, 2006 When a politician from the Northwest Territories threatened another member of the legislature last month, he was booted from cabinet the next day.

But when Liberal MPs signed affidavits swearing they heard Peter MacKay refer to fellow MP Belinda Stronach as a dog, the foreign affairs minister denied the accusations and the situation eventually boiled over.

In the legislatures of the Northwest Territories and Nunavut there are no party affiliations. Two governments. Two controversies. The Northwest Territories legislature voted to eject Michael Miltenberger from cabinet yet the House of Commons became embroiled in a lengthy 'he said, she said' dogfight. This may have something to do with two very different styles of government, says University of Toronto political science professor Graham White.

There are no political parties in the Northwest Territories Legislative Assembly. Instead, 19 independent MLAs sit in the legislature. The premier and six MLAs form the cabinet, which is perennially in a minority position and must work with the regular members to pass legislation.

"You don't get a lot of the mindless partisanship and mindless opposition mentality that you get in the south," White says. "It's not nearly as hard edged or as oppositional or adversarial as parliamentary systems in the south."

In the Northwest Territories, would be MLAs run as independents in the 19 constituencies. After the election, the newly elected MLAs hold a secret ballot to select one of them to serve as premier. The premier then chooses six other MLAs to form a cabinet. Regular members may opt to vote with or against the cabinet as they see fit. 'It's not nearly as hard edged or as oppositional or adversarial as parliamentary systems in the south.'

The debates tend to be centred more on issues that affect each of the constituencies, White says. "Most of the time it's much more civilized and respectful. People are actually listening and the debate actually matters."

Since the MLAs are not required by party discipline to support cabinet decisions, they are always free to do what they think is best for their constituents. White, who has studied northern consensus governments for years, describes the voting blocks as "much more fluid" than in party politics. "The fundamental political relationship is the member to the member's constituency." Nunavut has a consensus style government similar to its northern territorial neighbour. Both are hybrids of traditional aboriginal government and the British parliamentary system, White explains.

Willie Adams, a senator who represents Nunavut, says consensus style governments work better than party politics. In Ottawa, he says, he's had to vote along party lines for or against something he didn't agree with. Sometimes, Adams says, "I've got to vote for it because the prime minister wants it. I've got to vote for the Liberal party, even if I don't like it."

It might be easier to pass budgets in a consensus style government, he adds. But White says it's often hard in a consensus style government to get people to agree on anything. "It can be difficult to get everybody moving in the same direction because you don't have the party discipline and there may be a lot more compromises or lack of willingness to take on difficult issues," he says.

It's unlikely a consensus style government would work in federal politics, says Dennis Bevington, an MP for the Western Arctic. "Minority governments, by their nature, have to be more consensual." "We can't even form coalitions. We can't even make minority governments work. The thought that somehow Parliament would be able to operate on a consensual basis just doesn't stand up to any evidence," he says.

But that doesn't mean federal politicians can't learn anything from the Northwest Territories legislature, he adds. "Minority governments, by their nature, have to be more consensual. Just get people to support each other to make something pass," he says. If Canadians continue electing minority governments, he adds, parties will need to "learn better how to work together as coalitions. There are going to have to be more formal arrangements in Parliament so we don't have elections every 18 months."

One Justice System

The Justice System of Canada

From Wikipedia; lightly edited and formatted:

http://en.wikipedia.org/wiki/Government_of_Canada

http://en.wikipedia.org/wiki/Constitution_of_Canada

The Supreme Court of Canada

The sovereign is responsible for rendering justice for all her subjects, and is thus traditionally deemed the fount of justice. However, she does not personally rule in judicial cases; instead the judicial functions of the Royal Prerogative are performed in trust and in the Queen's name by Officers of Her Majesty's Court.

The Supreme Court of Canada, the country's court of last resort, has nine justices appointed by the Governor General and led by the Chief Justice of Canada. The Supreme Court hears appeals from decisions rendered by the various appellate courts from the provinces and territories. Below this is the Federal Court, which hears cases arising under certain areas of federal law, and works with the Federal Court of Appeal and Tax Court of Canada.

The Constitution Act, (England) 1867

This was an Act of the British Parliament, originally called the British North America Act 1867, that created the Dominion of Canada out of three separate provinces in British North America (Province of Canada, New Brunswick, and Nova Scotia) and allowed for subsequent provinces and colonies to join this union in the future. It outlined Canada's system of government, which combines Britain's Westminster model of parliamentary government with division of sovereignty (federalism). Although it is the first of twenty British North America Acts, it is still the most famous of these and is understood to be the document of Canadian Confederation (i.e. union of provinces and colonies in British North America). With the patriation of the Constitution in 1982, this Act was renamed Constitution Act, 1867. In recent years, the Constitution Act, 1867 has mainly served as the basis on which the division of powers between the provinces and federal government have been analyzed.

The Constitution Act, (Canada) 1982

The Constitution of Canada (La Constitution du Canada) is the supreme law in Canada; the country's constitution is an amalgamation of codified acts and uncodified traditions and conventions. It outlines Canada's system of government, as well as the civil rights of all Canadian citizens. Interpretation of the Constitution is called Canadian constitutional law.

The composition of the Constitution of Canada is defined in subsection 52(2) of the Constitution Act, 1982 as consisting of the Canada Act 1982 (including the Constitution Act, 1982), all acts and orders referred to in the schedule (including the Constitution Act, 1867, formerly the British North America Act), and any amendments to these documents. The Supreme Court of Canada held that the list is not exhaustive and includes unwritten components as well.

The patriation of the Canadian Constitution was achieved in 1982 when the British and Canadian parliaments passed parallel acts, the Canada Act 1982 in London, and the Constitution Act 1982 in Ottawa. Thereafter, the United Kingdom was formally absolved of any responsibility or jurisdiction over Canada; and Canada became responsible for her own destiny. In a formal ceremony on Parliament Hill in Ottawa, the Queen signed both acts into law on April 17, 1982.

The Canada Act / Constitution Act included the Canadian Charter of

Rights and Freedoms. Prior to the Charter, there were various statutes which protected an assortment of civil rights and obligations, but nothing was enshrined in the Constitution until 1982. The Charter has thus placed a strong focus upon individual and collective rights of the people of Canada.

Amendments to the Constitution Act, 1982

With the Constitution Act, 1982, amendments to the constitution must be made in accordance with Part V of the Constitution Act, 1982 which provides for five different amending formulas. Amendments may be brought forward under section 46(1) by any province or either level of the federal government. The general formula is set out in section 38(1), known as the "7/50 formula", requires: (a) assent from both the House of Commons and the Senate; (b) the approval of two-thirds of the provincial legislatures (at least seven provinces), representing at least 50% of the population (effectively, this would include at least Quebec or Ontario, as they are the most populous provinces). This formula specifically applies to amendments related to the proportionate representation in Parliament, powers, selection, and composition of the Senate, the Supreme Court and the addition of provinces or territories. The other amendment formulas are for exceptional cases as provided by in the Act:

- In the case of an amendment related to the Office of the Queen, the number of senators, the use of either official language (subject to section 43), the amending formula, or the composition of the Supreme Court, the amendment must be adopted by unanimous consent of all the provinces in accordance with section 41.

- However, in the case of an amendment related to provincial boundaries or the use of an official language within a province alone, the amendment must be passed by the legislatures affected by the amendment (section 43).

- In the case of an amendment that affects the federal government alone, the amendment does not need approval of the provinces (section 44). The same applies to amendments affecting the provincial government alone (section 45).

English Common Law

All provinces and territories within Canada, excluding Quebec, follow the common law legal tradition. Equally, courts have power under the provincial Judicature Acts to apply equity.

As with all common law countries, Canadian law adheres to the doctrine of "stare decisis". Lower courts must follow the decisions of higher courts by which they are bound. For instance, all Ontario lower courts are bound by the decisions of the Ontario Court of Appeal and, all British Columbia lower courts are bound by the decisions of the British Columbia Court of Appeal. However, no Ontario court is bound by decisions of any British Columbia court and no British Columbia court is bound by decisions of any Ontario court. Nonetheless, decisions made by a province's highest court (provincial Courts of Appeal) are often considered as "persuasive" even though they are not binding on other provinces.

Only the Supreme Court of Canada has authority to bind all courts in the country with a single ruling. The busier courts, such as the Court of Appeal for Ontario, for example, are often looked to for guidance on many local matters of law outside the province, especially in matters such as evidence and criminal law.

Quebec Civil Law

For historical reasons, Quebec has a hybrid legal system. Private law follows the civil law tradition, originally expressed in the Coutume de Paris as it applied in what was then New France. Today, the jus commune of Quebec is codified in the Civil Code of Quebec. As for public law, it was made that of the conquering British nation after the fall of New France in 1760, that is the common law. It is important to note that the distinction between civil law and common law is not based on the division of powers set out in the Constitution Act,

1867. Therefore, legislation enacted by the provincial legislature in matters of public law, such as the Code of Penal Procedure, should be interpreted following the common law tradition. Likewise, legislation enacted by the federal Parliament in matters of private law, such as the Divorce Act, is to be interpreted following the civil law tradition and in harmony with the Civil Code of Quebec. Because of Quebec's unique legal system, lawyers trained in either common law or civil law may not practice in Quebec without undergoing further training in one or the other legal system.

Losing Freedom by Government - (Catching Wild Pigs)

From Bozemantalks.com; lightly edited and formatted:
http://bozemantalks.com/2009/03/09/catching-wild-pigs

A chemistry professor in a large college had some exchange students in the class. One day while the class was in the lab the Professor noticed one young man (an exchange student) who kept rubbing his back and stretching as if his back hurt. The professor asked the young man what was the matter. The student told him he had a bullet lodged in his back. He had been shot while fighting communists in his native country who were trying to overthrow his country's government and install a new communist government.

In the midst of his story he looked at the professor and asked a strange question. He asked, 'Do you know how to catch wild pigs?'

The professor thought it was a joke and asked for the punch line. The young man said this was no joke. 'You catch wild pigs by finding a suitable place in the woods and putting corn on the ground. The pigs find it and begin to come everyday to eat the free corn.

When they are used to coming every day, you put a fence down one side of the place where they are used to coming. When they get used to the fence, they begin to eat the corn again and you put up another side of the fence. They get used to that and start to eat again. You continue until you have all four sides of the fence up with a gate in the last side. The pigs, who are used to the free corn, start to come through the gate to eat, you slam the gate on them and catch the whole herd.

Suddenly the wild pigs have lost their freedom. They run around and around inside the fence, but they are caught. Soon they go back to eating the free corn. They are so used to it that they have forgotten how to forage in the woods for themselves, so they accept their captivity.

The young man then told the professor that is exactly what he sees happening to America. The government keeps pushing us toward socialism and keeps spreading the free corn out in the form of programs such as supplemental income, tax credit for unearned income, tobacco subsidies, dairy subsidies, payments not to plant crops (CRP), welfare, medicine, drugs, etc.. While we continually lose our freedoms . . . just a little at a time.

One should always remember: There is no such thing as a free lunch! Also, a politician will never provide a service for you cheaper than you can do it yourself. Also, if you see that all of this wonderful government 'help' is a problem confronting the future of democracy in America, you might want to send this on to your friends. If you think the free ride is essential to your way of life then you will probably delete this email, but God help you when the gate slams shut! In this very important election year, listen closely to what the candidates are promising you. Just maybe you will be able to tell who is about to slam the gate on America.

'A government big enough to give you everything you want, is big enough to take away everything you have.' - Thomas Jefferson

---

The Napoleonic Code in Quebec

From Wikipedia; lightly edited and formatted:
http://en.wikipedia.org/wiki/Civil_Code_of_Quebec

The Civil Code of Quebec (French: Code civil du Québec) is the civil code in force in the province of Quebec, Canada. The Civil Code of

Quebec came into effect on January 1, 1994, except for certain parts of the book on the Law of the Family which were adopted by the National Assembly in the 1980s. It replaced the Civil Code of Lower Canada (French: Code civil du Bas-Canada) enacted by the Legislative Assembly of the Province of Canada in 1865, and which had been in force since July 1, 1866. The scope of the Code is summarized in its preliminary provision.

The Civil Code of Quebec, in harmony with the Charter of Human Rights and Freedoms and the general principles of law, governs persons, relations between persons, and property.

The Civil Code comprises a body of rules which, in all matters within the letter, spirit or object of its provisions, lays down the jus commune, expressly or by implication. In these matters, the Code is the foundation of all other laws, although other laws may complement the Code or make exceptions to it. Given its central place in the legal system, the Civil Code is frequently amended in order to reflect the evolution of the society. The Civil Code of Quebec comprises over 3000 sections and is structured into major divisions and subdivisions called books, titles, chapters and subsections. It comprises ten books:

1. Persons
2. The Family
3. Successions
4. Property
5. Obligations
6. Prior Claims and Hypothecs
7. Evidence
8. Prescription
9. Publication of Rights
10. Private International Law

History of the Civil Code of Quebec - During the French Colonial Era

From 1608 to 1664, the first colonists to New France followed the law, or "custom" (French: la coutume), that was in force in the province of France from which the colonists originated.

In 1664 the French King decreed in "l'Édit d'établissement de la compagnie des Indes occidentales" (art. XXXIII) that la Coutume de Paris was applicable throughout New France. Also added was "le droit français de la métropole". This included various royal legislation, royal ordinances ("ordonnances royales"), canon law for marriage and roman law for the law of obligations (les obligations, i.e. contracts and delicts). Also applicable were the ordinances of the Royal Intendants ("les ordonnances des intendants") and the decisions of the Conseil souverain ("les arrêts de règlement du Conseil souverain").

The Royal Intendant was responsible for the justice in the colony and lawyers were not allowed to practice in the colony. Most disputes were resolved by local notaries or local parish priests through arbitration in a manner much as had been done in ancient Rome. While French feudal law meant that New France was divided into seigneuries, the feudal lords (or seigneurs) did not possess the same judicial jurisdiction in New France that such lords enjoyed in France, as high (capital crimes)and low (minor offences) jurisdiction was reserved for the Intendant. Thus, while the Custom of Paris was the law of New France, there was little mechanism for residents of the colony to actually enforce that law.

Under the British Empire

Following France's abandonment of Canada in favour of Guadaloupe in the Treaty of Paris (1763), Canada came under British law. However, the seigneurial system of land tenure continued to be applied uniformly throughout the province. In 1774, the British Parliament passed the Quebec Act which restored the former French civil law for private relationships, while maintaining English common law for public administration, including the prosecution of crimes. As a result, modern-day Quebec is today one of only a handful of "bijural" countries in the world where two legal systems co-exist.

The Quebec Act was opposed by the English minority who believed that British citizens should be governed by English law. The Constitutional Act of 1791 resolved the dispute through the creation of Upper Canada west of the Ottawa River (subject to English common law) and Lower Canada around the St. Lawrence River (where civil law was maintained).

Adoption of the Civil Code of Lower Canada

The substantive law of the 1866 Civil Code of Lower Canada was derived primarily from the judicial interpretations of the law that had been in force to that date in Lower Canada. The work of the Commission on codification was also inspired by some of the modernizations found in the 1804 Napoleonic code. At the time of Canadian Confederation, the Civil Code of Lower Canada replaced most of the laws inherited from the Custom of Paris and incorporated some English law as it had been applied in Lower Canada such as the English law of trusts. The former Civil Code was also inspired by the Louisiana Civil Code, the Field Code movement in New York and the law of the Canton de Vaud.

The Revised Civil Code of Quebec

In 1955, the Government of Quebec embarked on a reform of the Civil Code with the passage of the Act respecting the revision of the Civil Code. The Civil Code Revision Office was established, which produced reports, held consultations, and presented a Draft Civil Code with commentaries to the Quebec National Assembly in 1978. After further consultations during the 1980s, portions of the Book on the Law of the Family were adopted. The consultation process continued through to the early 1990s, and the Civil Code of Quebec was passed into law in its entirety on December 18, 1991, coming into effect in 1994.

The Government of Canada undertook a review of all federal laws that deal with private law to ensure that they took into consideration the terminology, concepts and institutions of Quebec civil law and on January 31, 2001, tabled a Bill entitled A First Act to harmonize federal law with the civil law of the province of Quebec and to amend certain Acts in order to ensure that each language version takes into account the common law and the civil law.

The reform process that led to the replacement of the Civil Code of Lower Canada by the Civil Code of Quebec was one of the largest legislative recodification undertakings in any civil law jurisdiction. The Civil Code of Quebec was a complete restatement of the civil law in

Quebec as of the date of its adoption, including judicial interpretation of provisions that include privacy and personality rights protection and the adoption of a section on the patrimony of affectation.

Abolition of Slavery in Canada

From Wikipedia; lightly edited and formatted:
http://en.wikipedia.org/wiki/Slavery_in_Canada

Slavery in what now comprises Canada existed from prehistoric times to the 1830s, when slavery was officially abolished. Some slaves were of African descent, while others were aboriginal (typically called panis, likely a corruption of Pawnee). Slavery which was practised within Canada's current geography, was practised primarily by Aboriginal groups and the British and French empires. Slavery was practised by some aboriginal nations, who routinely captured slaves from neighbouring tribes. African slaves were forcibly brought as chattel by Europeans to Canada. Chattel slavery, a form of hereditary slavery, was established by European colonization and settlement of Canada during the 17th century. Legally, slaves were regarded as movable possessions and private property. Large scale plantation slavery of the sort that existed in warmer parts of the New World never existed because there were no plantations. Most of the slaves in Canada were domestic house servants, although some performed agricultural labour. Although pre-Confederation Canada has a history of slavery, it is often overshadowed by the more tumultuous kind featured in other areas in the Americas. Afua Cooper states that slavery is, "Canada's best kept secret, locked within the National closet."

Under indigenous rule

Slave owning people of what became Canada were, for example, the fishing societies, such as the Yurok, that lived along the Pacific coast from Alaska to California. Many of the indigenous peoples of the Pacific Northwest Coast, such as the Haida and Tlingit, were traditionally known as fierce warriors and slave traders, raiding as far as

California. Slavery was hereditary, the slaves being prisoners of war and their descendants were slaves. Among some Pacific Northwest tribes about a quarter of the population were slaves. One slave narrative was composed by an Englishman, John R. Jewitt, who had been taken alive when his ship was captured in 1802; his memoir provides a detailed look at life as a slave, and asserts that a large number were held.

Under French rule

In 1628 the first recorded slave in Canada was brought by a British Convoy to New France. Olivier le Jeune was the name given to the boy originally from Madagascar. His given name resonates with the Code Noir, although loosely established, the Code Noir forced baptisms and decreed the conversion of all slaves to Catholicism. By 1688, New France's population was 11,562 people, made up primarily of fur traders, missionaries, and farmers settled along the St. Lawrence Valley. To help overcome its severe shortage of servants and labourers, King Louis XIV granted New France's petition to import black slaves from West Africa. While slavery was prohibited in France, it was permitted in its colonies as a means of providing the massive labour force needed to clear land, construct buildings and (in the Caribbean colonies) work sugar plantation. New France soon established its own 'Code Noir,' defining the control and management of slaves. The Code in 1685 set the pattern for policing slavery. It required that all slaves be instructed as Catholics and not as Protestants. It concentrated on defining the condition of slavery, and established harsh controls. Slaves had virtually no rights, though the Code did enjoin masters to take care of the sick and old. The blacks were usually called "servants," and the harsh gang system was not used. Death rates among slaves was high.

Marie-Joseph Angélique was the black slave of a rich widow in Montreal. In 1734, after learning that she was going to be sold and separated from her lover, she set fire to her owner's house and escaped. The fire raged out of control, destroying forty-six buildings. Captured two months later, Marie-Joseph was paraded through the city, then tortured until she confessed her crime. The crowd watched as she was hanged, and her corpse was burned. Slavery continued after the British took control in 1760.

Under British rule

The 1763 Treaty of Paris made no reference to slavery in Canada, nor does the Quebec Act of 1774 or the Treaty of Paris of 1783, either to ban it or to permit it. After 1783, about 3,500 Black loyalists fled to Canada, mostly persons who had won their freedom by supporting the British by taking up arms during the U.S. War of Independence.

However many United Empire Loyalists brought their slaves with them to Canada after the American Revolution; they remained slaves and the Imperial Act of 1790 assured prospective immigrants that their slaves would remain their property. Some slaves fled Upper and Lower Canada to free states in America such as Massachusetts, Vermont, and Pennsylvania. Canadian First Nations owned or traded in slaves. Shawnee, Potawatomi, and other western tribes imported slaves from Ohio and Kentucky and sold them to Canadian settlers. Chief Joseph Brant of the Thayendenaga used blacks that he had captured during the American Revolution to build Brant House at Burlington Beach and a second home near Brantford. In all, Brant owned about forty black slaves.

By 1790 the abolition movement was gaining credence in Canada and the ill intent of slavery was evidenced by an incident involving a slave woman being violently abused by her slave owner on her way to being sold in the United States. In 1793 Chloe Clooey, in an act of defiance yelled out screams of resistance. The abuse committed by her slave owner and her violent resistance was witnessed by Peter Martin and William Grisely. Peter Martin, a former slave, brought the incident to the attention of Lieutenant Governor John Graves Simcoe. Under the auspices of Simcoe, The Slave Act of 1793 was legislated. The elected members of the executive council, many of whom were merchants or farmers who depended on slave labour, saw no need for emancipation.

White later wrote that there was "much opposition but little argument" to his measure. Finally the Assembly passed the Act Against Slavery that legislated the gradual abolition of slavery: no slaves could be imported;

slaves already in the province would remain enslaved until death, no new slaves could be brought into Upper Canada, and children born to female slaves would be slaves but must be freed at age 25. To discourage manumission, the Act required the master to provide security that the former slave would not become a public charge. The compromise Slave Act of 1793 stands as the only attempt by any Canadian legislature to act against slavery. This legal rule ensured the eventual end of slavery in Upper Canada, although as it diminished the sale value of slaves within the province it also resulted in slaves being sold to the United States. In 1798 there was an attempt by a lobby groups to rectify the legislation and import more slaves.

By 1797, courts began to rule in favour of slaves who complained of poor treatment from their owners. Slavery remained in Upper and Lower Canada until 1834 when the British Parliament's Slavery Abolition Act finally abolished slavery in all parts of the British Empire. Most of the emancipated slaves of African descent in Canada were in the 1830s sent to settle Freetown in Sierra Leone and those that remained primarily ended up in segregated communities such as Africville outside Halifax, Nova Scotia. Today there are four remaining slave cemeteries in Canada: in St. Armand, Quebec, Shelburne, Nova Scotia and Priceville and Dresden in Ontario.

Around the time of the Emancipation, the Underground Railroad network was established in the United States, particularly Ohio, where slaves would cross into the Northern States over the Ohio River en route to various settlements and towns in Upper Canada (now Ontario).

Abolition of the Chinese Head Tax

From Wikipedia; lightly edited and formatted:
http://en.wikipedia.org/wiki/Head_tax

In 1885 the Chinese Immigration Act authorized a fixed fee head tax for each Chinese person entering Canada to discourage Chinese immigration after completion of the Canadian Pacific Railway. The head tax was ended by the Chinese Immigration Act of 1923, which stopped Chinese immigration except for business people, clergy, educators, and students.

In 1993, Prime Minister Jean Chrétien refused to provide an apology or redress for the wrongs of the Chinese head tax. On June 22, 2006, Prime Minister Stephen Harper offered an apology and compensation only for the head tax once paid by Chinese immigrants. Survivors or their spouses will be paid approximately $20,000 CAD in compensation. There are only an estimated 20 Chinese Canadians who paid the tax still alive in 2006.

Currently, the major issues revolve around the content of any future settlement, with the leading groups demanding meaningful redress, not only for the handful of surviving "head tax" payers and widows/spouses, but first-generation sons/daughters who were direct victims. Some have proposed that the redress be based on the number of "Head Tax" Certificates (or estates) brought forward by surviving sons and daughters who are still able to register their claims, with proposals for individual redress, ranging from $10,000 to 30,000 for an estimated 4,000 registrants.

Abolition of Apartheid in South Africa

From Wikipedia; lightly edited and formatted:
http://en.wikipedia.org/wiki/South_Africa_under_apartheid

Apartheid (Afrikaans equivalent to English "apart+hood") was a system of legal racial segregation enforced by the National Party government in South Africa between 1948 and 1994. The rights of the majority black inhabitants of South Africa were curtailed and minority rule by whites was maintained.

Racial segregation in South Africa began in colonial times, but apartheid as an official policy was introduced following the general election of 1948. New legislation classified inhabitants into racial groups ("black", "white", "coloured", and "Indian"), and residential areas were segregated by means of forced removals. From 1958, Blacks were deprived of their citizenship, legally becoming citizens of one of ten tribally based self-governing homelands called Bantustans, four of which became nominally independent states. The government segregated education, medical care, and other public services, and provided black people with services inferior to those of whites.

Apartheid sparked significant internal resistance and violence as well as a long trade embargo against South Africa. A series of popular uprisings and protests were met with the banning of opposition and imprisoning of anti-apartheid leaders. As unrest spread and became more violent, state organizations responded with increasing repression and state sponsored violence. Reforms to apartheid in the 1980s failed to quell the mounting opposition, and in 1990 President Frederik Willem de Klerk began negotiations to end apartheid, culminating in multi-racial democratic elections in 1994, which were won by the African National Congress under Nelson Mandela. The vestiges of apartheid still shape South African politics and society.

Submission to Apartheid Law in Canada

From Wikipedia; lightly edited and formatted:
                    http://en.wikipedia.org/wiki/Indian_Act

The Indian Act is a statute that concerns registered Indians, their bands, and the system of Indian reserves. The Act was enacted in 1876 by Parliament under the provisions of Section 91(24) of the Constitution Act 1867, which gives the federal government exclusive authority to legislate regarding "Indians and Lands Reserved for Indians". The Indian Act is administered by the Minister of Indian Affairs and Northern Development.

The Act defines who is an "Indian" and contains certain legal disabilities and legal rights for registered Indians. The rights exclusive to Indians in the Indian Act are beyond legal challenge under of the Canadian

Charter of Rights and Freedoms. Section 25 of the Canadian Charter of Rights and Freedoms provides that the charter shall not be interpreted as negating specific aboriginal treaties and their corresponding rights and freedoms. Section 35 of the Constitution Act, 1982 also recognizes and affirms the legal validity of aboriginal treaties.

An Indian whose name was in the Indian Register established by the act was said to have Indian status or treaty status. An Indian who was not registered was said to be a non-status Indian. Prior to 1985, Indians could lose status in a variety of ways, including:

- marrying a man who was not a Status Indian
- enfranchisement (until 1960, Indians could vote only by renouncing Indian status)
- having a mother and paternal grandmother who did not have status before marriage
- being born out of wedlock to a mother with status and a father without.

In Attorney General of Canada v. Lavell (1974), these laws were upheld despite arguments made under the Canadian Bill of Rights. The Indian Act was amended in 1985 (Bill C-31) to restore status to people who had lost it in one of these ways, and to their children.

Imposition of The Indian Act in Canada

From Wikipedia; lightly edited and formatted:
http://en.wikipedia.org/wiki/Indian_Act

The Indian Act ("An Act respecting Indians"), R.S., 1985, c. I-5, is a Canadian statute that concerns registered Indians (that is, First Nations peoples of Canada), their bands, and the system of Indian reserves. The Indian Act was enacted in 1876 by the Parliament of Canada under the provisions of Section 91(24) of the Constitution Act, 1867, which provides Canada's federal government exclusive authority to legislate in relation to "Indians and Lands Reserved for Indians". The Indian

Act is administered by the Minister of Indian Affairs and Northern Development.

The Indian Act defines who is an "Indian" and contains certain legal disabilities and legal rights for registered Indians. The rights exclusive to Indians in the Indian Act are beyond legal challenge under of the Canadian Charter of Rights and Freedoms. Section 25 of the Canadian Charter of Rights and Freedoms provides that the charter shall not be interpreted as negating specific aboriginal treaties and their corresponding rights and freedoms. Section 35 of the Constitution Act, 1982 also recognizes and affirms the legal validity of aboriginal treaties.

The Act was extensively amended after World War II and was again under study in the mid-1960's. The 2-volume Hawthorne Report vividly portrayed the Indian fact in Canada and, after a national consultation with Chiefs, government advanced the 1969 White Paper Policy which would abolish Indian status, Indian reserves, Indian Treaties, the Indian Department and the Indian Act. Indian resistance to this initiative, coupled with favourable court decisions, forced government to re-think its policies. In 1973, the White Paper was formally withdrawn and government began to deal seriously -- if somewhat intermittently -- with land claims. Its resistance to such claims was apparent when, in the Guerin case, (1984) 2 S.C.R. 335, it denied any legal responsibility for leasing reserve lands on terms much less favourable than those discussed with a Band before the formal surrender. The Supreme Court of Canada confirmed the fiduciary duties of the Crown, derivable from the nature of Indian title and from the Indian Act, and held Canada liable for its breach of duty in that case. Claims policy is still problematic and there has been no statutory initiative to deal with those problems.

Indian Status

An Indian whose name is in the Indian Register established by the act is said to have Indian status or treaty status. An Indian who is not registered is said to be a non-status Indian. Prior in 1985 status was often lost in ways that are now considered unfair. In Attorney General of Canada v. Lavell (1974), these discriminatory laws were upheld despite arguments made under the Canadian Bill of Rights. The act was nevertheless amended in 1985 to restore status to people who had lost it in one of these ways, and to their children. Before the amendment, the ways in which status were lost were:

- marrying a man who was not a Status Indian
- enfranchisement (until 1960, Indians could vote only by renouncing Indian status)
- having a mother and paternal grandmother who did not have status before marriage
- being born out of wedlock to a mother with status and a father without.

Section 88

Section 88 of the Indian Act states that provincial laws may affect Aboriginals if they are of "general application", meaning that they affect other people as well as Aboriginals. Hence, provincial laws are incorporated into federal law, since otherwise the provincial laws would be unconstitutional. In Kruger et al. v. The Queen (1978), the Supreme Court found provincial laws with a more significant impact on Aboriginals than other people can be upheld, as "There are few laws which have a uniform impact."

Constitutional scholar Peter Hogg argues that in Dick v. The Queen (1985), the Supreme Court "changed its mind about the scope of s. 88." Section 88 could now protect provincial laws relating to primary Aboriginal laws and even limiting Aboriginal rights.

Amendments

1881: Amended to make officers of the Indian Department, including Indian Agents, legal justices of the peace, able to enforce regulations. The following year they were granted the same legal power as magistrates. Further amended to prohibit the sale of agricultural produce by Indians in Prairie Provinces without an appropriate permit from an Indian agent. This prohibition is, as of 2008 (update), still included in the Indian Act though not enforced.

1884: Amended to prevent elected band leaders deposed from office from being re-elected.

1885: Amended to prohibit religious ceremonies (such as potlatches) and dances (such as Tamanawas dances).

1894: Amended to remove band control of non-natives living on reserve. This power now rested *(rests ?)* exclusively in the hands of the Superintendent General of Indian Affairs.

1895: Amended to outlaw all dances, ceremonies and festivals that involved the wounding of animals or humans, or the giving away of money or goods.

1905: Amended to allow aboriginal people to be removed from reserves near towns with more than 8,000 residents.

1906: Amended to allow 50 per cent of the sale price of reserve lands to be given to band members, following the surrender of that land.

1911: Amended to allow municipalities and companies expropriate portions of reserves, without surrender, for roads, railways, and other public works. Further amended to allow a judge to move an entire reserve away from a municipality if it was deemed "expedient." These amendments were also known as the Oliver Act.

1914: Amended to require western Indians to seek official permission before appearing in "aboriginal costume" in any "dance, show, exhibition, stampede or pageant."

1918: Amended to allow the Superintendent-General to lease out uncultivated reserve lands to non-aboriginals if the new lease-holder would use it for farming or pasture.

1920: Amended to allow the Department of Indian Affairs to ban hereditary rule of bands. Further amended to allow for the involuntary enfranchisement (and loss of treaty rights) of any status Indian considered fit by the Department of Indian Affairs without the possession of land previously required for those living off reserve. Repealed two years later, but reintroduced in a modified form in 1933.

1927: Amended to prevent anyone (aboriginal or otherwise) from soliciting funds for Indian legal claims without a special license from the Superintendent-General. This effectively prevented any First Nation from pursuing aboriginal land claims.

1930: Amended to prevent a pool hall owner from allowing entrance to an Indian who "by inordinate frequenting of a pool room either on or off an Indian reserve misspends or wastes his time or means to the detriment of himself, his family or household". The owner could face a fine or a one-month jail term.

1936: Amended to allow Indian agents to direct band council meetings, and to cast a deciding vote in the event of a tie.

1951: Amended to allow the sale and slaughter of livestock without an Indian Agent permit. Status women are allowed to vote in band elections. Attempts to pursue land claims, and the use of religious ceremonies (such as potlatches) are no longer prohibited by law. Further amended for the compulsory "enfranchisement" of First Nations women who married non-status men (including Metis, Inuit, non-status Indian, and non-aboriginal men) thus removing their status and that of any children from the marriage.

1961: Amended to end the compulsory "enfranchisement" of men or bands.

1985: Amended to allow First Nations women the right to keep or regain their status even after "marrying out", and to grant status to the children (but not grandchildren) of such a marriage. This amendment was debated in Parliament as Bill C-31. Under this amendment, full status Indians are referred to as 6-1. A child of a marriage between a status (6-1) person and a non-status person would qualify for 6-2 (half) status, but if his/her child in turn married another 6-2 or a non-status person, the child will be non-status. If a 6-2 marries a 6-1 or another 6-2, their children will revert to 6-1 status. Blood quantum is disregarded, or rather, replaced with a "two generation cut off clause". According to Thomas King, around half of status Indians are currently marrying non-status people, meaning this legislation will accomplish complete legal assimilation in a matter of a few generations.

2000: Amended to allow band members living off reserve to vote in elections and referendums.

Indian Case law

The 1895 Amendment of the Indian Act (Section 114) criminalized many Aboriginal ceremonies which resulted in the arrest and conviction of many Aboriginal people. These arrests were based on their participation in festivals, dances and ceremonies that involved the wounding of animals or humans, or the giving away of money or goods. The Dakota people (Sioux) who settled in Oak River, Manitoba in 1875 were known to conduct "Give Away Dances", also known as the "Grass Dance". The dance ceremony involved the giving away and exchange of blankets and horses and therefore breached Section 114 of the Indian Act. As a result, Wanduta, an elder of the Dakota community, was sentenced to four months of hard labour and imprisonment on January 26th, 1903.

According to Canadian historian Constance Backhouse, the Aboriginal "Give Away Dances" were ceremonies that connected entire communities politically, economically and socially. These Dances affirmed kinship ties, provided elders with opportunities to pass on insight, legends and history to the next generation, and were a core part of aboriginal resistance to assimilation. It is estimated that between 1900 and 1904, fifty Aboriginal people were arrested and twenty were convicted for their involvement in such dances. The Indian Act was amended in 1951 to re-allow religious ceremonies including the "Give Away Dance". In R. v. Jim (1915), the B. C. Supreme Court found that Aboriginal hunting on Indian reserves should be considered federal jurisdiction under the Constitution and the Indian Act. The case involved provincial game laws.

The act was at the centre of the 1969 Supreme Court case R. v. Drybones regarding the conflict of a clause forbidding Indians to be drunk off the reserve with the Bill of Rights. The case is remembered for being one of the few in which the Bill of Rights prevailed. In Corbiere v. Canada (1999), voting rights on reserves were extended under Section Fifteen of the Canadian Charter of Rights and Freedoms.

Discriminatory definition issues

Bonita Lawrence (2003) discusses a feminist position on the relationship between federal definition and Indian identity in Canada. Until 1985, section 12(1)(b) of the Act "discriminated against Indian women by stripping them and their descendants of their Indian status if they married a man without Indian status". Under Section 12(2) of the act, "'illegitimate' children of status Indian women could also lose status if the alleged father was known not to be a status Indian and if the child's status as an Indian was "protested" by the Indian Agent." Further, Section 12(1)(a)(iv), which Lawrence calls the "double mother" clause, "removed status from children when they reached the age of 21 if their mother and paternal grandmother did not have status before marriage." Much of the discrimination stems from the Indian Act modifications in 1951.

She discusses the struggles of Jeannette Corbiere Lavell and Yvonne

Bedard in the early 1970s, two women who had both lost their status for marrying white men. The Canadian Supreme Court ruled that the Indian Act was not discriminatory as the pair gained the legal rights of white women at the same time they lost the status of Indian women. Finally, in 1981, Sandra Lovelace, a Maliseet woman from Tobique—Mactaquac forced the issue by taking her case to the United Nations Human Rights Committee. The Canadian law was amended in 1985.

The Indian Reserve System

The National Post, 2007/10/24   By Jonathan Kay

The reserve system is Canada's worst moral failing. Let's do the right thing and get rid of it.

When it comes to what needs fixing, every problem in this country pales beside our signature disgrace: the state of Canada's native reserves. The worst are bastions of truly Third World style poverty and decrepitude, infectious disease and stomach churning social pathologies.

In strictly numerical terms, the problem is not large. There are about 400,000 natives living on reserves - just 1.3% of the Canadian population. It would be a simple thing to cap this wellspring of misery if we had the right policies in place. But that's the problem: We don't.

Every time the native file makes the news, the proposed solutions are the same: more money and more self government. Each year the federal government spends over $8 billion on reserve resident natives, or $80,000 per reserve resident household (a statistic I never get tired of quoting, because it puts to rest the idea that natives are somehow being nickel and dimed under the current system). We have handed over all sorts of powers to native bands, even creating a new extra constitutional order of government in the process.

None of this has worked, and the reason is simple: Our policy of propping up reserves with massive government subsidies flies in the

211

face of three well observed empirical truths learned the hard way in societies around the world.

- The modern global economy is driven by cities, which serve as hubs for high value knowledge industries, skilled workers and transportation networks. Rural economies have been dying since the Second World War. No government would pay white Canadians to confine themselves to the jobless outback, hundreds of miles from the country's universities and job centres (unless, perhaps, they lived in Atlantic Canada, a subject for a separate "Fixing Canada" column). Yet that is exactly what we do with our native population.

- One of the great lessons of the 20th century was that collective land ownership is a recipe for economic disaster. Behind the Iron Curtain, agricultural productivity exploded once people were given the right to own their own parcels of land outright, and sell the proceeds for profit. As Peruvian economist Hernando de Soto has definitively shown, denying land title to slum dwellers is one of the main impediments to prosperity in poor societies.

  Yet almost two decades after the Iron Curtain fell, our reserves are still run literally like Marxist workers' collectives (to the extent anyone actually works). Every once in a while a Canadian reporter wanders around a reserve and writes shocked dispatches about the run down quality of housing stock. Question: Would you pay good money to take care of your house if you couldn't sell it, couldn't use it to acquire mortgage financing, and you knew someone else would build you a new one as soon as the old one collapsed?

- Welfare destroys societies. Temporary government entitlements such as EI *(Employment Insurance)* are fine for helping people get back on their feet. But when they become the permanent income source for an entire community, be it an inner city American ghetto or a Canadian native reserve, civic life unravels. In a welfare society, the discipline and pride of workaday life are absent, men lose their social function, alcoholism carries no price (the cheque arrives whether you're drunk or sober) and people are encouraged to view the government as nothing but a platform for doling out booty.

All three of these principles have guided Western policymakers for generations. Yet when it comes to natives, we pretend we never learned them. Many aboriginal advocates claim that racism is the main barrier facing natives. I would say it's the opposite: We somehow have convinced ourselves that native societies have the collective, superhuman ability to resist the gravitational socioeconomic forces governing every other society on Earth. Like all utopian experiments, this one has led to disaster and heartache, played out in everything from water contamination to glue sniffing to abused children.

My fix for Canada is to make life better for natives by treating them like real human beings who are governed by the same empirically observed weaknesses and incentives as the rest of humanity, not Rousseauvian noble savages.

A proper native policy would bel guided by the three principles listed above. The most decrepit and remote reserves, such as Kashechewan and Natuashish, would simply be torn down, their inhabitants installed at government expense in population centres of the residents' choice. The hundreds of millions of dollars that go into running these hell holes would be used to teach job skills, detox the drunks, educate the children, and otherwise integrate the families into the mainstream of Canadian life.

Those reserves that have a fighting chance at developing a self sustaining local economy, either through proximity to urban centres, tourism, agri-business or resource extraction, would be reorganized as municipal corporations. Land would be privatized and turned over to individuals, who would then own it in fee simple. Natives would stay if they chose, but only if they could find the employment necessary to feed them selves: Aside from treaty mandated entitlements and regular government social programs, they would be cut off from the dole.

Self-government would be possible, but only in the same limited way that any Canadian city or town is self governing. The conceit that native reserves can be re-conceived as culturally distinct "nations" would be given up in favour of a model that promotes integration.

All this, of course, would represent a massive legal and political undertaking . . . requiring not only the destruction of the Indian Act, but also, possibly, a rewriting of the Constitution. Even the act of parcelling out reserve land to band members would itself be a decades long exercise, requiring armies of land surveyors and bureaucrats to accomplish. This is a radical fix I am proposing, and I have no illusions about how wrenching the experience of cultural dislocation would be for the affected communities.

That said, it is a trauma that need be inflicted only once . . . as opposed to the status quo, under which every generation of our reserve resident natives suffers under our dysfunctional system afresh. Which, I ask, is the more inhumane?

The Majority of Indians Live in Cities

From CBC News, 2010/04/06; lightly edited and formatted:
http://www.cbc.ca/canada/story/2010/03/31/
urban-aboriginal-peoples-hope-city.html

Hope in the City

Almost half of Canadian aboriginal people are city dwellers, and a new study released to the CBC by the Environics Institute suggests many have no plans to return to their home reserve. The national Urban Aboriginal Peoples Study of 2,614 self identified aboriginal people found that while many native Canadians maintain ties with their home communities, only three in 10 first generation urban aboriginal people have moved back to their home communities since moving to the city.

"Notwithstanding the sense of connection majorities of urban aboriginal peoples have to their communities of origin, the large majority of urban aboriginal peoples feel their current city of residence is home," the study said. "When asked 'where is home for you?' seven in 10 (71 per cent) UAPS participants say it is their current city of residence."

Native Canadians in 11 urban centres across the country participated in the study, which included person to person interviews conducted from March to October 2009. The Urban Aboriginal Peoples Study set out to examine the attitudes of native Canadians who call the city home. Non-aboriginal people were also interviewed in a separate poll.

Half of the country's 1,172,790 aboriginal Canadians lived in urban centres, according to the 2006 census. Nine in 10 of those interviewed in the study said they liked living in their city at least somewhat. "Within Canada's cities, urban aboriginal peoples are seeking to become a significant and visible part of the urban landscape," the study said. "They like living in their cities and majorities feel they can make a positive difference in their urban homes. Notably, they are as likely as non-aboriginal people to feel this way."

Eighty-two per cent of participants said they were "very proud" of their specific aboriginal identity, that is, First Nations, Métis or Inuk. Slightly fewer (70%) said the same about being Canadian. And most are confident that they can retain cultural ties in an urban setting. Six in 10 were completely or somewhat unworried about losing contact with their culture, while a minority were totally (17%) or somewhat (21%) concerned.

Perceptions of racism

'It's so weird to say I'm an urban aboriginal because no matter where I go, I say I'm from Indian Brook, Nova Scotia, and that's my home community. But when I'm talking to people from home, they ask where I'm from, and I say that I'm from Halifax.'   Ashley Julian, Halifax

'Self determination, that is the motivating factor. So the question off reserve and in cities is 'what form does that take over time?' We're not going to get there overnight but we're certainly on that path.
'
                                        Damon Johnston, Winnipeg

215

'When my mother came to Montreal she didn't want to take the bus, she'd rather walk everywhere because she was afraid of white people. People who come here know about mainstream culture only by what they saw on TV.'   Tina Pisutkie, Montreal

Participants in the study did note, however, that while they have a strong sense of pride in their culture and their country, a majority continue to experience negative stereotypes. "If there is a single urban aboriginal experience, it is the shared perception among First Nations peoples, Métis and Inuit, across cities, that they are stereotyped negatively," the report said. "Indeed, most report that they have personally experienced negative behaviour or unfair treatment because of who they are."

Almost 9 in 10 of those native Canadians interviewed said they believe others behave unfairly or negatively toward aboriginal people. Seventy per cent said they had been teased or insulted because of their background. Many of the aboriginal respondents also believe other Canadians hold negative stereotypes against them. Almost three in four perceive assumptions about addiction problems in the aboriginal community, while many felt negative stereotypes about laziness (30%), lack of intelligence (20%) and poverty (20%).

One participant in the study said the stereotypes tend to be twofold, aboriginal peoples as both romantic ideals and troublemakers. "There's that impression of (the) noble savage, there's like the exotic romantic view, and generally we're viewed as problematic," one participant said. "You know, blocking bridges, protesting and always looking for a free lunch."

In contrast, the survey of non-aboriginal city dwellers found generally good impressions of native Canadians. Researchers labelled 45% of urban non-native Canadians as "cultural romantics" who believe in the artistic and cultural contributions of aboriginal people to Canadian society. As well, these survey respondents are optimistic that the lives of aboriginal people will improve in the next generation. However, the survey found 24% could be described as "dismissive nay sayers" who tend to hold more negative impressions.

Education a top priority

Participants in the study were also asked about their goals, which closely mirrored those of many Canadians. For example, respondents said their top aspirations are to complete their education (28%), start or raise a family (24%) and have a satisfying career (22%). Many participants also saw education as a top priority for themselves and future generations, but reported financial cost as a major obstacle to post-secondary studies.

Schooling is a top hope for future generations. When asked how they would like their children's and grandchildren's lives to be different from their own, one in five mentioned education. Slightly fewer hoped for a solid cultural connection (18%) and a life without racism (17%).

The Environics Institute

The study suggests that many aboriginal people are clearly concerned about how to pay for that future. Money was cited as the No. 1 barrier to getting a post secondary education among 36% of those planning to attend, and 45% of those already enrolled in, a university or college.

Little faith in justice system

One out of every two urban native Canadians interviewed say they have had serious involvement with the Canadian justice system in the past decade: 52% have been a crime witness or a victim, or have been arrested or charged. Of these, nearly 4 in 10 believe they have been treated unfairly by the system, while 57% believed they received a fair shake.

The participants also tended to lack faith in the justice system. More than half of aboriginal respondents have little (33%) to no (22%) confidence, while 6% have a great deal. A majority of respondents (56%) supported the idea of creating an aboriginal only justice system separate from mainstream Canadian courts.

One Economy

The Economy of Canada

From Wikipedia; lightly edited and formatted:
http://en.wikipedia.org/wiki/Economy_of_Canada

Canada has the tenth largest economy in the world (measured in US dollars at market exchange rates) is one of the world's wealthiest nations, and a member of the Organization for Economic Co-operation and Development (OECD) and Group of Eight (G8). As with other developed nations, the Canadian economy is dominated by the service industry, which employs about three quarters of Canadians. Canada is unusual among developed countries in the importance of the primary sector, with the logging and oil industries being two of Canada's most important. Canada also has a sizable manufacturing sector, centred in Central Canada, with the automobile industry especially important.

Canada has one of the highest levels of economic freedom in the world. Today Canada closely resembles the U.S. in its market oriented economic system, and pattern of production. As of June 2009, Canada's national unemployment rate stood at 8.6% as the effect of the world economic crisis settled in and more people looked for work. Provincial unemployment rates vary from a low of 3.6% in Alberta to a high of 15.6% in Newfoundland and Labrador; however, Newfoundland and Labrador was the only province with employment gains in June of 2009, up 2,500. At the same time, the unemployment rate edged up to 15.6% from previous lows as more people entered the labour force. According to the Forbes Global 2000 list of the world's largest companies in 2008, Canada had 69 companies in the list, ranking 5th

218

next to France. As of 2008, Canada's total government debt burden is the lowest in the G8.

International trade makes up a large part of the Canadian economy, particularly of its natural resources. The United States is by far its largest trading partner, accounting for about 76% of exports and 65% of imports as of 2007. Canada's combined exports and imports ranked 8th among all nations in 2006.

Economic sector: Canada has considerable natural resources spread across its varied regions. In British Columbia, the forestry industry is of great importance, while the oil industry is important in Alberta and Newfoundland and Labrador. Northern Ontario is home to a wide array of mines, while the fishing industry has long been central to the character of the Atlantic provinces, though it has recently been in steep decline. Canada has mineral resources of coal, copper, iron ore, and gold.

These industries are increasingly becoming less important to the overall economy. Only some 4% of Canadians are employed in these fields, and they account for less than 6% of GDP. They are still paramount in many parts of the country. Many, if not most, towns in northern Canada, where agriculture is difficult, exist because of a nearby mine or source of timber. Canada is a world leader in the production of many natural resources such as gold, nickel, uranium, diamonds and lead. Several of Canada's largest companies are based in natural resource industries, such as EnCana, Potash, Cameco, Goldcorp, and Barrick Gold. The vast majority of these products are exported, mainly to the United States. There are also many secondary and service industries that are directly linked to primary ones. For instance one of Canada's largest manufacturing industries is the pulp and paper sector, which is directly linked to the logging industry.

The relatively large reliance on natural resources has several effects on the Canadian economy and Canadian society. While manufacturing and service industries are easy to standardize, natural resources vary greatly by region. This ensures that differing economic structures developed in each region of Canada, contributing to Canada's strong regionalism. At the same time the vast majority of these resources are exported, integrating Canada closely into the international economy. Howlett and Ramesh argue that the inherent instability of such industries also contributes to greater government intervention in the economy, to reduce the social impact of market changes.

Such industries also raise important questions of sustainability. Despite many decades as a leading producer, there is little risk of depletion. Large discoveries continue to be made, such as the massive nickel find at Voisey's Bay. The far north remains largely undeveloped as producers await higher prices or new technologies as many operations in this region are not yet cost effective. In recent decades Canadians have become less willing to accept the environmental destruction associated with exploiting natural resources. High wages and Aboriginal land claims have also curbed expansion. Instead many Canadian companies have focussed their exploration and expansion activities overseas where prices are lower and governments more accommodating. Canadian companies are increasingly playing important roles in Latin America, Southeast Asia, and Africa.

It is the renewable resources that have raised some of the greatest concerns. After decades of escalating overexploitation the cod fishery all but collapsed in the 1990s, and the Pacific salmon industry also suffered greatly. The logging industry, after many years of activism, have in recent years moved to a more sustainable model.

Canada is one of the few developed nations that is a net exporter of energy. Most important are the large oil and gas resources centred in Alberta and the Northern Territories, but also present in neighbouring British Columbia and Saskatchewan. The vast Athabasca Tar Sands give Canada the world's second largest reserves of oil after Saudi Arabia according to USGS. In British Columbia and Quebec, as well as Ontario, Saskatchewan, Manitoba and the Labrador region, hydroelectric power is an inexpensive and relatively environmentally friendly source of abundant energy. In part because of this, Canada is also one of the world's highest per capita consumers of energy. Cheap energy has enabled the creation of several important industries, such as the large aluminum industry in Quebec, Alberta and British Columbian.

Historically, an important issue in Canadian politics is that while Western Canada is one of the world's richest sources of energy, the industrial heartland of Southern Ontario has fewer sources of power. It is, however, cheaper for Alberta to ship its oil to the western United States than to eastern Canada. The eastern Canadian ports thus import significant quantities of oil from overseas, and Ontario makes significant use of nuclear power.

In times of high oil prices, the majority of Canada's population suffers, while the West benefits. The National Energy Policy of the early 1980s attempted to force Alberta to sell low priced oil to eastern Canada. This policy proved deeply divisive, and quickly lost its importance as oil prices collapsed in the mid-1980s. One of the most controversial sections of the Canada - United States Free Trade Agreement of 1988 was a promise that Canada would never charge the United States more for energy than fellow Canadians.

Agriculture in Canada

Canada is also one of the world's largest suppliers of agricultural products, particularly of wheat and other grains. Canada is a major exporter of agricultural products, to the United States but also to Europe and East Asia. As with all other developed nations the proportion of the population and GDP devoted to agriculture fell dramatically over the 20th century.

As with other developed nations, the Canadian agriculture industry receives significant government subsidies and supports. However, Canada has been a strong supporter of reducing market influencing subsidies through the World Trade Organization. In 2000, Canada spent approximately CDN $4.6 billion on supports for the industry. Of this, $2.32 billion was classified under the WTO designation of "green box" support, meaning it did not directly influence the market, such as money for research or disaster relief. All but $848.2 million were subsidies worth less than 5% of the value of the crops they were provided for, which is the WTO threshold. Consequently, Canada used only $848.2 million of its $4.3 billion subsidy allowance granted by the WTO.

Manufacturing

The general pattern of development for wealthy nations was a transition from a primary industry based economy to a manufacturing based one, and then to a service based economy. Canada did not follow this pattern; manufacturing has always been secondary, though certainly not unimportant. Partly because of this, Canada did not suffer as greatly from the pains of de-industrialization in the 1970s and 1980s.

Central Canada is home to branch plants to all the major American and Japanese automobile makers and many parts factories owned by Canadian firms such as Magna International and Linamar Corporation. Central Canada today produces more vehicles each year than the neighbouring U.S. state of Michigan, the heart of the American automobile industry. Manufacturers have been attracted to Canada due to the highly educated population with lower labour costs than the United States. Canada's publicly funded health care system is also an important attraction, as it exempts companies from the high health insurance costs they must pay in the United States.

Much of the Canadian manufacturing industry consists of branch plants of United States firms, though there are some important domestic manufacturers, such as Bombardier Inc.. This has raised several concerns for Canadians. Branch plants provide mainly blue collar jobs, with research and executive positions confined to the United States. (citation needed)

De-industrialization in Canada has become a serious problem, especially in Ontario (which is very dependent on the automotive industry), with foreign businesses closing plants across the board. The economic crisis is only worsening the situation, with even more plants closing, Oshawa and Windsor, Ontario being especially hard hit.

Service Sector

The service sector in Canada is vast and multifaceted, employing some three quarters of Canadians and accounting for over two thirds of GDP. The largest employer is the retail sector, employing almost 12% of Canadians. The retail industry is mainly concentrated in a relatively small number of chain stores clustered together in shopping malls. In recent years the rise of big box stores, such as Wal-Mart (of the United States) and Future Shop (a subsidiary of the US based Best Buy), have led to fewer workers in this sector and a migration of retail jobs to the suburbs.

The second largest portion of the service sector is the business services, employing only a slightly smaller percentage of the population. This includes the financial services, real estate, and communications industries. This portion of the economy has been rapidly growing in recent years. It is largely concentrated in the major urban centres, especially Toronto and Calgary (see Banking in Canada).

The education and health sectors are two of Canada's largest, but both are largely under the purview of the government. The health care industry has been rapidly growing, and is the third largest in Canada. Its rapid growth has led to problems for governments who must find money to fund it.

Canada has an important high tech industry, and also an entertainment industry creating content both for local and international consumption. Tourism is of increasing importance, with the vast majority of international visitors coming from the United States. Though the recent strength of the Canadian Dollar has hurt this sector, other nations such as China have increased tourism to Canada.

Regional imbalances

The Canadian economy differs greatly from region to region. Traditionally Central Canada has been the economic engine of Canada, home to more than half of its population and much of its industry.

223

Recent years have seen rapid growth in Western Canada as trade with Asia has enriched British Columbia and oil wealth provided a major boost to Alberta and Saskatchewan.

The four Atlantic provinces, though once the centre of economic activity, underwent a major decline in the late 19th century and have traditionally been significantly poorer than the rest of Canada, especially after the recent collapse of the fishing industry. Recent years have seen some significant moves towards diversification, especially as offshore oil and gas wealth have begun to flow into the region. Quebec has also traditionally been poorer than the Canadian average although by a lesser margin than the Atlantic provinces. In more recent years Newfoundland and Labrador have started to see a change in their economy, being called the "Celtic tiger of Canada," (in a comparison to the economic transformation in Ireland); it has also been called a "mini Alberta" because of new oil and gas exploration. While many inhabitants of Newfoundland and Labrador still emigrate to Alberta for higher paying jobs, the provinces population has been rising in recent years with people deciding to move back home.

Canada – United States Relations

Canada and the United States share a deep and common trading relationship. Canada's job market continues to perform well along with the U.S., reaching a 30 year low in the unemployment rate in December 2006, following 14 consecutive years of employment growth. Disputes over trade tariffs, multilateral military action and controversial Canadian legislation such as same sex marriage, disability rights, racism, immigration law, and legal medical marijuana have raised tensions and cooled relations between these two countries.

Despite these differences, the United States is by far Canada's largest trading partner, with more than $1.7 billion CAD in trade per day in 2005. 81% of Canada's exports go to the United States, and 67% of Canada's imports are from the United States. Trade with Canada makes up 23% of America's exports and 17% of its imports. By comparison, in 2005 this was more than U.S. trade with all countries in the European

Union combined, and well over twice U.S. trade with all the countries of Latin America combined. Just the two way trade that crosses the Ambassador Bridge between Michigan and Ontario equals all U.S. exports to Japan. Canada's importance to the United States is not just a border state phenomenon: Canada is the leading export market for 35 of 50 U.S. states, and is the United States' largest foreign supplier of energy.

Bilateral trade increased by 52% between 1989, when the US - Canada Free Trade Agreement (FTA) went into effect, and 1994, when the North American Free Trade Agreement (NAFTA) superseded it. Trade has since increased by 40%. NAFTA continues the FTA's moves toward reducing trade barriers and establishing agreed upon trade rules. It also resolves some long standing bilateral irritants and liberalizes rules in several areas, including agriculture, services, energy, financial services, investment, and government procurement. NAFTA forms the largest trading area in the world, embracing the 406 million people of the three North American countries.

The largest component of US - Canada trade is in the commodity sector. The U.S. is Canada's largest agricultural export market, taking well over half of all Canadian food exports. Similarly, Canada is the largest market for U.S. agricultural goods with nearly 20% of American food exports going to its Northern neighbour. Nearly two-thirds of Canada's forest products, including pulp and paper, are exported to the United States; 72% of Canada's total newsprint production also is exported to the U.S.

At $73.6 billion in 2004, U.S. - Canada trade in energy is the largest U.S. energy trading relationship, with the overwhelming majority ($66.7 billion) being exports from Canada. The primary components of U.S. energy trade with Canada are petroleum, natural gas, and electricity. Canada is the United States' largest oil supplier and the fifth largest energy producing country in the world. Canada provides about 16% of U.S. oil imports and 14% of total U.S. consumption of natural gas. The United States and Canada's national electricity grids are linked and both countries share hydro power facilities on the borders.

While most of the U.S. - Canada trade flows smoothly, there are bilateral trade disputes occasionally, particularly in the agricultural and cultural fields. Usually these issues are resolved through bilateral consultative forums or referral to World Trade Organization (WTO) or NAFTA dispute resolution. In May 1999, the U.S. and Canadian Governments negotiated an agreement on magazines that provides increased access for the U.S. publishing industry to the Canadian market. The United States and Canada also have resolved several major issues involving fisheries. By common agreement, the two countries submitted a Gulf of Maine boundary dispute to the International Court of Justice in 1981; both accepted the Court's 12 October 1984 ruling which demarcated the territorial sea boundary. A current issue between the United States and Canada is the softwood lumber dispute, as the U.S. alleges that Canada unfairly subsidizes its forestry industry.

In 1990, the United States and Canada signed a bilateral Fisheries Enforcement Agreement, which has served to deter illegal fishing activity and reduce injury during fisheries enforcement incidents. The U.S. and Canada signed a Pacific Salmon Agreement in June 1999 that settled differences over implementation of the 1985 Pacific Salmon Treaty for the next decade.

Canada and the United States signed an aviation agreement during Bill Clinton's visit to Canada in February 1995, and air traffic between the two countries has increased dramatically as a result. The two countries also share in operation of the St. Lawrence Seaway, connecting the Great Lakes to the Atlantic Ocean.

The U.S. is Canada's largest foreign investor and the most popular destination for Canadian foreign investments; at the end of 2007, the stock of U.S. direct investment in Canada was estimated at $293 billion while Canadian direct investment (stock) in the United States was valued at $213 billion. The U.S. accounts for 59% of total foreign direct investment (FDI) in Canada, while Canadian FDI in the U.S. accounts for 10% (5th largest foreign investor). The U.S. investments are primarily in Canada's mining and smelting industries, petroleum, chemicals, the manufacture of machinery and transportation equipment, and finance while Canadian investment in the United States is concentrated in manufacturing, wholesale trade, real estate, petroleum, finance, and insurance and other services.

Electrical Power & the BNA

From The Freedom Party; lightly edited and formatted:
http://www.freedomparty.ca/htm/en/constitution1867.htm

"Non-Renewable Natural Resources, Forestry Resources and Electrical Energy 92A.

(1) Laws respecting non-renewable natural resources, forestry resources and electrical energy. In each province, the legislature may exclusively make laws in relation to

   (a) exploration for non-renewable natural resources in the province;
   (b) development, conservation and management of non-renewable resources natural resources and forestry resources in the province, including laws in relation to the rate of primary production therefrom; and
   (c) development, conservation and management of sites and facilities in the province for the generation and production of electrical energy.

(2) In each province, the legislature may make laws in relation to the export from the province to another part of Canada of the primary production from non-renewable natural resources and forestry resources in the province and the production from facilities in the province for the generation of electrical energy, but such laws may not authorize or provide for discrimination in prices or in supplies exported to another part of Canada.

(3) Nothing in subsection (2) derogates from the authority of Parliament to enact laws in relation to the matters referred to in that subsection and, where such a law of Parliament and a law of a province conflict, the law of Parliament prevails to the extent of the conflict.

(4) In each province, the legislature may make laws in relation to the raising of money by any mode or system of taxation in respect of

    (a) non-renewable natural resources and forestry resources in the province and the primary production therefrom, and

    (b) sites and facilities in the province for the generation of electrical energy and the production therefrom, whether or not such production is exported in whole or in part from the province, but such laws may not authorize or provide for taxation that differentiates between production exported to another part of Canada and production not exported from the province.

(5) The expression "primary production" has the meaning assigned by the Sixth Schedule.

(6) Nothing in subsections (1) to (5) derogates from any power or rights that a legislature or government of a province had immediately before the coming into force of this section.

Banks & Brokerages in Canada

From Wikipedia; lightly edited and formatted:
http://en.wikipedia.org/wiki/Banking_in_Canada

Banking in Canada is widely considered the most efficient and safest banking system in the world, ranking as the world's soundest banking system according to a 2008 World Economic Forum report. According to the Department of Finance, Canada's banks, also called chartered banks, have over 8,000 branches and almost 18,000 automated teller machines (ATMs) across the country. In addition, Canada has the highest number of ABMs per capita in the world and benefits from the highest penetration levels of electronic channels such as debit cards, Internet banking, and telephone banking.

Despite various loss events (such as the Latin American debt crisis, the collapse of Olympia and York, Enron related liabilities, and the U.S. sub-prime mortgage crisis), the big five banks have thus far proven to be safe and stable companies. For example, in securities prospectuses the Royal Bank of Canada says it has paid a common share dividend in every year since 1870, the year after it received its banking charter. According to the Department of Finance, two small regional banks failed in the mid-1980s, the only such failures since 1923, which is the year Home Bank failed. There were no bank failures during the Great Depression.

Recent History

In the 1980s and 1990s, the largest banks acquired almost all significant trust and brokerage companies in Canada. They also started their own mutual fund and insurance businesses. As a result, Canadian banks broadened out to become supermarkets of financial services. After large bank mergers were ruled out by the federal government, some Canadian banks turned to international expansion, particularly in various U.S. markets such as banking and brokerage. Two other notable developments in Canadian banking were the launch of ING Bank of Canada (which relies mostly on a branchless banking model), and the slow emergence of non-bank mortgage origination companies.

A survey conducted in 2008 by the World Economic Forum called the Global Competitiveness Report of twelve thousand corporate executives concluded that Canada has the best banking system in the world, receiving a score of 6.8 out of possible seven.

The "Big Five" Banks

The five largest banks in Canada are:

- Royal Bank of Canada (RBC),
- Toronto Dominion Bank (TD),
- Bank of Montreal (BMO),
- Bank of Nova Scotia (BNS), and
- Canadian Imperial Bank of Commerce (CIBC).

Notable second tier banks include the National Bank of Canada, the Mouvement Desjardins (technically not a bank but an alliance of credit unions), HSBC Bank Canada, and ING Bank of Canada. These second tier organizations are largely Canadian domestic banking organizations. Insurance companies in Canada have also created deposit taking bank subsidiaries.

Unlike the smaller Canadian banks, the Big Five are not just Canadian banks, but are instead better described as international financial conglomerates, each with a large Canadian banking division. In fiscal 2007, RBC's Canadian segment called "Personal Financial Services" (the segment most related to what was traditionally thought of as retail banking) had revenue of only CAD$5,082 million (or 22.6%) of a total revenue of CAD$22,462 million.

Canadian retail operations of the Big Five comprise other activities that do not need to be operated from a regulated bank. These other activities include mutual funds, insurance, credit cards, and brokerage activities. In addition, they have large international subsidiaries. The Canadian banking operations of the Big Five are largely conducted out of each parent company, unlike U.S. banks that use a holding company structure to hold their primary retail banking subsidiaries.

Islamic Banking & Canadian Banks

From Richard Dawkins.net   http://richarddawkins.net/articles/2183

From the Globe and Mail (Thanks to Dd Fd for the linl)
http://www.theglobeandmail.com/servlet/story/RTGAM.20080125.
wcomment0125/BNStory/National/home

Banks are helping sharia make a back door entrance
Tarek Fatah

It seems only yesterday that Premier Dalton McGuinty declared: "There will be no sharia law in Ontario." Many of us, who witnessed the medieval nature of manmade sharia laws in our countries of birth, heaved a sigh of relief back in September of 2005. We thought this was the end of the attempt by Islamists to sneak sharia into a Western jurisdiction. We were wrong.

The campaign to introduce sharia is back. Last time, the campaign took a populist approach, invoking multiculturalism. This time, the pro-sharia lobby is dangling the carrot of new niche markets and has the backing of Canada's major banks. Such icons of the corporate world as Citibank NA, HSBC Holdings PLC, and Barclays PLC have endorsed sharia banking and have started offering Islamic financing products to a vulnerable Muslim population.

In May, 2007, The Globe reported that "Several Canadian financial institutions are preparing sharia compliant mortgages, insurance, taxi licensing and investment funds to help serve the country's fastest growing part of the population." Recently, the Toronto Star's business section reported that an unnamed bank may offer sharia loans as early as this summer; Le Journal de Montreal disclosed that Canada Mortgage and Housing Corporation(CMHC) was also getting in on the act. Stephanie Rubec, spokesperson for the CMHC, said the Crown corporation had launched a tender worth $100,000 to study Islamic mortgages for Muslim Canadians. Could she be oblivious to the fact that almost all Muslim Canadians currently have home mortgages through banks and don't feel they are living in sin? In fact, CMHC has gone a step further: it has quietly entered into a partnership with a Saudi company, AaYaan Holdings, to develop sharia compliant mortgage lending systems.

The origin of Islamic banking has its roots in the 1920s, but did not start until the late 1970s and owes much of its foundation to the Islamist doctrine of two people, Abul Ala Maudoodi of the Jamaat e Islami in Pakistan and Hassan al Banna of the Muslim Brotherhood in Egypt. The theory was put into practice by Pakistani dictator General Zia ul Haq who established sharia banking law in Pakistan.

Proponents of sharia banking rest their case on many verses of the Holy Koran that outlaw usury, not interest. Verses that address the question of loans and debts include:

Al Baqarah (2:275): God hath permitted trade and forbidden usury;

Al Baqarah (2:276): Allah does not bless usury, and He causes charitable deeds to prosper, and Allah does not love any ungrateful sinner.

Every English language translation of the Koran has translated the Arabic word "riba" as usury, not interest. Yet, Islamists have deliberately portrayed bank interest as usury and labelled the current banking system as un-Islamic. Instead, these Islamists have created exotic products with names that are foreign to much of the world's Muslim population. This is where they mask interest under the niqab of Mudraba, Musharaka, Murabaha, and Ijara. Two authors, both senior Muslim bankers, have written scathing critiques of sharia banking, one labelling the practice as nothing more than "deception," with the other suggesting the entire exercise was "a convenient pretext for advancing broad Islamic objectives and for lining the pockets of religious officials." Why Canadian banks would contribute to this masquerade is a question for all ordinary Canadians to ask.

Muhammad Saleem is a former president and CEO of Park Avenue Bank in New York. Prior to that, he was a senior banker with Bankers Trust where, among other responsibilities, he headed the Middle East division and served as adviser to a prominent Islamic bank based in Bahrain. In his book, Islamic Banking, *A $300 Billion Deception*, Mr. Saleem not only dismisses the founding premise of sharia and Islamic banking, he says, "Islamic banks do not practise what they preach: they all charge interest, but disguised in Islamic garb. Thus they engage in deceptive and dishonest banking practises."

Another expert, Timur Kuran, who taught Islamic Thought at the University of Southern California, mocks the very idea. In his book, *Islam and Mammon: The Economic Predicaments of Islamism*, Prof. Kuran writes that the effort to introduce sharia banking "has promoted the spread of anti-modern currents of thought all across the Islamic world. It has also fostered an environment conducive to Islamist militancy."

Dozens of Islamic scholars and imams now serve on sharia boards of the banking industry. Moreover, a new industry of Islamic banking conferences and forums has emerged, permitting hundreds of sharia scholars to mix and mingle with bankers and economists at financial centres around the globe. In the words of Mr. Saleem, who attended many such meetings, they gather "to hear each other praise each other for all the innovations they are making." He gives examples of how sharia scholars care only for the money they get from banks, willing to rubberstamp any deal where interest is masked.

No sooner had CMHC announced its plans to study sharia compliant mortgages, than an imam from Montreal's Noor Al Islam mosque offered his services to Canada's banks, claiming Muslims are averse to conventional mortgages because "it goes against their beliefs," a claim that would not withstand the slightest scrutiny.

Other academics who have studied the phenomenon have reached similar conclusions. Two New Zealand business professors, Beng Soon Chong and Ming-Hua Liu of Auckland University, in an October, 2007, study on the growth of Islamic banking in Malaysia, wrote: "Only a negligible portion of Islamic bank financing is strictly 'profit and loss sharing' based. Our study however, provides new evidence which shows that in practice Islamic deposits are not interest free." They concluded that the rapid growth in Islamic banking was "largely driven by the Islamic resurgence worldwide."

In the name of Islam, deception and dishonesty is being practised while ordinary Muslims are being made to feel that their interaction with mainstream banks is un-Islamic and sinful. As Mr. Saleem asks, "If Islamic banks label their hamburger a Mecca Burger, as long as it still has the same ingredients as a McDonald's burger, is it really any different in substance?"

Tarek Fatah is the author of Chasing a Mirage: The Tragic Illusion of an Islamic State, to be published in March.

Security Exchanges & Commissions

From the Department of Finance; lightly edited and formatted:
http://www.fin.gc.ca/n08/data/08-049_1-eng.asp

Designated Stock Exchanges

With the integration of global financial markets, the rapid growth in Canadian Registered Retirement Savings Plan (RRSP) and Deferred Profit Sharing Plan (DPSP) assets, the removal of the foreign content limit on tax deferred retirement assets enacted in 2005, and technological advances in securities trading systems, Canadian investors are increasingly looking to foreign securities listed on foreign stock exchanges for return enhancement and portfolio diversification. New domestic exchanges are also being created, expanding the range of publicly listed Canadian securities available to Canadian investors. This has contributed to a rise in the number of requests from domestic and foreign stock exchanges to be qualified under the Income Tax Act for RRSP and DPSP purposes.

Budget 2007 updated the concept of "prescribed stock exchange", used for a variety of purposes under the Income Tax Act, in order to make the prescription process more transparent and flexible to meet evolving market needs. In place of the two former lists of prescribed stock exchanges (domestic and foreign), there are now three categories of stock exchange: Designated Stock Exchange, Recognized Stock Exchange and Stock Exchange. A description of each category of exchange and their Income Tax Act implications are presented in Annex 5 of Budget 2007 (http://www.budget.gc.ca/2007/plan/bpa5a-eng.html).

Under the new system, securities listed on a Designated Stock Exchange are eligible to be held in an RRSP and a DPSP. Designated Stock Exchanges include all prescribed exchanges as of December 13, 2007, and additional exchanges designated by the Minister of Finance by way of public notice since this date (see Annex). This document presents some considerations against which additional exchanges will be evaluated for designation status as well as the process under which exchanges may seek to be designated by the Minister of Finance.

The Minister of Finance's role is to ensure that investments, given their tax deferred status for policy purposes, trade on well governed, regulated and transparent markets. Designated Stock Exchanges must therefore be explicitly designated, by public notice, by the Minister of Finance. Designated Stock Exchanges are also considered to be Recognized Stock Exchanges and Stock Exchanges for the purposes of the Income Tax Act. Recognized Stock Exchanges are determined by definition under that Act. "Stock Exchange" is not defined in the tax law; it is intended that the general legal and commercial meaning of the term will apply.

The new designation process and the kinds of considerations described herein will expedite the review of applications from exchanges and provide more transparency around the factors used to evaluate such applications. Designation status is not an endorsement or recommendation of individual securities listed and traded on the exchange.

Canadian Securities Commissions

From Wikipedia; lightly edited and formatted:
http://en.wikipedia.org/wiki/Canadian_securities_regulation

Canadian securities regulation is managed through laws and agencies established by Canada's 13 provincial and territorial governments. Each province and territory has a securities commission or equivalent authority.

Unlike other major federations, Canada does not have a securities regulatory authority at the federal government level. Provincial governments began to establish regulatory agencies in 1912 (in Manitoba), and the Privy Council decided in Lymburn and Mayland,

(1932) A.C. 318 that such legislation is more properly authorized under the provincial property and civil rights power, since it seeks to ensure that the sale of securities is done honestly and openly, rather than under the federal trade and commerce power. Notwithstanding the lack of a federal regulator, the provincial security commissions operate under a passport system, so that the approval of one commission essentially allows for registration in another province.

The federal and Ontario governments, most (but not all) national industry groups, and many media commentators argue that the current structure has resulted in operational inefficiencies, although no actual evidence of such inefficiencies has been provided. These groups argue that governments should consolidate the provincial regulatory bodies into a single combined entity. Over the past fifteen years, there have been repeated efforts to create a single regulator but all have failed.

Federal Finance Minister Jim Flaherty was reported in July 2008 to say that he was certain that Canada would soon have a single securities regulator. However, there is still no agreement from provinces other than Ontario. The Quebec National Assembly passed a unanimous resolution in October 2007 asking the federal government to abandon the single regulator project. The Quebec government has said it will never agree to it. The Expert Panel on Securities Regulation released its report in January 2009.

Designated Stock Exchanges & TFSAs

From the Department of Finance; lightly edited and formatted:
http://www.fin.gc.ca/n08/08-049-eng.asp

New Rules for Designated Stock Exchanges

The Honourable Jim Flaherty, Minister of Finance, today released new guidelines for stock exchanges that seek to become Designated Stock Exchanges for income tax purposes. The guidelines will provide greater transparency and increased opportunities for investors, and will improve the ability of Canadian capital markets to respond to global market developments.

"With today's release of principles that will guide our government's official designation of domestic and foreign stock exchanges, Canadians can make informed investment decisions confident that securities trade on well governed, regulated and transparent markets," said Minister Flaherty. "At the same time, foreign exchanges can now rely on clear rules in their efforts to attract Canadian investments."

Designation Status for TFSAs

In Budget 2007, the Government updated and streamlined the identification of stock exchanges for purposes of the Income Tax Act. The new three tiered system includes Designated Stock Exchanges, Recognized Stock Exchanges and Stock Exchanges. Designation status is particularly important for Registered Retirement Savings Plan (RRSP) investors, as securities listed on designated exchanges are eligible RRSP investments. They are also eligible investments for Deferred Profit Sharing Plans (DPSP), and will be eligible for the recently announced Tax Free Savings Account (TFSA).

Also released today is a complete list of current Designated Stock Exchanges, which include all former prescribed exchanges under the previous Income Tax Act provisions. Under the income tax rules, any future additions to the list will be approved by the Minister of Finance. Approvals will follow the process and criteria set out today.

Canada's Founding Values

Excerpt from Globe and Mail 2009/09/11   by Neil Reynolds

Demographics dictate a return to traditional values.

In his illuminating new book, economist Brian Lee Crowley anticipates a historic restoration of the principles by which the country governed

237

itself in the past - among them, the classically liberal principles of limited government and personal responsibility. Entitled Fearful Symmetry: The Fall and Rise of Canada's Founding Values, Mr. Crowley's contrarian assessment explains (he holds this belief), why demographic step by demographic step.

The fading of Quebec nationalism will combine with an eroding population to reverse the dysfunctional trends of the past 50 years. Put simply, Canada will soon lack the workers necessary to fund Big Government. The only alternative will be less government and more personal responsibility.

The two facts that will most significantly determine Canada's economic future, Mr. Crowley says, are the fact that Canadians do not have nearly enough babies to sustain Canada's approaching peak population and the fact that immigrants can't make up the difference. The probable consequences are: (1) Canada gradually loses influence in the world as its population shrinks and (2) Canada's standard of living stagnates.

Mr. Crowley, most recently the Clifford Clark Visiting Economist with the Department of Finance, says that people will need to work longer and harder, which (though difficult for people desperate to retire at 55) will restore the work ethic that once made Canadians an extraordinarily productive people. Canadians may expect less government because government won't be able to subsidize people who choose not to work harder and longer, he says. We can expect more personal responsibility because economic survival will require it.

But Canadians won't increase the country's birth rate merely by working longer and harder. Nor will government. The implications are dramatic - especially when contrasted to the United States, whose population will expand as Canada's falters. By 2050, Canada's projected population will be 44 million; the U.S. projected population will be as high as 550 million, reflecting a birth rate that The Economist magazine has described as "astonishing."

Canada and the U.S. will diverge in other ways. Canadians are already massing into three or four big cities; Americans are dispersing to outer suburbs and to the countryside, but places more distant from the U. S.-Canada border. In 2050, the median Canadian age will be 42; the median American age will be 36. The "shape" of the Canadian population will be like a vase - narrow at the bottom (reflecting the lack of children), wide at the shoulders (reflecting the higher percentage of older people); the "shape of the American population will be almost cylindrical. (By 2020, the proportion of children in the U.S. population will surpass China's.)

Canadians must anticipate that the "prosperity gap" between the two countries will grow much larger. Mr. Crowley observes: "Half a billion Americans, with the highest productivity in the world; a relatively young, flexible and highly educated work force, and a willingness to spend a significant share of GDP on defence would be a superpower perhaps even more formidable in 2050 than today - and possibly less inclined to pay attention to Canada's interests." (In these circumstances, Canada might be wise to negotiate a mobility-rights treaty with the U.S., either to give Canadians an escape route or to give Americans easy entry to our labour force.)

Canada's falling birth rate, Mr. Crowley suggests, has many causes, but he adds a couple of his own to the usual list (the Zeitgeist, the contraceptives, the two-worker family). "Over weaning government," he says, "has undermined families for the last 50 years." He attributes part of Canada's falling birth rate to the struggle to keep Quebec in Confederation and the creation of "pseudo-jobs" to absorb the surplus workers of the Baby Boom generation. Government, he says, has itself operated as a contraceptive.

All this sounds serious and sombre. Mr. Crowley's profound optimism, however, arises from the inevitable withering of the state that lies directly ahead, a withering already under way. "We are on the cusp of a tremendous renaissance," he says, "if we want to seize the moment." The disappearance of surplus workers will bring with it the disappearance of the government programs that purported to create jobs, "pulling hundreds of thousands of people out of dependency, pseudo-work and premature retirement." Real work will once more become the norm. Family will become important again, as will marriage.

Governments will increasingly revert to "The kinds of policies that underpinned our great success as a nation in our first century." The ensuing power shift will diminish the influence of Quebec and increase the influence of British Columbia and Alberta; in this way, the country will move "closer to the traditional values of our founders." Other provinces will move in the same direction: "Saskatchewan will almost certainly become more like Alberta," he writes. "In a few short years, the values of the left-liberal welfare state will seem a quaint echo of a receding past," Mr. Crowley says. "Politically, any party that can capture the high ground of Canada's traditional values will likely become the country's dominant party . . . The low rumble that you hear is the traditionalist juggernaut gathering force across the land . . . It will leave nothing as it was." We can only hope.

The Purpose of Stock Markets

From the National Post 2008/12/27   by William Hanley
(Lightly edited and formatted)

The Market was not established to manage savings
     . . . investors learned a hard lesson this year.

A man who barely made it through a particularly brutal day in the market called his financial advisor the next day; "May I please speak to Artie, my advisor?" The operator replied: "I'm sorry. Artie is deceased. Can anyone else help you?" The man said no and hung up. He called again ten minutes later and asked for Artie, his advisor. The operator said: "You just called a few minutes ago, didn't you? Artie has died. I'm not making this up." The man hung up again. Fifteen minutes later he called a third time and asked for Artie. By this time, the operator was fuming. "I've told you twice already. Artie is dead. He's not here! Why do you keep asking for him when I tell you he's dead?" The man replied: "I just like hearing it."

If there had been no mordant humour this past year in the markets, there would have been no humour at all - nothing whatsoever to laugh about. Even those out of stocks could barely manage a wan smile at the thought of getting negligible returns on their money market funds and government bonds. You were damned if you did and damned if you didn't, caught in limbo.

It was a market year to forget that will always be remembered by investors tested mightily by the second stock crash in a decade and by the bursting of the resource bubble against a toxic backdrop of a financial meltdown and recession triggered by the U.S. housing debacle. After a year that had everything in terms of high drama, most Canadian investors will be reflecting on what was and what might have been. While regret is a basically useless emotion, an exercise in self doubt, many people will be examining their behaviour in 2008 and wondering if they really do know themselves and their human capacity for risk.

With just a few days of trading left in the year, the S&P/TSX composite index is down 40% for 2008 and down 45% from its peak above 15,000 in June. Now, sadly for many buy and holders, most of the gains hard won since the tech crash of 2000 and market recovery beginning in 2002 have evaporated. Equally sadly, those investors who tip-toed back into the market late in the heady run-up have been handed their heads.

The stock market can be a cruel place for people to invest their life savings, as millions discovered in this annus horribilis. Millions upon millions worldwide are feeling hard done by right now and perhaps even a little sheepish, having been bushwhacked twice in just a decade. Investors everywhere should know that the stock market was not set up to manage their savings. It was established as the supposedly most efficient way of marshalling capital for companies. Wall Street, Bay Street and financial districts the world over, facilitate this process, taking handsome fees in the bargain.

After the grinding markets of the 1970s and since the market rebound of the 1980s, equities have become the investment vehicle of choice for the majority of savers, with mutual funds taking an ever bigger role in portfolios. The place of stocks in portfolios was questioned bitterly after the tech wreck of 2000 and is being questioned more bitterly still after this year's crash as the Bernie Madoff scandal and various other shenanigans have cast Wall Street - indeed, the entire financial industry - in an even more negative light.

Rightfully, investors feel betrayed, believing they have kept their part of the bargain - putting their savings in what they thought were safe hands. The Street, they believe, has not kept its part of the bargain - good, solid stewardship of assets.

The problem is that, at heart, the Street is not there to be a good steward, but a gatherer of capital for business with no end of self interest. Witness the billions in bonuses still being paid this Christmas despite the fact that trillions of paper assets have been vaporized. Witness the inability of regulators to regulate.

Investors and savers everywhere will surely now know that they are at the bottom of the investment industry food chain. That's the way it has been and always will be, protestations from the Street notwithstanding. As investors await their year-end quarterly statements with dread, some will be able to take a little comfort from the fact that in 2008 they've learned more about the markets and their own tolerance for risk. Financial Post whanley@nationalpost.com

---

Reforming Canadian Securities Regulation

Canada Library of Parliament (PRB 05-28E)
by Tara Gray & Andrew Kitching
http://www.parl.gc.ca/information/library/PRBpubs/prb0528-e.pdf

Introduction

Each day, several billion dollars are traded on Canadian capital markets. In an era in which capital flows effortlessly across borders, the effective regulation of these markets is crucial to the country's economic well-being. Efficient capital markets allocate resources rationally, focussing investment on the most constructive uses possible. This paper provides a general overview of the regulation of Canadian securities markets, their evolution, the benefits and costs of the current system, and possible reforms that would improve market efficiency.

Securities law exists primarily to protect investors from being deceived or defrauded by the companies that issue capital and the brokers who trade on capital markets. The protection offered under securities law is designed to create investor confidence in the markets. If the investing members of the public have faith in the integrity of capital markets, they will be more willing to invest. Shareholders who witness corporate scandals, or perceive that the only people who benefit are those with insider knowledge or connections, withdraw their money, depriving Canadian companies of much needed capital.

While the regulation of securities in Canada has historically fallen under provincial jurisdiction, some legal opinions have found that the federal government has the constitutional authority to pass comprehensive legislation regulating capital market activity within Canada. However, at present, the sale of securities is subject to the rules and regulations of 13 different provincial and territorial securities regulators. Navigating through these regulations is often time consuming and costly. It is argued, moreover, that over regulated capital markets hamper foreign investment in Canada and limit the opportunities available to Canadian investors. Additional costs associated with excessive regulation hurt Canadian companies trying to raise money in Canada and reduce their international competitiveness.

The profusion of regulation has led many analysts to argue that the current structure of capital markets is unsustainable without the enactment of uniform securities laws across Canada. The debate is whether harmonization can be achieved through coop~ration by provincial regulators or whether a more radical solution is necessary: the imposition of a single national securities regulator by the federal government. While this latter option is still under consideration, recent reform efforts have focussed on working within the current system.

Historical Background

In the early 19th century, deceitful eastern capitalists were increasingly defrauding people wishing to invest in America's frontier states. Unwitting investors were sold worthless stock in "fly by night concerns, visionary oil wells, distant gold mines and other like fraudulent exploitations." It was stated that these speculative ventures were backed up by nothing but the blue skies of Kansas, and in 1911 that state became the first North American jurisdiction to enact a securities law, later known as the "blue-sky law." Canadian provinces began passing their own securities legislation shortly afterwards. Manitoba enacted its first securities law in 1912, a modification of the Kansas law, and other Canadian provinces followed. Ontario overhauled its securities legislation in 1945, 1966, and again in 1978, introducing stiffer licensing requirements and new measures designed to prevent fraud. After each reform, many Canadian provinces followed the Ontario legislation and enacted similar laws.

For a more complete history of Canadian securities regulation, see Mark Gillen, Securities Regulation in Canada, 2nd ed., Carswell, Scarborough, 1998.

The Wise Persons' Committee and Recommendations for Reform

In December 2003, the Wise Persons' Committee (WPC), an independent body formed by the federal government and chaired by Michael Phelps and Harold MacKay, released its report on Canadian securities regulation. The WPC's mandate was to recommend a securities regulatory system that best supports competitiveness, innovation and growth in Canada's capital markets, responds to the requirements of regional capital markets and emerging public companies, and at the same time inspires and maintains investor confidence. The report, entitled It's Time, recommends that Canada adopt a single regulator administering a single code. This proposed new structure would be cooperatively created and overseen by the federal and provincial governments.

There appeared to be considerable support in the financial industry for a national securities commission. The presidents of the IDA and the Canadian Bankers Association both cited efficiency and a better match between markets and regulators as reasons for adopting a national body.

Provincial reaction to the idea of a national securities commission, however, was mixed. The Ontario Securities Commission supported it, but the Quebec Securities Commission opposed it. The Alberta and British Columbia commissions, for their part, had strong reservations, expressing fear that centralizing securities policy would impose uniform rules that ignore the varying needs of each provincial capital market.

A. Jurisdiction Over Securities Regulation

The Canadian Constitution does not explicitly assign securities regulation to either level of government. Regulation has traditionally fallen to the provinces under the "property and civil rights" power of the Constitution (subsection 92). The federal government also has jurisdiction over capital markets pursuant to its power to legislate in respect of "trade and commerce" under subsection 91 (2) of the Constitution Act.

In 2003, the WPC commissioned three legal opinions on this issue, all of which said that the federal government has the constitutional authority to pass comprehensive legislation regulating capital market activity within Canada. The WPC found that provincial cooperation would facilitate the process; but it also found that, in the absence of agreement, the federal government could impose a single national regulator to govern securities law in Canada, under the constitutional doctrine of federal paramountcy. It should be noted, however, that the jurisdiction of the federal government to override provincial securities law has never been tested in a court, and is not assured.

B. Recommendation for a Single National Securities Administrator

While the WPC report acknowledged that Canada's existing system of 13 provincial and territorial regulators has positive attributes, it claimed that the weaknesses of the system are serious and outweigh its strengths. According to the WPC, Canada suffers from inadequate enforcement and inconsistent investor protection. The Committee felt that the existing system also contributed to sluggish policy development, needless duplication, inefficiencies and costs, and regulatory complexities. The WPC concluded that these weaknesses make Canada less competitive than it must be at a time of increasing global competition.

The WPC also found the passport system was an inadequate solution to the weaknesses inherent in provincial regulation, for two reasons. First, the WPC claimed that the system would not improve the enforcement of laws. Provincial commissions would still have divergent enforcement priorities, with smaller provinces lacking the resources to properly enforce laws. Provincial commissions would also continue to have limited power to impose sanctions on breaches of the law in different jurisdictions. Second, the WPC believed that policy development under the passport system would continue to be sluggish and unresponsive, since it would continue to rely on the ability of provincial commissions to reach a consensus.

The WPC believed that a single securities commission, m which provincial governments electing to participate would pool some or all of their authority in a single regulator administering one set of rules, would be a considerable improvement on the existing system and would best achieve the objectives of an ideal securities regulatory structure. The Committee argued that the recommended national model would:

- significantly strengthen enforcement through more efficient allocation of resources, better coordination, and uniform investment protection across the country;
- facilitate better and, when needed, more timely policy innovation and development;

- address the disproportionate regulatory burden that the current system places on small and emerging companies;
- enhance the "brand" of Canada's securities regulation internationally;
- eliminate additional compliance costs resulting from multiple regulators;
- ensure responsiveness to local and regional needs through the participation of the provinces and capital market participants in its governance structure and regional offices;
- establish clear accountability and governance mechanisms; and
- simplify the current system by reducing the number of regulators from 13 to 1.

The report proposed that reform would begin through the enactment of a Canadian Securities Act that would provide a comprehensive scheme of capital markets regulation for Canada. The new legislation would be administered by a single Canadian Securities Commission consisting of nine full time, regionally representative commissioners two from each of Ontario and Quebec, one from each of British Columbia and Alberta, two from the remaining provinces and territories, and a ninth commissioner to be selected without regional restrictions. The federal Minister of Finance would be responsible for appointing the commissioners, based on nominees put forward by a Nominating Committee consisting of members from each province.

The report also proposed a Securities Policy Ministerial Committee made up of the federal Minister of Finance and provincial ministers responsible for securities regulation. This Ministerial Committee would provide a forum for policy and administrative input. The new structure would ensure responsiveness to Canada's capital markets and regions by locating the Commission's head office in the National Capital Region and by establishing "strong, functionally empowered regional offices" in Vancouver, Calgary, Winnipeg, Toronto, Montreal, and Halifax. A Capital Markets Advisory Committee would allow issuers and investors (the users of the system) to provide their input, and would preserve regional representation.

Conclusion

Since the release of the WPC report, the provinces and territories (with the exception of Ontario) have endorsed a passport system that would keep the existing infrastructure of 13 securities regulators intact. Ontario has rejected the agreement and continues to strongly endorse a single securities commission, similar to that proposed by the WPC. The federal government, in the March 2004 Budget, also endorsed a single national securities regulator.

Without Ontario's support, it is unlikely that the passport system will lead to significant improvements in the regulatory environment. A major reform of Canada's securities regulation system may require stronger intervention at the federal level.

The Courts & A National Securities Regulator

Nov 13, 2009, Bloomberg Press; lightly edited and formatted

By Joe Schneider

http://www.bloomberg.com/apps/news?pid=20601082&sid=aZXy3Wr.drig

The Canadian government will probably win approval at the country's highest court to create a national securities regulator, constitutional experts say. "The federal government has a pretty good case," Jean-Francois Gaudreault-DesBiens, professor of constitutional law at the Universite de Montreal, told a Toronto audience yesterday. "It will change the constitutional landscape."

Justice Minister Rob Nicholson said last month he will seek the opinion of the Supreme Court of Canada on whether the federal government can set up a national securities regulator. Finance Minister Jim Flaherty has sought to replace the 13 regional agencies that govern the securities industry to reduce costs and improve enforcement. Canada is the only member of the Group of Seven nations without a national securities watchdog. The government's efforts to create one have been opposed by provinces including Quebec and Alberta.

Quebec said in July it would seek an opinion from the provincial court of appeal on the legality of the plan. The federal government responded, saying it will ask the Supreme Court for an opinion when the legislation is ready in the second quarter of 2010.

The federal government will rely on a 1989 Supreme Court ruling upholding the validity of a federal anti-competition law known as the Combines Investigation Act, said law professor Peter Hogg. The Supreme Court, in General Motors of Canada Ltd. v. City National Leasing, said the law intrudes on provincial powers but "because the regulation of competition is so clearly of national interest" it must be upheld "without heed to the provincial legislation."

Uphold Law

"I believe that the court will uphold that," said Hogg, author of Constitutional Law of Canada, the single most cited book in decisions of the Supreme Court, according to the Osgoode Hall Law School.

Quebec will probably argue that the federal securities law doesn't meet the GM test, Gaudreault-DesBiens said. In order to move into provincial jurisdiction, the federal government is required to prove that provinces can't constitutionally enact the law, the Supreme Court said in the GM case. The provinces have had jurisdiction over securities for more than 100 years. They've simplified regulation with a so- called "passport" system, under which registrants filing in one province are automatically recognized in other provinces that adopted the passport. "The passport system works relatively well," he said.

Opt Out

A proposed provision in the national securities law, allowing provinces to opt out and maintain their regulatory power, will also help the federal government in arguing its case, former Supreme Court Judge John Major said. "So long as provinces can opt out, the federal government can regulate," Major told a group of lawyers and students at the symposium, hosted by the Blake, Cassels & Graydon LLP law firm.

Supreme Court judges might be reluctant to "push a stick in the eye of Quebec" by transferring powers from the province to the federal government and enflaming the nationalistic movement in the mostly French speaking population, Major said. Quebec twice held referenda on a proposal to separate from Canada, with federalists winning the 1995 vote by a margin of less than 1 percent.

Although Supreme Court judges insist they comply strictly with the law, they are affected by the prospect of splitting the country and that might factor into their decision, Major said in an interview following the discussion. "This has transcended the legal debate and has become a political holy grail," Gaudreault-DesBiens said.

Flat Rate Taxes and VATs

From Wikipedia; lightly edited and formatted:
http://en.wikipedia.org/wiki/Flat_tax

A flat tax (short for flat rate tax) is a tax system with a constant tax rate. Usually the term flat tax refers to household income (and sometimes corporate profits) being taxed at one marginal rate, in contrast with progressive taxes that vary according to parameters such as income or usage levels. Flat taxes offer simplicity in the tax code, which has been reported to increase compliance and decrease administration costs.

Flat tax schemes that allow a tax exemption for household income below a cutoff level are not true proportional taxes, because, for household incomes below the cutoff level, taxable income is less than total income.

Tax Distribution

Tax distribution is a hotly debated aspect of flat taxes. The relative fairness hinges crucially on what tax deductions are abolished when a flat tax is introduced, and who profits the most from those deductions.

Proponents of the flat tax claim it is fairer than stepped marginal tax rates, since everybody pays the same proportion. Opponents of the flat tax, on the other hand, claim that since the marginal value of income declines with the amount of income (the last $100 of income of a family living near poverty being considerably more valuable than the last $100 of income of a millionaire), taxing that last $100 of income the same amount despite vast differences in the marginal value of money is unfair.

Administration and enforcement

A flat tax taxes all income once at its source. Hall and Rabushka (1995) includes a proposed amendment to the US Revenue Code implementing the variant of the flat tax they advocate. This amendment, only a few pages long, would replace hundreds of pages of statutory language. As it now stands, the USA Revenue Code is over 9 million words long and contains many loopholes, deductions, and exemptions which, advocates of flat taxes claim, render the collection of taxes and the enforcement of tax law complicated and inefficient. It is further argued that current tax law retards economic growth by distorting economic incentives, and by allowing, even encouraging, tax avoidance. With a flat tax, there are fewer incentives to create tax shelters and to engage in other forms of tax avoidance.

Under a pure flat tax without deductions, companies could simply, every period, make a single payment to the government covering the flat tax liabilities of their employees and the taxes owed on their business income. For example, suppose that in a given year, ACME earns a profit of 3 million, pays 2 million in salaries, and spends an added 1 million on other expenses the IRS deems to be taxable income, such as stock options, bonuses, and certain executive privileges. Given a flat rate of 15%, ACME would then owe the IRS (3M + 2M + 1M) x0.15 = 900,000. This payment would, in one fell swoop, settle the tax liabilities of ACME's employees as well as taxes it owed by being a firm. Most employees throughout the economy would never need to interact with the IRS, as all tax owed on wages, interest, dividends, royalties, etc. would be withheld at the source. The main exceptions would be employees with incomes from personal ventures. The Economist claims that such a system would reduce the number of entities required to file returns from about 130 million individuals, households, and businesses, as at present, to a mere 8 million businesses and self-employed.

This simplicity would remain even if realized capital gains were subject to the flat tax. In that case, the law would require brokers and mutual funds to calculate the realized capital gain on all sales and redemptions. If there were a gain, 15% of the gain would be withheld and sent to the IRS. If there were a loss, the amount would be reported to the IRS, which would offset gains with losses and settle up with taxpayers at the end of the period.

Under a flat tax, the government's cost of processing tax returns would become much smaller, and the relevant tax bodies could be abolished or massively downsized. The people freed from working in administering taxes will then be employed in jobs that are more productive. If combined with a provision to allow for negative taxation, the flat tax itself can be implemented in an even simpler way.

It is invariably argued that a flat tax will greatly simplify tax compliance and administration. In fact, simplicity does not so much stem from the structure of tax rates as from the definition of what is subject to tax. Tax simplification - getting rid of all the deductions, exemptions, and special rules added over the years, is an issue wholly separable from that of the rate structure. A nation can vastly simplify its tax code while keeping its rate structure progressive. Similarly, a nation could establish a flat tax rate while retaining inordinately complex rules defining the nature of income.

Economic efficiency

A common approximation in economics is that the economic distortion or excess burden from a tax is proportional to the square of the tax rate. A 20 percent tax rate thus causes four times the excess burden or deadweight loss of a 10 percent tax, since it is twice the rate. Broadly speaking, this means that a low uniform rate on a broad tax base will be more economically efficient than a mix of high and low rates on a smaller tax base.

Revenues

Some claim the flat tax will increase tax revenues, by simplifying the tax code and removing the many loopholes currently exploit to pay less tax. The Russian Federation is a claimed case in point; the real revenues from its Personal Income Tax rose by 25.2% in the first year after the Federation introduced a flat tax, followed by a 24.6% increase in the second year, and a 15.2% increase in the third year. The Laffer curve predicts such an outcome, but attributes the primary reason for the greater revenue to higher levels of economic growth. The Russian example is often used as proof of this, although an IMF study in 2006 found that there was no sign "of Laffer-type behavioural responses generating revenue increases from the tax cut elements of these reforms" in Russia or in other countries.

Overall structure

Some taxes other than the income tax (for example, taxes on sales and payrolls) tend to be regressive. Hence, making the income tax flat could result in a regressive overall tax structure. Under such a structure, those with lower incomes tend to pay a higher proportion of their income in total taxes than the affluent do. The fraction of household income that is a return to capital (dividends, interest, royalties, profits of unincorporated businesses) is positively correlated with total household income. Hence a flat tax limited to wages would seem to leave the wealthy better off. Modifying the tax base can change the effects. A flat tax could be targeted at income (rather than wages), which could place the tax burden equally on all earners, including those who earn income primarily from returns on investment. Tax systems could utilize a flat sales tax to target all consumption, which can be modified with rebates or exemptions to remove regressive effects.

Border adjustable

A flat tax system and income taxes overall are not inherently border adjustable; meaning the tax component embedded into products via taxes imposed on companies (including corporate taxes and payroll taxes) are not removed when exported to a foreign country. Taxation systems such as a sales tax or value added tax can remove the tax component when goods are exported and apply the tax component on imports. The domestic products could be at a disadvantage to foreign products (at home and abroad) that are border adjustable, which would impact the global competitiveness of a country. Though, it's possible that a flat tax system could be combined with tariffs and credits to act as border adjustments. Implementing an income tax with a border adjustment tax credit is a violation of the World Trade Organization agreement. Tax exemptions (allowances) on low income wages, a component of most income tax systems could mitigate this issue for high labour content industries like textiles that compete Globally.

Tax rates around the world

Eastern Europe

Advocates of the flat tax argue that the former Communist states of Eastern Europe have benefited from the adoption of a flat tax. Most of these nations have experienced strong economic growth of 6% and higher in recent years, some of them, particularly the Baltic countries, experience exceptional GDP growth of around 10% yearly.

Lithuania, which levies a flat tax rate of 24% (previously 27%) on its citizens, has experienced amongst the fastest growth in Europe. Advocates of the flat tax speak of this country's declining unemployment and rising standard of living. They also state that tax revenues have increased following the adoption of the flat tax, due to a subsequent decline in tax evasion and the Laffer curve effect. Others point out, however, that Lithuanian unemployment is falling at least partly as a result of mass emigration to Western Europe. The argument is that Lithuania's comparatively very low wages, on which a non-progressive flat tax is levied, combined with the possibility now to work legally in Western Europe since accession to the European Union, is forcing people to leave the country en masse.

The Ministry of Labour estimated in 2004 that as many as 360,000 workers may have left the country by the end of that year, a prediction that is now thought to have been broadly accurate. The impact is already evident: in September 2004, the Lithuanian Trucking Association reported a shortage of 3,000 - 4,000 truck drivers. Large retail stores have also reported some difficulty in filling positions. However, the emigration trend has recently stopped as enormous real wage gains in Lithuania (presumably due to the shortage of workers) have caused a return of many migrants from Western Europe. In addition, it is clear that countries not levying a flat tax such as Poland also temporarily faced large waves of emigration after EU membership in 2004.

Whilst in most countries the introduction of a flat tax has coincided with strong increases in growth and tax revenue, there is no proven causal link between the two. For example, it is also possible that both are due to a third factor, such as new government that may institute other reforms along with the flat tax.

In Estonia, which has had a 26% (24% in 2005, 23% in 2006, 22% in 2007, 21% in 2008, 21% in 2009, planned 20% in 2010, 19% in 2011, 18% in 2012) flat tax rate since 1994, studies have shown that the significant increase in tax revenue experienced was caused partly by a disproportionately rising VAT revenue. Moreover, Estonia and Slovakia have high social contributions, pegged to wage levels. Both matters raise questions regarding the justice of the flat tax system, and thus its long term viability. The Estonian economist and former chairman of his country's parliamentary budget committee Olev Raju, stated in September 2005 that "income disparities are rising and calls for a progressive system of taxation are getting louder, this could put an end to the flat tax after the next election". However, this did not happen, since after the 2007 elections a right wing coalition was formed which has stated its will to keep the flat tax in existence. However, critics argue that the tax rates these countries have are actually more progressive than flat.

Countries that have flat tax systems

These are countries, as well as minor jurisdictions with the autonomous power to tax, that have adopted tax systems that are commonly described in the media and the professional economics literature as a flat tax.

Bulgaria	Albania	Czech Republic	Estonia
Georgia	Guernsey	Kazakhstan	Iceland
Iraq	Jersey	Kyrgyzstan	Latvia
Lithuania	Macedonia	Mongolia	Montenegro
Mauritius	Romania	Russia	Serbia
Slovakia	Ukraine		

Note: There is more detailed information available on this website.

Canada's GNP in 1939

From Le Quebecois Libre October 25, 2003

by Chris Leithner

http://www.quebecoislibre.org/031025-6.htm

Equally importantly, during the 1920s and 1930s Canada's external relations were commendably limited and non-interventionist. The Dominion, according to King, was "not inclined to organise or join in crusades on other continents (...) We are not asking and will not receive any help from outside in meeting (our) difficulties and we are unlikely to have any surplus of statesmanship or good fortune to bestow elsewhere." On the eve of war in 1939 he affirmed that "the idea that every twenty years this country should automatically and as a matter of course take part in a war overseas (...) to save, periodically, a continent that cannot run itself, and to these ends risk the lives of its people, bankruptcy and disunion, seems to many a nightmare and sheer madness." In that year Dominion, provincial and municipal governments consumed 19.5% of Canada's GNP; in the U.S., the corresponding levels of government consumed 22.5%.

Canadian & American Economies by Mark Steyn

Eco - Canadian & American Economies.wpd

From Hillsdale College / Imprimis; lightly edited and formatted:
http://www.immigrationwatchcanada.org/index.
php?module=pagemaster&PAGE_user_op=view_
printable&PAGE_id=2857&lay_quiet=1

Mark Steyn was invited by Hillsdale College to speak at the Free Market Forum Sept. 29, 2007. This month's edition of Imprimis presents an abridged version of that speech. Two Economies - One is Canadian, One Isn't; by Mark Steyn in Imprimis, February 09, 2008

Is Canada's Economy a Model for America?

Mark Steyn's column appears in the New York Sun, the Washington Times, Philadelphia's Evening Bulletin, and the Orange County Register. In addition, he writes for The New Criterion, MacLean's in Canada, the Jerusalem Post, The Australian, and Hawke's Bay Today in New Zealand. The author of National Review's Happy Warrior column, he also blogs on National Review Online and appears weekly on the Hugh Hewitt Radio Show. He is the author of several books, most recently America Alone: The End of The World as We Know It, a New York Times best seller and a number one best seller in Canada. A Canadian citizen, Mr. Steyn lives with his family in New Hampshire.

The following is abridged from a lecture delivered on the Hillsdale College campus September 29, 2007, at the second annual Free Market Forum, sponsored by the College's Centre for the Study of Monetary Systems and Free Enterprise. I was a bit stunned to be asked to speak on the Canadian economy. "What happened?" I wondered. "Did the guy who was going to talk about the Belgian economy cancel?" It is a Saturday night, and the Oak Ridge Boys are playing the Hillsdale

County Fair. Being from Canada myself, I am, as the President likes to say, one of those immigrants doing the jobs Americans won't do. And if giving a talk on the Canadian economy on a Saturday night when the Oak Ridge Boys are in town isn't one of the jobs Americans won't do, I don't know what is.

Unlike America, Canada is a resource economy: The U.S. imports resources, whereas Canada exports them. It has the second largest oil reserves in the world. People don't think of Canada like that. The Premier of Alberta has never been photographed in Crawford, Texas, holding hands with the President and strolling through the rose bower as King Abdullah of Saudi Arabia was. But Canada is nonetheless an oil economy-a resource economy. Traditionally, in America, when the price of oil goes up, Wall Street goes down. But in Canada, when the price of oil goes up, the Toronto stock exchange goes up, too. So we are relatively compatible neighbours whose interests diverge on one of the key global indicators.

As we know from 9/11, the Wahabbis in Saudi Arabia use their oil wealth to spread their destructive ideology to every corner of the world. And so do the Canadians. Consider that in the last 40 years, fundamental American ideas have made no headway whatsoever in Canada, whereas fundamental Canadian ideas have made huge advances in America and the rest of the Western world. To take two big examples, multiculturalism and socialized health care both pioneered in Canada, have made huge strides down here in the U.S., whereas American concepts, such as non- confiscatory taxation, remain as foreign as ever.

My colleague at National Review, John O'Sullivan, once observed that post-war Canadian history is summed up by the old Monty Python song that goes, "I'm a Lumberjack and I'm OK." If you recall that song, it begins as a robust paean to the manly virtues of a rugged life in the north woods. But it ends with the lumberjack having gradually morphed into a kind of transvestite pickup who likes to wear high heels and dress in women's clothing while hanging around in bars. Of course, John O'Sullivan isn't saying that Canadian men are literally cross dressers certainly no more than 35-40 percent of us . . . but rather that a once manly nation has undergone a remarkable psychological make over.

If you go back to 1945, the Royal Canadian Navy had the world's third largest surface fleet, the Royal Canadian Air Force was one of the world's most effective air forces, and Canadian troops got the toughest beach on D-Day. But in the space of two generations, a bunch of tough hombres were transformed into a thoroughly feminized culture that prioritizes all the secondary impulses of society welfare entitlements from cradle to grave over all the primary ones. And in that, Canada is obviously not alone. If the O'Sullivan thesis is flavoured, it's only because the lumberjack song could stand as the post-war history of almost the entire developed world.

Today, the political platforms of at least one party in the United States and pretty much every party in the rest of the Western world are nearly exclusively about those secondary impulses such as government health care, government day care, government this, and government that. And you have government health care, you not only annex a huge chunk of the economy, you also destroy a huge chunk of individual liberty. You fundamentally change the relationship between the citizen and the state into something closer to that of junkie and pusher, and you make it very difficult ever to change back. Americans don't always appreciate how far gone down this path the rest of the developed world is. In Canadian and Continental cabinets, the defence ministry is now a place where an ambitious politician passes through on his way up to important jobs like running the health department. And if you listen to recent Democratic presidential debates, it is clear that American attitudes toward economic liberty are being Canadianized.

To some extent these differences between the two countries were present at their creations. America's Founders wrote of "life, liberty and the pursuit of happiness." The equivalent phrase at Canada's founding was "peace, order and good government' - which words are not only drier and desiccated and stir the blood less, but they also presume a degree of statist torpor. Ronald Reagan famously said, "We are a nation that has a government, not the other way around." In Canada it too often seems the other way around.

All that being said, if you remove health care from the equation, the differences between our two economies become relatively marginal. The Fraser Institute's "Economic Freedom of the World 2007 Annual Report" ranks the U.S. and Canada together, tied in fifth place along with Britain. And here's an interesting point. The top ten most free economies in this report are Hong Kong, Singapore, New Zealand, Switzerland, United States, United Kingdom, Canada, Estonia, Ireland, and Australia: With the exception of Switzerland and Estonia, these systems are all British derived. They're what Jacques Chirac dismissively calls *"les anglo-saxon"*. And he and many other Continentals make it very clear that they regard free market capitalism as some sort of kinky Anglo-Saxon fetish. On the other hand, Andrew Roberts, the author of *A History of the English-Speaking Peoples since 1900*, points out that the two most corrupt jurisdictions in North America are Louisiana and Quebec-both French derived. Quebec has a civil service that employs the same number of people as California, even though California has a population nearly five times the size.

In the province of Quebec, it's taken more or less for granted by all political parties that collective rights outweigh individual rights. For example, if you own a store in Montreal, the French language signs inside the store are required by law to be at least twice the size of the English signs. And the government has a fairly large bureaucratic agency whose job it is to go around measuring signs and prosecuting offenders. There was even a famous case a few years ago of a pet store owner who was targeted by the Office De La Langue Francaise for selling English-speaking parrots. The language commissar had gone into the store and heard a bird saying, "Who's a pretty boy, then?" and decided to take action. I keep trying to find out what happened to the parrot. Presumably it was sent to a re-education camp and emerged years later with a glassy stare saying in a monotone voice, "Qui est un joli garçon, hein?".

The point to remember about this is that it is consonant with the broader Canadian disposition.

A couple of years ago it emerged that a few Quebec hospitals in the eastern townships along the Vermont border were, as a courtesy to their English speaking patients, putting up handwritten pieces of paper in the corridor saying "Emergency Room This Way" or "Obstetrics Department Second on the Left." But in Quebec, you're permitted to offer health care services in English only if the English population in your town reaches a certain percentage. So these signs were deemed illegal and had to be taken down. I got a lot of mail from Canadians who were upset about this, and I responded that if you accept that the government has a right to make itself the monopoly provider of health care, it surely has the right to decide the language in which it's prepared to provide that care. So my point isn't just about Quebec separatism. It's about a fundamentally different way of looking at the role of the state.

The Two Economies

So, granted the caveat that the economically freest countries in the world are the English speaking democracies, within that family there are some interesting differences, and I would say between America and Canada there are five main ones.

First, the Canadian economy is more unionized. According to the Fraser Institute report, since the beginning of this century the unionized proportion of the U. S. work force has averaged 13.9 percent. In Canada it has averaged 32 percent. That is a huge difference. The least unionized state in America is North Carolina, at 3.9 percent, whereas the least unionized province in Canada is Alberta, with 24.2 percent. . . a higher percentage than any American state except Hawaii, Alaska, and New York. In Quebec, it is 40.4 percent. If you regard unionization as a major obstacle to productivity, this is a critical difference.

I drive a lot between Quebec and New Hampshire, and you don't really need a border post to tell you when you've crossed from one country into another. On one side the hourly update on the radio news lets you know that Canada's postal workers are thinking about their traditional pre Christmas strike - the Canadians have gotten used to getting their Christmas cards around Good Friday and its part of the holiday tradition now - or that employees of the government liquour store are on strike, nurses are on strike, police are on strike, etc. Whereas you could listen for years to a New Hampshire radio station and never hear the word "strike"except for baseball play-by-play.

In a news item from last year, an Ottawa panhandler said that he may have to abandon his prime panhandling real estate on a downtown street corner because he is being shaken down by officials from the panhandlers union. Think about that. There's a panhandlers' union which exists to protect workers' rights . . . or in this case . . . non-workers rights. If the union negotiated work contracts aren't honoured, the union panhandlers will presumably walk off the job and stand around on the sidewalk. No, wait . . . they'll walk off the sidewalk! Anyway, that's Canada: Without a Thatcher or a Reagan, it remains over unionized and with a bloated public sector.

Not that long ago, I heard a CBC news anchor announce that Canada had "created 56,100 new jobs in the previous month." It sounded like good news. But looking at the numbers, I found that of those 56,100 new jobs, 4,200 were self employed, 8,900 were in private businesses, and the remaining 43,000 were on the public payroll. In other words, 77 percent of the new jobs were government jobs paid for by the poor slobs working away in the remaining 23 percent. So it wasn't good news, it was bad news about the remorseless transfer of human resources from the vital dynamic sector to the state.

The second difference between our economies is that Canada's is more protected. I was talking once to a guy from the Bay area who ran a gay bookstore, and he swore to me that he'd had it with President Bush and that he was going to move to Vancouver and reopen his bookstore there. I told him that would be illegal in Canada, and he got very huffy and said indignantly, "What do you mean it's illegal? It's not illegal for a gay man to own a bookstore in Canada."

I said, "No, but it's illegal for a foreigner to own a bookstore in Canada." He could move to Canada, yes, but he'd have to get a government job handing out benefit checks. His face dropped, and I thought of pitching one of those soft-focus TV movie-of-the week ideas to the Lifestyle Channel, telling the heartwarming story of a Berkeley gay couple who flee Bush's regime to live their dream of running a gay bookstore in Vancouver, only to find that Canada has ways of discriminating against them that the homophobic fascists in the United States haven't even begun to consider.

The third difference is that Canada's economy is more subsidized. Almost every activity amounts to taking government money in some form or other. I was at the Summit of the Americas held in Canada in the summer of 2001, with President Bush and the presidents and prime ministers from Latin America and the Caribbean. And, naturally, it attracted the usual anti-globalization anarchists who wandered through town lobbing bricks at any McDonald's or Nike outlet that hadn't taken the precaution of boarding up its windows. At one point I was standing inside the perimeter fence sniffing tear gas and enjoying the mob chanting against the government from the other side of the wire, when a riot cop suddenly grabbed me and yanked me backwards, and a nanosecond later a chunk of concrete landed precisely where I had been standing. I bleated the usual "Oh my God, I could have been killed" for a few minutes and then I went to have a café au lait. And while reading the paper over my coffee, I learned that not only had Canadian colleges given their students time off to come to the Summit to riot, but that the Canadian government had given them $300,000 to pay for their travel and expenses. It was a government-funded anti-government riot! At that point I started bleating "Oh my God, I could have been killed at taxpayer expense." Say what you like about the American trust-fund babies who had swarmed in to demonstrate from Boston and New York, but at least they were there on their own dime. Canada will and does subsidize anything and everything.

Fourth point. The Canadian economy is significantly more dirigiste (i.e., centrally planned).

A couple of years ago it was revealed that the government had introduced a fast track immigration program for exotic dancers (otherwise known as strippers). Now as a general rule, one of the easiest things to leave for the free market to determine is the number of strippers a society needs. But for some reason, the government concluded that the market wasn't generating the supply required and introduced a special immigration visa. To go back to President Bush's line, maybe this is one of those jobs that Canadians won't do, so we need to get some Ukrainians in to do it. Naturally, the exotic dancers are unionized, so it's only a matter of time before the last viable industry in Quebec grinds to a halt and American tourists in Montreal find themselves stuck in traffic because of huge numbers of striking strippers. What governmental mind would think of an exotic dancer immigration category?

Fifth and obviously, the Canadian economy is more heavily taxed: Total revenue for every level of government in the U.S. is approximately 27 percent of GDP, while in Canada it's 37 percent And yes, that 37 percent includes health care, but you would have to be having an awful lot of terminal illnesses each year to be getting your money's worth from what you're giving to the treasury for that.

Canadian Dependence on the U.S.

Yet, having criticized Canada's economy in various features, let me say something good about it: It doesn't have the insanely wasteful federal agricultural subsidies that America has . . . in fact, if a Canadian wants to get big-time agriculture subsidies, he's more likely to get them from the U.S. government I'm sure most people here know that very few actual farmers . . . that's to say, guys in denim overalls and plaid shirts and John Deere caps with straws in the stumps of their teeth . . . get any benefit from U.S. agricultural subsidies. Almost three-quarters of these subsidies go to 20,000 multi-millionaire play farmers and blue chip corporations.

Farm subsidies are supposed to help the farm belt. But there's a map of where the farm subsidies go that you can find on the Internet. And judging from the beneficiaries, the farm belt runs from Park

Avenue down Wall Street, out to the Hamptons, and then by yacht over to Martha's Vineyard, which they really ought to rename Martha's Barnyard. Among the farmers piling up the dollar bills under the mattress are Ted Turner, Sam Donaldson, the oil company Chevron, and that dirt poor, hardscrabble share cropper David Rockefeller. But what you may not know is that also among their number is Edgar Bronfman Sr., who isn't any old billionaire, he's the patriarch of Montreal's wealthiest family, owner of Seagram's Whiskey, which subsequently bought Universal Pictures. So the U.S. taxpayer, in his bound less generosity is subsidizing the small family farms of Canadian billionaires. As a Canadian and a broken down New Hampshire tree farmer myself, I wondered whether I could get in on the U.S. farm program, but as I understand it, it would only pay me for a helicopter pad on top of my barn and a marble bathroom in my grain silo.

Edgar Bronfman's dependence on U.S. taxpayers is symbolic of more than just the stupidity of federal agriculture subsidies. In the end, there's no such thing as an independent Canadian economy. It remains a branch plant for the US. Over 80 percent of Canadian exports come to America. From time to time, nationalist politicians pledge to change that and start shipping goods elsewhere. But they never do because they don't have to - they've got the world's greatest market right next door. So when people talk about the Canadian model as something that should be emulated, they forget that it only works because it's next to the American model The guy who invented the Blackberry email device is Canadian but it's not been a gold mine for him because he's selling a lot of them in Labrador or Prince Edward Island. It's been a gold mine because he's selling a lot of them in New York and California and in between.

Canadian dependence on the United States is particularly true in health care, the most eminent Canadian idea looming in the American context. That is, public health care in Canada depends on private health care in the U.S. A small new"S story from last month illustrates this:

A Canadian woman has given birth to extremely rare identical quadruplets. The four girls were born at a U.S. hospital because there was no space available at Canadian neonatal intensive care units. Autumn, Brook, Calissa, and Dahlia are in good condition at Benefice Hospital in Great Falls, Montana. Health officials said they checked every other neonatal intensive care unit in Canada, but none had space. The Jepps, a nurse, and a respiratory technician were flown 500 kilometres to the Montana hospital, the closest in the U.S., where the quadruplets were born on Sunday.

There you have Canadian health care in a nutshell. After all, you can't expect a G-7 economy of only 30 million people to be able to offer the same level of neonatal intensive care coverage as a town of 50,000 in remote, rural Montana. And let's face it, there's nothing an expectant mom likes more on the day of delivery than 300 miles in a bumpy twin prop over the Rockies. Everyone knows that socialized health care means you wait and wait and wait six months for an MRI, a year for a hip replacement and so on. But here is the absolute logical *"reductio ad absurdum"* of a government monopoly in health care: the ten month waiting list for the maternity ward.

In conclusion, I'm not optimistic about Canada for various reasons . . . from the recent Chinese enthusiasm for buying up the country's resources to the ongoing brain drain . . . but also for a reason more profound. The biggest difference between Canada and the U.S. is not that you crazy, violent, psycho Yanks have guns and we caring, progressive Canucks have socialized health care, but that America has a healthy fertility rate and we don't. Americans have 2.1 children per couple, which is enough to maintain a e population, whereas according to the latest official figures, Canadian couples have only1.5. This puts us on the brink of steep demographic decline. Consider the math: 10 million parents have 7.5 million children, 5.6 million grandchildren, and 4.2 million great-grandchildren. You can imagine what shape those lavish Canadian social programs will be in under that scenario, and that's before your average teenage burger flipper gets tired of supporting entire gated communities and decides he'd rather head south than pay 70 percent tax rates.

So, to produce the children we couldn't be bothered having ourselves, we use the develop world as our maternity ward. Between 2001 and 2006,Canada's population increased by 1.6 million. 400,000 came from natural population growth kids, while 1.2 million came from immigration. Thus native Canadians . . . already only amounting to 25 percent of the country's population growth . . . will become an ever smaller minority in the Canada of the future. It's like a company in which you hold an ever diminishing percentage of the stock. It might still be a great, successful company in the years ahead, but if it is, it won't have much if anything to do with you.

In that most basic sense, American progressives who look to Canada are wrong. Not only is Canada's path not a model for America, it's not a viable model for Canada. As Canadians are about to discover, the future belongs to those who show up for it.

Detroit 3 Auto Makers - Union Wages

From Guru Focus; lightly edited and formatted:
http://www.gurufocus.com/forum/read.php?2,41757

According to Forbes Magazine:
Labour cost per hour, wages and benefits for hourly workers.

Ford:	$70.51 ($141,020 per year)
GM:	$73.26 ($146,520 per year)
Chrysler:	$75.86 ($151,720 per year)
Toyota, Honda, Nissan (in U.S.):	$48.00 ($96,000 per year)

According to AAUP and IES, the average annual compensation for a college professor in 2006 was $92,973 (average salary nationally of $73,207 + 27% benefits). Bottom Line: The average UAW worker with a high school degree earns 57.6% more compensation than the average university professor with a PhD, and 52.6% more than the average worker at Toyota, Honda or Nissan.

Many industry analysts say the Detroit Three, must be on par with Toyota and Honda to survive. This year's contract, they say, must be "transformational" in reducing pension and health care costs. What would "transformational" mean? It would mean that UAW workers, most with a high school diploma, would have to accept compensation equal to that of the average university professor with a PhD.

Then there's the "Job Bank". When a D3 (Detroit 3 car maker) lays an employee off, that employee continues to receive all benefits - medical, retirement, etc., etc., PLUS an hourly wage of $31/hour. Here's a typical story . . .

Ken Pool is making good money. On weekdays, he shows up at 7 a.m. at Ford Motor Co.'s Michigan Truck Plant in Wayne, signs in, and then starts working . . . on a crossword puzzle. Pool hates the monotony, but the pay is good: more than $31 an hour, plus benefits. "We just go in and play crossword puzzles, watch videos that someone brings in or read the newspaper," he says. "Otherwise, I just sit."

Pool is one of more than 12,000 American auto workers who, instead of installing windshields or bending sheet metal, spend their days counting the hours in jobs bank set up by Detroit automakers as demanded by the United Auto Workers Union (UAW), as part of an extraordinary job security agreement. Now the D3 wants Joe Taxpayer to pick up this tab in a $25 Billion bailout package . . . soon to be increased to $45 Billion if Nancy Pelosi and Hillary Clinton have their way.

The "Big 3" want this money . . . not to build better autos. No. They want it to pay the tab for Medical and Retirement benefits for RETIRED auto workers. Not ONE PENNY would be used to make them more competitive, or to improve the quality of their cars. We ALL have problems paying for our Medical Insurance . . . but the Democrat leaders in Congress now want us to pay the Medical Insurance premiums of folks who have RETIRED from Ford, GM and Chrysler. Not a good deal for us. How about Chapter 11 . . . and getting rid of these ridiculous union contracts?

Interprovincial Trade Barriers

From the National Post, 2008/11/11   by John Ivison

An ambush of provincial premiers gathered in Ottawa yesterday to demand the Prime Minister fix the global financial crisis. The wish list, as usual, was long and unaffordable - regional aid packages, increased agricultural subsidies and loans to most sectors of manufacturing industry. But since Jean Charest, the Quebec Premier and chief negotiator for the provinces, is in the midst of an election campaign, in which his main pitch is blame Ottawa for everything, and the expectations for the meeting were low. It did not disappoint.

Then again, it was not completely without merit, either. "This crisis presents some opportunities," said Brad Wall, the Saskatchewan Premier. His fellow first ministers agreed, namely the opportunity to get their mitts on federal infrastructure dollars more quickly, and without the need to back up their cash grab with a sound business case. It seems that the one thing everyone agreed on was that the long-term goal of shoring up Canada's crumbling infrastructure should be supplanted by the short-term goal of keeping shovels in the ground and construction workers in jobs. The phrase "billion-dollar boondoggle" and the image of the "Ding wall" around Cape Breton University, won't go away for some reason.

John Baird, the new Transport Minister, said his department is going to try hard to expedite the due diligence process. "I have a sign on my desk that says 'It can be done' and I gave one to my deputy minister when I arrived here," he said, with typical chutzpah. In reality though, there's not much the feds can do to speed up the process - they don't write the cheques, they merely reimburse municipalities when they receive an invoice after the job is finished.

But Mr. Wall is right - there are opportunities in a crisis. The current credit crunch offers up a chance to overcome what Premier Gordon Campbell of British Columbia called "the institutional inertia" that has built up in federal-provincial system over the last few decades. In setting the agenda yesterday, Stephen Harper indicated that one of his priorities is going to be to enact a pledge made in the Conservative Party's election platform - namely that this government is going to break down internal trade barriers, with or without the consent of the provinces. In its platform, the government said that it will target barriers that restrict or impair trade, investment or labour mobility between provinces by 2010. In last year's Speech from the Throne, the government said it was prepared to use the federal trade and commerce power to strengthen the economic union to impose a solution. Yesterday, Mr. Harper placed the issue of a common securities regulator and the need for improved labour mobility between provinces at the top of his agenda.

The issue might seem arcane but government has the power to eliminate barriers that impede the free movement of goods and people. Ottawa has the same power, in the form of the trade and commerce clause in the British North America Act, but in practice, the provinces have wrestled the responsibility from the federal government. The provinces did agree to the Agreement on Internal Trade in 1995 but anyone who thinks it has been effective should try to employ a construction crew from Ontario to build a house in Quebec.

There has been progress. In 2006, BC and Alberta signed a trade, investment and labour mobility agreement, which phased out many barriers between the two provinces. Last year, the premiers announced moves they said would strengthen domestic trade flows - namely, making professional credentials acceptable across the country and developing a more effective enforcement mechanism to resolve disputes.

But, Mr. Harper seems to have concluded that the U.S. example of internal free trade can only be guaranteed when national interests are placed ahead of regional considerations - and that means the Prime Minister has to take charge. The issue is likely to come to a head next month when a panel headed by former federal Cabinet minister Tom Hockin reports on the shape of Canada's securities regulatory system.

Privatization of Crown Corporations

From the National Post 2009/04/03
by Charles Lammam and Niels Veldhuis

Time to Privatize

While many Canadians were undoubtedly dismayed by the federal government's 2009 budget and its about-face regarding the state's role in the economy, one positive may yet result from the massive spending spree. In an effort to control ballooning deficits, the federal government has initiated a review of its "corporate assets" with an eye to privatization.

Potentially up for sale are assets such as Canada Post, Via Rail and the Canadian Air Transport Security Authority. Property such as the CN Tower and others held by Canada Lands could also be sold. The fact is Canadians would benefit tremendously from sweeping privatization of Crown assets.

The benefits of privatization are well established in the academic literature. Overwhelmingly, research finds that privatization improves the economic and service performance of divested state owned enterprises.

Renowned privatization experts, Professors William Megginson and Jeffry Netter, provided the most comprehensive review of worldwide privatizations in a 2001 study published in the prestigious Journal of Economic Literature. They found both short and long term benefits to economies undertaking privatizations.

Governments should begin selling off assets immediately.

In the short term, taxpayers gained through one-time revenues from the sale of government assets. In the longer term, privatization improved firm performance and increased economic growth.

Megginson and Netter concluded their extensive review by stressing that "privatization 'works,' in the sense that divested firms almost always become more efficient, more profitable, financially healthier and increase their capital investment spending." There is a host of academic work that buttresses the Megginson and Netter study.

Most recently, in a 2009 study published in the *Journal of Banking & Finance*, Narjess Boubakri and colleagues analyzed the impact of privatization on the performance of189 state-owned enterprises operating in 39 countries. Overall, they found that "privatization is associated with significant improvements in profitability, operating efficiency and capital expenditures." Canadian-based research finds much the same: privatization would improve the performance of Crown corporations.

In a comprehensive study, University of British Columbia Professor Anthony Boardman and colleagues analyzed the performance of major Canadian Crown corporations privatized between 1985 and 1996, including;

> Air Canada,
> CN Railway,
> Petro Canada,
> Fishery Products International,
> Potash Corporation of Saskatchewan,
> Eldorado Nuclear Limited,
> Saskatchewan Mining Development Corporation (now Cameco),
> Alberta Government Telephones (now Telus),
> Suncor, and
> Nova Scotia Power.

The results showed that privatized firms increased profitability, efficiency and dividends while reducing debt ratios. Privatization also had a positive impact on capital expenditures. Industry specific research also points to significant benefits from privatization.

Consider the postal services industry. *The Mail Monopoly*, a seminal in depth analysis of Canada's postal service, found that the Crown failed to provide Canadians with expedient and reliable services. A more recent study by University of Toronto Professor Edward Iacobucci and colleagues concluded that privatizing Canada Post would produce efficiency gains and improvements in service quality. Evidence of postal deregulation in other countries shows that companies increased service quality, adapted products and services to demand, introduced several mail related innovations, reduced employment, and improved labour performance after deregulation.

The benefits of privatization result from key differences between how the private and public sectors behave, and the incentives each faces. For example, the public sector generally uses less capital and is more labour intensive than the private sector. As a result, state owned enterprises tend to be less productive.

Another essential difference is that governments are preoccupied with fulfilling political goals rather than pursuing economic or business objectives. Instead of allocating capital where it garners the highest economic return, governments typically allocate capital to areas that maximize their chances for re-election.

In addition, government businesses usually operate in a state-provided monopoly shielded from competitive discipline. This means they are not required to constantly update their technologies and production processes and/or offer innovative products and services to their customers. In the private sector, competition forces firms to regularly invest in new capital and meet consumer demand in order to survive and grow profitably.

Finally, government budgets are "soft" since it is impossible for them to go broke. Private sector businesses, however, face "hard" budget constraints. If they incur sustained losses the decline of capital will push them into bankruptcy. The private sector must therefore provide its customers with the quality goods and services they demand, in a timely manner, and at affordable prices. The public sector simply does not face the same pressures.

While some might balk at selling assets in a weak economy, preferring to wait for a more ideal environment, reports from Canada's Auditor General repeatedly highlight that the government has a difficult time performing the most routine tasks efficiently:

- issuing checks (as was the case in the heating expense relief program),
- managing databases (SINs, Firearm Registry) and
- using (misusing) credit cards (RCMP).

Waiting for the "ideal environment" could be a long wait. Most financial and investment professionals are not able to time the markets; why should we have any faith that the government can? Moreover, it will take time to decide what assets will be sold, to prepare them for sale, and then to actually sell them. Associated time lags may see Canada in recovery by the time sales actually occur.

The sooner assets are sold, the sooner Canadians will see benefits. Privatized assets will be more efficient and productive. They will provide citizens with higher quality goods and services. Most importantly, privatizations would generate more economic activity through increased investment, a welcome undertaking in these tough economic times.

Financial Post: Charles Lammam is a policy analyst and Niels Veldhuis is director of fiscal studies with The Fraser Institute.

Low Retirement Income

From The National Post 2007/10/24   by Jonathan Chevreau

In financial planning circles it's long been axiomatic that retirees can get by on 70% of the income generated in their working years. But a survey of 2,200 households from Fidelity Investments Canada suggests 80% or 85% might be a more realistic target. True, it's in the interests of a mutual-fund company to scare working Canadians to invest as much as they can.

The scary statistic Fidelity cites in its just-released 2007 Retirement Index Survey is that Canadians are on track to replace only 50% of their pre-retirement income. The picture is bleaker in western Canada, where Albertans may replace only 45% of their working income. It's 53% in Quebec and 52% in Atlantic Canada.

Washington-based pension consultants Watson Wyatt Worldwide argued in 2002 that a 105% replacement ratio may be more realistic, at least for Americans. However, Mercer consultant and actuary Malcolm Hamilton still says Canadians can get by with a replacement ratio of 50%. He reasons that once mortgages are gone, children educated and employment expenses removed, retirees won't need as much as when they worked.

Also, they won't need to be saving for retirement any more and won't have to pay the top rate of income tax to meet all those displaced expenses. While 50% may not be an opulent lifestyle, Canadians are taxed so heavily when working that they don't have a high lifestyle either, Hamilton said yesterday. "If the objective is to maintain people in their accustomed manner, then 50% is not far off": Hamilton disagrees with Fidelity's 80% figure, saying the firm offers little to back it up.

Studies have shown Canadian retirees live on less than 80% of their working incomes and report missing those salaries less than they thought, Hamilton said. "No one who hits 80% will be complaining but sending a message that everyone needs to try for 80% is a disservice." Fidelity says Baby Boomers don't plan to slow down in retirement so neither will their spending. It argues longer life expectancy coupled with early retirement means they will be retired longer than previous generations. In a video shown by Manulife Financial to promote Income Plus, professor Moshe Milevsky said many will live 30 years or more in retirement. The risk they face is outliving their money. Fidelity says Boomers "have no intention of reducing their lifestyle dramatically at retirement". Fully 37% of those surveyed expect to maintain their pre-retirement lifestyle, though only 17% are on track to replace 70% of their working income, and less than 10% will replace 80% of it.

According to Statistics Canada, the median retirement age in Canada is 61. As Fidelity puts it, retirees "may spend as much time drawing income from their retirement assets as they did accumulating them". If that's not scary enough, Fidelity says the percentage of the labour force covered by traditional defined benefit pensions has dropped from 33% in 1992 to 26% in 2006. Canadians 55 and older are on track to replace 59% of their working incomes, versus 44% for Canadians 25 to 40. But 20% of workers have no retirement savings.

Those with financial advisors are, not surprisingly, better prepared. One is Warren Baldwin of T. E. Wealth, who says the focus should be on meeting expenses, not income. He says new measures like pension income splitting and lower tax rates on dividends or capital gains should reduce the tax bite in retirement. So "a lower overall income may work fine" but "certainly we cannot be complacent".

If reality seems out of whack with expectations, the solution for many will be to continue working in retirement - 60% told Fidelity they expect to do so. Fidelity suggests governments can help by ending mandatory retirement, and should let Canadians contribute to RRSPs beyond age 71.

Fixing Canada's Pension Plans

From the National Post Blogs; lightly edited and formatted:

By Keith Ambachtsheer

http://network.nationalpost.com/np/blogs/fpcomment/archive/
tags/Keith+Ambachtsheer/default.aspx

Pension funds have no business investing in stocks. So opined Terence Corcoran in last Friday's Financial Post editorial entitled "Pension funds still gambling on stocks". Is he right? The answer is yes and no.

He is right in the sense that traditional defined benefit (DB) pension plans have serious property rights problems embedded in them. The claims and obligations that various stakeholder groups (i.e. pensioners, workers, shareholders, taxpayers) have on, and to, each other are often not well-defined. "Fuzzy" would be a better word.

Now add the popular mantra that equity investments offer high returns at only modest risk in the long run and you have the makings of a serious gaming situation. Why? Because by investing part of a DB plan balance sheet in stocks, each stakeholder group believes that it will share in the rewards when asset returns are good, but will be able to deflect asset shortfalls to other groups when they are bad. Facts confirm what game theory predicts. During the high equity return period of the 1990s, pensions were happily increased and contribution rates cut. Everyone was a winner.

Now the tables have turned. The September-October free fall in stock prices punched gaping holes in DB balance sheets that were still recovering from the funding shortfalls caused by lower interest rates and the 2000-03 stock market problems. So how will these gaping holes now be plugged? Willing volunteers have yet to step forward. Pensioners are insisting that they be paid their full pensions.

Workers won't take pay cuts to allow more money to be diverted into now seriously underfunded pension plans. Corporations say they can't fill the funding holes because they have to conserve cash to continue operating as going concerns, and are now lobbying to have the funding rules relaxed. Public sector employers have their own cash flow concerns as tax receipts start to go flat and possibly fall next year.

So what is the "out" here for all these players? Again, game theory provides the answer. Load the whole problem on the only stakeholder groups not at the bargaining table today: future generations of workers and taxpayers. In other words, delay taking corrective actions now, and hope that somehow the future will take care of itself.

Does all this prove Mr. Corcoran's point that pension funds have no business investing in stocks? Actually, no.

His point should have been that the fuzzy property rights/ gaming problem embedded in traditional DB pension plans makes them poor mechanisms to accumulate retirement savings and generate adequate, reliable streams of pension payments in a fair manner. But let me add that while traditional defined contribution (DC) and RRSP based plans solve the fuzzy property rights problem, they are equally dysfunctional for different reasons. Theory suggests, and research confirms, that forcing workers to choose their own contribution rates, select their own investment policies and figure out how to manage their own longevity risk is highly problematical. The typical worker has no clue how to do this, and has no interest in learning.

Further, if the savings to pensions intermediation process now involves some combination of commission driven financial advisors and retail investment products, that same typical worker will likely be paying too much in fees for too little value. Research suggests that in such situations, the high intermediation costs can easily cut a worker's future pension in half relative to much lower cost alternatives.

So how do we solve the traditional DB and DC pension design problems that the recent stock market crash have made glaringly obvious? The answer is surprisingly simple. We must move beyond the current "either DB or DC" to a more creative, integrative "best of both" mind set.

We need a more creative, integrative mind set that works for young and old alike. We need a new pension design that permits younger workers with many years of retirement saving ahead of them to take equity risk in their personal pension accounts. These younger Canadians would be well served if their pension savings were acquiring pieces of good companies, commercial real estate and infrastructure projects today at what are likely to be bargain prices.

At the same time, this new pension plan design must also recognize that older workers and pensioners need a steady stream of reliable pension payments that will continue as long as they live. Can the differing needs of younger and older workers be met under the roof of a single pension plan? And can we build institutions that can convert these needs in a manner that is expert and low cost at the same time? The answer is a resounding yes.

The widely accepted theories of life cycle personal finance, and of integrative investment intermediation, create a solid theoretical foundation. Their practical validity has been confirmed through empirical research, and their implementation in the Netherlands and Australia have made them the top two pension countries in the world. Even in North America the giant US college pension system TIAA CREF, and Saskatchewan's smaller Cooperative Superannuation Society Pension Plan have operated successfully on these principles for decades.

A final question. If we know how to design and operate sustainable 21st century workplace pension plans in Canada, why haven't we done it already? Because knowing is not enough. There must also be a consensus that the traditional DB and DC pension models should be discarded, and that the time has come to move to a model that is superior in both theory and practice. Malcolm Gladwell has observed that such change requires a tipping point. The confluence of three events is now creating a Canadian pensions tipping point.

The first is the stock market crash which has sharply focussed minds on the flaws of current pension arrangements. The second is the imminent arrival of the recommendations of pension reform commissions in Ontario, Alberta, BC and Nova Scotia. This sets the stage for a Canadian Pensions Summit in 2009. The third is the recent C. D. Howe Institute commentary, *The Canada Supplementary Pension Plan: Towards an Adequate, Affordable Pension for All Canadians*, which sets out the better pension model in detail, and shows how it could be implemented at the national level to cover all Canadian workers without a pension plan. The commentary also points out that the same better pension model could be implemented at the regional, industry or even individual employer levels. Is there a role for equity investing in this better model? Absolutely. But only by those willing and able to bear the risks involved.

Employment Insurance Lessons from the USA

From the Financial Post 2009/06/12   By John Williamson

John Williamson is a Chevening scholar studying at the London School of Economics, a senior fellow with the Fraser Institute and a fellow with the Manning Centre for Building Democracy.

If Canada's Employment Insurance program is made more generous, as opposition parties in Ottawa are demanding, the result will be a permanent increase in the unemployment rate. There's no two ways about it. The rejoinder, to any politician, columnist or economist that scoffs at the suggestion that an economy can be derailed by easier social assistance, is the region of Atlantic Canada.

Federal government changes in the 1970s to EI made leisure more attractive by paying richer benefits in areas of high unemployment. The result was predictable. Some people decided collecting pogey was preferable to extra work. It was a rational response to lousy public policy. The result is that the Atlantic region has continued to suffer from two conflicting problems at the same time, high unemployment and a labour shortage.

Implementing these looser EI rules across Canada would have the same damaging result. It isn't a question of a unique east-coast culture that favours idleness. We should not forget that in the mid-1990s, an astounding one in nine people in Ontario were on welfare as a result of generous payments.

EI is a byzantine system with different rules for workers. In parts of the country with relatively low unemployment, 6% or less, it can take about 18 weeks (700 hours) of work to qualify for assistance. In places where joblessness is over 13%, benefits can flow after working as little as 10.5 weeks (420 hours). All said, Canada has 58 different EI zones.

Opposition leader Michael Ignatieff is calling on the Conservatives to dramatically reduce the EI qualification period. The Liberals think even the current minimum 420 hours of work is already too punitive. Instead, they are proposing a mere 360 hours of work to qualify. As economist Jack Mintz has written on these pages, "Under (Ignatieff 's) proposal, someone could virtually work each summer (about 45 days) to claim benefits for the rest of the year." The result of such generosity would be an increase in the number of people working less.

Consider New Brunswick and the U. S. state of Maine. These two neighbouring jurisdictions have much in common. Both are located in the eastern periphery of the continental market, they each rely on a large resource sector and they have below-average incomes. Where they differ is with jobless benefits and long-term unemployment.

According to a report published by the Fraser Institute in 2006, sourced from a National Bureau of Economic Research paper, Canada's more generous benefits had a "dramatic impact" on the use of EI and the province's labour market. People in New Brunswick claimed more unemployment and worked less than workers in Maine. The combination of seasonal benefits and larger payments caused a large gap to emerge between the Maine and New Brunswick unemployment rates in the mid-1970s.

The report, entitled "The Long-Term Effects of Generous Income Support Program: Unemployment Insurance in New Brunswick and Maine, 1940-1991," found only 5.7% of male workers and 3.3% of female workers in Maine collected benefits in 1990. Cross the northern border into Canada and 29.5% of male workers and 29.7% of female workers were on the dole. The authors estimated more liberal benefits in New Brunswick accounted for two thirds of this difference. They also found that since 1982, the jobless rate in New Brunswick has consistently been above 12% whereas the rate in Maine has routinely been below 8%.

The Atlantic provinces can afford such a rich system because workers in the rest of Canada pay for it. EI payroll taxes paid by central and

Western Canadians make it possible. These workers transfer more than $500-million in benefits annually to the East Coast. But that's not the worst part. The Atlantic EI scheme retards job creation by making it more costly for business to hire workers.

Companies that have, in the past, been ready to hire could not find enough workers willing to trade leisure for regular work. This choice is influenced by generous EI payments and explains the paradox of both high unemployment and a labour shortage in the region. As a result, companies invest less in Atlantic Canada or leave in search of more willing workers in New England or central and Western Canada. The result is more unemployment and an exodus of young people to the United States or other parts of the country. It is a vicious circle with less economic growth, more dependency and declining opportunity.

People assume that higher unemployment rates necessitate more EI. But it is worth considering to what degree generous EI has caused chronic unemployment. Indeed, if EI rules were similar across provinces, it would be an incentive for workers in areas with high unemployment to move to locations with more jobs. That EI should be reformed is not disputed. But lowering the eligibility rate to 360 or even 420 hours would blow a permanent hole in Ottawa's balance sheet, damage Canada's labour market and be costly to future job creation.

EI should operate as an insurance program. Frequent users should either pay higher premiums or receive lower benefits. Similarly, businesses that routinely abuse the system by "laying off" workers and hiring them back weeks later should pay more. But a recession is hardly the time to make these changes. If benefits are inadequate in the current economy, the solution might be to provide temporary payments outside EI. Indeed, it is regrettable the government dedicated a $10.5 billion bailout to subsidize the jobs of auto workers instead of making that money available to unemployed Canadians.

The Conservatives' program of massive deficit spending is bad news for taxpayers because it will mean paying more interest to service the national debt. But Ottawa's reckless fiscal expansion should not hurt employment growth prospects in long term, provided government expenditures are curtailed and taxes are not increased. The same cannot be said about a more generous EI system. It would be detrimental to labour market growth. Mr. Ignatieff's proposal is ill conceived and the government should ignore him.

Employment Insurance vs Private Savings Accounts

From the Ottawa Citizen 20090727

by Colin Busby: CD Howe Institute

The Employment Insurance (EI) Review Panel named by Stephen Harper and Michael Ignatieff as part of a deal to avoid a summer election, must decide on some prickly issues before reporting this fall. All eyes are on fairness of access, but one superficially attractive recent proposal to offer EI benefits to the self employed looms as the big danger. The EI program, seemingly boundless already, owing to its coverage of sickness, maternity, parental and adoption leave, would face nearly insurmountable issues and function even more poorly than it now does, were it to be extended to the self employed.

Over the last 30 years, the growth of self-employment has reshaped the Canadian labour market. The self-employed represented 12 per cent of total employment in 1980, but have since risen to 16 per cent. Over this time frame, the number of self-employed has expanded by a surprising 93 (33?) per cent. The debate over the inclusion of all self-employed workers cuts right to the issue of fairness in EI access. Currently, self-employed fishermen, who do not pay into the program, get access to EI benefits while other groups of self-employed Canadians do not. But why should self-employed fishermen qualify for extended EI benefits, yet those who are self-employed and in the service sector cannot? Are grain farmers not equally dependent upon the regular rainfall to develop their crops, just as fishermen are dependent on the seasonal spawning patterns and regeneration of fish?

Given the remarkable expansion of self employed Canadians in the last

30 years, their inability to access social supports other than welfare, and the favourable treatment given to some kinds of seasonally self employed, it is not surprising the issue has become important to Canada's policy agenda. But is El the right program for the task at hand?

No. The problem is the moral hazard; insuring activities that are likely to cause the insured to draw on the insurance; which in turn creates conditions that increase the likelihood of collecting benefits. So if the self-employed were covered by El, they would engage in excessively riskier behaviour and be less likely to pursue self-sufficiency.

Administratively the problems are equally complex. For example, who will decide that one person's self-termination is a legitimate outcome and not the consequence of mis-conduct? Also, how can records of employment properly verify the hours worked and the level of wages paid? Further, many employees of the self-employed are family members, which poses yet another conflict.

Artists are a notable group of the self-employed. What is challenging about their situation, like that of many other self-employed Canadians, is the infrequent flow of income from their jobs. Writers, for example, may struggle through years of adversity to finally craft a coveted piece of fiction. Then, as income comes all at once, they must face the probability of never producing another hot-seller.

The underlying issue then, in this case and in many others, is the lack of a predictable and recurring, income stream, complicating the case for El coverage. If they joined the current El system, should they then have to pay El premiums, say 35 years' worth, all at once? But if they paid the current maximum annual individual amount, about $735, with windfall earnings, this would only add to the inequities of the program by shifting costs elsewhere.

A better option would be an individual savings account, which functions separately from the El program, that could be set up by the government but leaves the individual in charge of investing. Such an account could have a high annual contribution limit, say $35,000, with a maximum size at roughly the same level. While this may not seem high, considering the maximum one can earn from collecting EI benefits is about $22,350 over 50 weeks, it is a reasonable plan. The government should offer some tax shelter to such a fund, thereby increasing the appeal to contribute and allowing it to function much like an RRSP. So, should self-employed workers not face any job loss over their careers, they can cash out their savings as retirement income later on.

A simpler option but with a similar end would allow self-employed individuals to contribute a larger percentage of annual earned income to RRSPs, instead of the current 18 per cent. True, self-employed individuals can count only on social assistance as a social safety net. Yet given the troubles with making EI work for them, perhaps concern over the self-employed highlights the idea that what Canada needs is a separate national income supplement program. If so it's, time for a different debate.

Participation in Pensions & Insurance

Employment Insurance (EI)

From The Canadian Encyclopedia; lightly edited and formatted:
    http://www.thecanadianencyclopedia.com/index.cfm?PgNm=
    TCE&Params=A1ARTA0008203

Employment insurance (Unemployment Insurance up to 1996) refers to government benefit payments during a period of unemployment. In Canada, the employment insurance system is financed by premiums paid by employers and employees and by federal government contributions. Unemployment rates in Canada reached levels of about 20% during the great depression and hastened the adoption of unemployment insurance, as did the mobilization effort of WWII. To aid the organization of the work force for war, employment bureaus were expanded and used to administer the unemployment insurance system.

To qualify for employment insurance benefits, applicants must show that they were previously employed for between 420 and 700 hours depending on the local unemployment rate. To receive benefits, they must file a claim stating that they are without work, are willing to work and are registered at the Human Resource Centre. Following a waiting period of 2 weeks (new claims only), individuals are eligible to receive 55% of average weekly insured earnings up to a maximum in 1997 of $413, *($457 in 2010)* per week. The number of weeks for which benefits can be claimed varies, depending on the length of previous employment, previous employment insurance claims, and the national and regional unemployment rate.

The employment insurance system is an important component of the economic safety net provided by government and there is little disagreement, in principle, that it has provided greater income security for Canadians. Among economists, however, there is substantial concern that specific features of the existing system may create unemployment. For example, it has been argued that the relatively short qualifying period may encourage individuals who would not choose to work, were it not for the prospect of also collecting benefits, to enter the labour force; and that unemployment is higher than it should be among those employed in seasonal industries because it may be easier to collect benefits than to look for other work during the off season.

Public Service Pension Plan (PSPP)

From the Federal Treasury Board Secretariat; lightly edited and formatted:
http://www.tbs-sct.gc.ca/pubs_pol/hrpubs/Pensions/yppl-eng.asp

(In the Introduction on the website), The Public Service Superannuation Act provides pensions for public service employees, and has been in effect since January 1, 1954. Part II of the Act, the Supplementary Death Benefit Plan, which provides decreasing term life insurance coverage to pension plan contributors, was added a year later. Since then, the Act and its supporting regulations have been amended many times to respond to changes in the employees' and the employer's needs and to reflect changes in other federal and provincial laws.

The Canada Pension Plan (CPP)

From Wikipedia; lightly edited and formatted:
http://en.wikipedia.org/wiki/Canada_Pension_Plan

The Canada Pension Plan (CPP) is a contributory, earnings-related social insurance program. It forms one of the two major components of Canada's public retirement income system, the other component being Old Age Security (OAS). Other parts of Canada's retirement system are private pensions, either employer-sponsored or from tax-deferred individual savings (known in Canada as a Registered Retirement Savings Plan (RRSP)).

The CPP program mandates all employed Canadians who are 18 years of age and over to contribute a prescribed portion of their earnings income to a nationally administered pension plan. The plan is administered by Human Resources and Social Development Canada on behalf of employees in all provinces and territories except Quebec, which operates an equivalent plan, the Quebec Pension Plan (QPP).

The CPP is funded on a "steady state" basis, with its current contribution rate set so that it will remain constant for the next 75 years, by accumulating a reserve fund sufficient to stabilize the asset/expenditure and funding ratios over time. Such a system is a hybrid between a fully funded plan, and a "pay as you go" plan. In other words, assets held in the CPP fund are by themselves insufficient to pay for all future benefits accrued to date but sufficient to prevent contributions from rising any further. While a sustainable path for this particular plan, given the indefinite existence of a government, it is not typical of other public or private sector pension plans. A study published in April 2007 by the CPP's chief actuary showed that this type of funding method is "robust and appropriate" given reasonable assumptions about future conditions. The chief actuary submits a report to Parliament every three years on the financial status of the plan.

Public Service Health Care Plan (PSHCP)

From the Public Service Health Care Plan; lightly edited and formatted:
http://www.pshcp.ca/english/introduction/default.shtml

(In the Plan Details;) The purpose of the PSHCP is to reimburse Plan participants for all or part of costs they have incurred for eligible services and products, as identified in the Plan Document, only after they have taken advantage of benefits provided by their provincial/ territorial health insurance plan or other third party sources of health care expense assistance to which the participant has a legal right. Unless otherwise specified in the Plan Document, all eligible services and products must be prescribed by a physician or a dentist who is licensed, or otherwise authorised in accordance with the applicable law, to practice in the jurisdiction in which the prescription is made.

Contributions to Pensions & Insurance

Employment Insurance (EI) Contributions 2009

From University of Toronto, Human Resources and Equity; lightly edited and formatted:
http://www.hrandequity.utoronto.ca/payroll/ei.htm

Employee and employer contributions to Employment Insurance (EI) are based on all eligible earnings beginning with the first pay each January. Contributions cease during the calendar year once the maximum contributions are reached. For those employees who earned more than $41,100.00 in the calendar year 2008, the maximum contributions would probably have been reached prior to the December pay period.

For 2009, EI contributions begin January 1 on all eligible earnings, and will continue throughout the year until the maximum contribution levels are reached. The new rates and maximums are provided below.
- Maximum Annual Insurable Earnings - $42,300.00

- Premium/Contribution Rate (employee) - 1.73%
- Annual Maximum Premium (employee) EI - $731.79

Public Service Pension Plan (PSPP) Contributions 2009

From the federal Treasury Board Secretariat; lightly edited and formatted:
http://www.tbs-sct.gc.ca/pubs_pol/hrpubs/pensions/nppm-aprp01-eng.asp

Contribution rates

2005	2006	2007	2008	2009	2010	2011	2012	2013
On earnings up to the maximum covered by the CPP/QPP								
4.0%	4.3%	4.6%	4.9%	5.2%	5.5%	5.8%	6.1%	6.4%
On any earnings over the maximum covered by the CPP/QPP								
7.5%	7.8%	8.1%	8.4%	8.4%	8.4%	8.4%	8.4%	8.4%

Canada Pension Plan (CPP) Contributions 2009

From University of Toronto, Human Resources and Equity; lightly edited and formatted:
http://www.hrandequity.utoronto.ca/payroll/cpp.htm

Employee and employer contributions to the CPP are based on all eligible earnings beginning with the first pay each January. Contributions cease during the calendar year once the maximum contributions are reached. For those employees who earned more than $44,900.00 in the calendar year 2008, the maximum contributions would probably have been reached prior to the December pay period.

For 2009, CPP contributions begin January 1 on all eligible earnings, and will continue throughout the year until the maximum contribution levels are reached. The new rate and maximum are provided below:

- Year's Maximum Pensionable Earnings - $46,300.00
- Year's Basic Exemption - $3,500.00
- Contribution Rate - 4.95%
- Maximum Contribution - $2,118.60

Public Service Health Care Plan (PSHCP) Contributions 2009

From the National Joint Council, Schedule V; lightly edited and formatted: http://www.njc-cnm.gc.ca/directive/index.php?sid=87&hl=1&lang=eng

Monthly Contribution Rates, Employees Supplementary Coverage, Appendix A April 2009

	Hospital Level I			Hospital Level II			Hospital Level III		
	EE $	ER $	Total $	EE $	ER $	Total $	EE $	ER $	Total $
Single	0.00	95.08	95.08	1.09	95.13	96.22	5.30	95.13	100.43
Family	0.00	95.09	95.09	3.52	95.13	98.65	10.33	95.13	105.46
Exec							0.00	95.10	95.10

One Religion (Official)

Paragraphs have been lightly edited and formatted:
http://en.wikipedia.org/wiki/Religion_in_Canada

Religions in Canada

Religion in Canada encompasses a wide range of groups, and Canada has no official religion. The preamble to the Canadian Charter of Rights and Freedoms mentions "God" but no specific beliefs are specified, and support for religious pluralism is an important part of Canada's political culture. However, most people report they are Christians.

In the Canada 2001 Census, 72% of the Canadian population list Roman Catholicism or Protestantism as a religion. The Roman Catholic Church in Canada is the country's largest single denomination. Those of no religion account for 16% of total respondents. In British Columbia, however, 35% of respondents reported no religion - more than any single denomination and more than all Protestants combined. For further information on historically significant religions in Canada, please see Canadian census results on religion.

Religious Denominations in Canada

	2001 Number	%	1991 Number	%	% change (in numbers)
Christian		77		80	
Roman Catholic	12,936,905	43.6	12,203,625	45.2	+4.8
Total Protestant	8,654,850	29.2	9,427,675	34.9	-8.2
United	2,839,125	9.6	3,093,120	11.5	-8.2
Anglican	2,035,495	6.9	2,188,110	8.1	-7.0
Christian	780,450	2.6	353,040	1.3	+121.1
Baptist	729,475	2.5	663,360	2.5	+10.0
Lutheran	606,590	2.0	636,205	2.4	-4.7
Protestant	549,205	1.9			
Presbyterian	409,830	1.4	636,295	2.4	-35.6
Christian Orthodox	479,620	1.6	387,395	1.4	+23.8
Coptic Orthodox	10,285	0.03	5,020	0.02	+104.9
Romanian Orthodox	4,675	0.02	4,570	0.02	+2.3
No religion	4,796,325	16.2	3,333,245	12.3	+43.9
Other					
Muslim	579,640	2.0	253,265	0.9	+128.9
Jewish	329,995	1.1	318,185	1.2	+3.7
Buddhist	300,345	1.0	163,415	0.6	+83.8
Hindu	297,200	1.0	157,015	0.6	+89.3
Sikh	278,415	0.9	147,440	0.5	+88.8

[1] Includes who report Christian, Apostolic, Born-again Christian, and Evangelical

[2] Includes persons who report only Protestant.

* For comparability purposes, 1991 data are presented according to 2001 boundaries.

Non-Christian religions in Canada

Non-Christian religions in Canada are overwhelmingly concentrated in metropolitan cites such as Montreal, Toronto and Vancouver, and to a much smaller extent in mid-sized cities such as Ottawa, Quebec, Calgary, Edmonton, Winnipeg and Halifax. A possible exception is Judaism, which has long been a notable minority even in smaller centres. Much of the increase in non-Christian religions is attributed to changing immigration trends in the last fifty years. Increased immigration from Asia, the Middle East and Africa has created ever-growing Muslim, Buddhist, Sikh, and Hindu communities. Canada is also home to smaller communities of the Bahá'í Faith, Unitarian Universalists, Pagans, and subscribers to First Nations religions.

Islam in Canada

The Muslim community in Canada is almost as old as the nation itself. Four years after Canada's founding in 1867, the 1871 Canadian Census found 13 Muslims among the population. The first Canadian mosque was constructed in Edmonton in 1938, when there were approximately 700 Muslims in the country. This building is now part of the museum at Fort Edmonton Park. The years after World War II saw a small increase in the Muslim population. However, Muslims were still a distinct minority. It was only with the removal of European immigration preferences in the late 1960s that Muslims began to arrive in significant numbers. According to 2001 census, there were 579,640 Muslims in Canada, just under 2% of the population. In 2006, Muslim population is estimated to be 783,700 or about 2.5%.

Sikhism in Canada

Sikhs have been in Canada since 1897. One of the first Sikh soldiers arrived in Canada in 1897 following Queen Victoria's Diamond Jubilee. Sikhs were one of the few Asian immigrant communities who were loyal members of the British Empire. The irony was that greater entry restrictions were placed on prospective Sikh immigrants as compared to the Japanese and Chinese. While Canadian politicians, missionaries, unions and the press did not want Asian labour, British Columbia industrialists were short of labour and thus Sikhs were able to get an early foothold at the turn of the century in British Columbia. Of the nearly 5,000 East Indians in Canada by 1907, 98% were Sikhs, mostly retired British army veterans. Sikh immigration to Canada was banned in 1908, and the population began to shrink.

With the advent of World War II and the internment of Japanese Canadians, Sikhs were able to prosper. Before going to the internment camps Japanese preferred to sell their homes and properties to their

293

Sikh neighbours who they had known for so long. As the war economy picked up speed and moved into high gear, Sikhs were given positions of greater responsibility on the factory floors across the country as well as sharpening their skills as successful businessmen. Just as the war helped to emancipate North American women, showing that they were capable of doing a man's job, Sikhs were showing that they were just as talented as their European counterparts. One of the last major roadblocks remained the right to vote. The year was 1947, fifty years since the first Sikh immigrants had arrived, yet they were still denied this fundamental right. A right that was long overdue and Sikhs rallied to the cause, holding town hall meetings and lobbying local politicians and the government in Ottawa to change the law.

After the 1960s Canada's immigration laws were liberalized and racial quotas were removed, allowing far more Sikhs to immigrate to Canada. The Sikh population has rapidly increased in the decades since. Major Sikh communities exist in most of the major cities of British Columbia and Ontario. Sikhs have become an integral part of Canada's economy and culture.

Canadians with no religious affiliation

Non-religious Canadians are common throughout all provinces and territories. Non-religious Canadians include atheists, agnostics, humanists as well as other non-theists. In 1991, they made up 12.3 percent of the population which increased to 16.2 percent in 2001 according to the 2001 census. Some non-religious Canadians have formed some associations, such as the Humanist Association of Canada or the Toronto Secular Alliance. In 1991, some non-religious Canadians signed a petition, tabled in Parliament by Svend Robinson, to remove "God" from the preamble to the Canadian Constitution, after which he was relegated to the backbenches by his party leader. Shortly afterwards, the same group petitioned to remove "God" from the Canadian national anthem, "O Canada", but to no avail. Among the estimated 4,900,095 Canadians of no religion, an estimated 18,605 would specify atheist, 17,815 would specify agnostic, and 1,245 humanist. (See also www. religioustolerance.org)

Christianity in Canada

The majority of Canadian Christians attend church infrequently. Cross-national surveys of religiosity rates such as the Pew Global Attitudes Project indicate that, on average, Canadian Christians are less observant than those of the United States but are still more overtly religious than their counterparts in Britain or in western Europe. In 2002, 30% of Canadians reported to Pew researchers that religion was "very important" to them. This figure was similar to that in the United Kingdom (33%) and Italy (27%). In the United States, the equivalent figure was 59%, in France, a mere 11%.

Regional differences within Canada exist, however, with British Columbia and Quebec reporting especially low metrics of traditional religious observance, as well as a significant urban-rural divide, while Alberta and rural Ontario saw high rates of religious attendance. The rates for weekly church attendance are contested, with estimates running as low as 11% as per the latest Ipsos-Reid poll and as high as 25% as per Christianity Today magazine. This American magazine reported that three polls conducted by Focus on the Family, Time Canada and the Vanier Institute of the Family showed church attendance increasing for the first time in a generation, with weekly attendance at 25 per cent. This number is similar to the statistics reported by premier Canadian sociologist of religion Prof. Reginald Bibby of the University of Lethbridge, who has been studying Canadian religious patterns since 1975. Although lower than in the US, which has reported weekly church attendance at about 40% since the Second World War, weekly church attendance rates are higher than those in Northern Europe (for example, Austria 9%, Germany 6%, France 8%, Netherlands 6% and UK 10%).

As well as the large churches—Roman Catholic, United, and Anglican, which together count more than half of the Canadian population as nominal adherents—Canada also has many smaller Christian groups, including Orthodox Christianity. The Egyptian population in Ontario and Quebec (Greater Toronto in particular) has seen a large influx of the Coptic Orthodox population in just a few decades. The relatively large Ukrainian population of Manitoba and Saskatchewan has produced many followers of the Ukrainian Catholic and Ukrainian Orthodox Churches, while southern Manitoba has been settled largely by Mennonites. The concentration of these smaller groups often varies greatly across the country. Baptists are especially numerous in the Maritimes. The Maritimes and prairie provinces have significant numbers of Lutherans. Southwest Ontario has seen large numbers of German and Russian immigrants, including many Mennonites and Hutterites, as well as a significant contingent of Dutch Reformed. Alberta has seen considerable immigration from the American plains, creating a significant Mormon minority in that province. The Church of Jesus Christ of Latter-day Saints claims 178,102 members (73,630 of those are in Alberta) as of year-end 2007. And according to the Jehovah witness year report there are 111,963 active members in Canada.

Age and religion

According to the 2001 census, adherents to the major religions in Canada have the following median age in years. Canada has a median age of 37.3 years.

* Presbyterian   46.0
* United Church   44.1
* Anglican   43.8
* Lutheran   43.3
* Jewish   41.5
* Greek Orthodox   40.7
* Baptist   39.3
* Buddhist   38.0
* Roman Catholic   37.8
* Pentecostal   33.5
* Hindu   31.9
* No religion   31.1
* Sikh   29.7
* Muslim   28.1

Government and religion

Canada today has no official church, and the government is officially committed to religious pluralism. In some fields Christian influence remains.

Christmas and Easter are nationwide holidays, and while Jews, Muslims, and other groups are allowed to take their holy days off work they do not share the same official recognition. The French version of "O Canada", the official national anthem, contains a Catholic reference to "carrying the cross". In some parts of the country Sunday shopping is still banned, but this is steadily becoming less common. There was an ongoing battle in the late 20th century to have religious garb accepted throughout Canadian society, mostly focussed on Sikh turbans. Eventually the Royal Canadian Mounted Police, the Royal Canadian Legion, and other groups accepted members wearing turbans.

Canada is a Commonwealth realm in which the head of state is shared with 15 other countries, including the United Kingdom. The UK's succession laws forbid Roman Catholics and their spouses from occupying the throne, and the reigning monarch is also ex officio Supreme Governor of the Church of England, but Canada is not bound by these laws. Within Canada, the Queen's title include the phrases "By the Grace of God" and "Defender of the Faith."

While the Canadian government's official ties to Christianity are few, it more overtly recognizes the existence of God and even the supremacy of God. Both the preamble to the Canadian Charter of Rights and Freedoms and the national anthem in both languages refer to God.

In 1957, Parliament declared Thanksgiving, "a day of general thanksgiving to almighty God for the bountiful harvest with which Canada has been blessed.", stating that God is almighty and that Canada is blessed. Some religious schools are government-funded. See Section Twenty-nine of the Canadian Charter of Rights and Freedoms.

Religions by Age since Origin

Name	Origin	Adherents	Document	Reincarnation
Buddhism	520 BC	360 M	Tripitaka	Yes
Hinduism	~3000 BC	900 M	Vedas	Yes
Islam	622 AD	1.3 B [940 M Sunni]	Qur'an	
Judaism	1300 BC	14 M	Talmud	
Sikhism	1500 AD	23 M	Adi Granth	
Taoism	550 BC	400 M	Tao Te Ching	

One Language (Official)

Languages of Canada

From Wikipedia: lightly edited and formatted:
http://en.wikipedia.org/wiki/Demographics_of_Canada#
Visible_minorities

Language used most often at work according to 2006 census:

- English: 78.3%
- French: 21.7%
- Non-official languages: 2.0%

Languages by mother tongue:

- English: 58.2%
- French: 21.7%
- Non-official: 19.0%
- Chinese: 3.1%
- Italian: 1.4%
- German   1.2%
- Spanish   1.2%
- Punjabi: 1.1%
- Tagalog: 0.9%
- Tamil: 0.8%

The English Language

From Wikipedia; lightly edited and formatted:
http://en.wikipedia.org/wiki/English_language

English is a West Germanic language that developed in England and south eastern Scotland during the Anglo Saxon era. As a result of the military, economic, scientific, political, and cultural influence of the British Empire during the 18th, 19th, and early 20th centuries, and of the United States since the mid 20th century, it has become the lingua franca in many parts of the world, and the most prominent language in international business and science. It is used extensively as a second language and as an official language in Commonwealth countries and many international organizations.

Historically, English originated from several dialects, now collectively termed Old English, which were brought to the eastern coast of the island of Great Britain by Anglo Saxon settlers beginning in the 5th century. English was further influenced by the Old Norse language of Viking invaders.

At the time of the Norman conquest, Old English developed into Middle English, borrowing heavily from the Norman (Anglo French) vocabulary and spelling conventions. The etymology of the word "English" is a derivation from the 12th century Old English englisc or Engle, plural form Angles ("of, relating to, or characteristic of England").

Modern English developed with the Great Vowel Shift that began in 15th-century England, and continues to adopt foreign words from a variety of languages, as well as coining new words. A significant number of English words, especially technical words, have been constructed based on roots from Latin and Greek.

Significance

Modern English, sometimes described as the first global lingua franca, is the dominant language or in some instances even the required international language of communications, science, business, aviation, entertainment, radio and diplomacy. Its spread beyond the British Isles began with the growth of the British Empire, and by the late nineteenth century its reach was truly global. Following the British colonisation of North America, it became the dominant language in the United States and in Canada. The growing economic and cultural influence of the United States and its status as a global superpower since World War II have significantly accelerated the language's spread across the planet.

A working knowledge of English has become a requirement in a number of fields, occupations and professions such as medicine and computing; as a consequence over a billion people speak English to at least a basic level (see English language learning and teaching). It is also one of six official languages of the United Nations.

Linguists such as David Crystal recognise that one impact of this massive growth of English, in common with other global languages, has been to reduce native linguistic diversity in many parts of the world, most particularly in Australasia and North America, and its huge influence continues to play an important role in language attrition. Similarly, historical linguists, aware of the complex and fluid dynamics of language change, are always aware of the potential English contains through the vast size and spread of the communities that use it and its natural internal variety, such as in its creoles and pidgins, to produce a new family of distinct languages over time.

History of the English Language

English is a West Germanic language that originated from the Anglo-Frisian and Lower Saxon dialects brought to Britain by Germanic settlers and Roman auxiliary troops from various parts of what is now northwest Germany, Denmark and the Netherlands in the 5th century. One of these Germanic tribes was the Angles, who may have come from Angeln, and Bede wrote that their whole nation came to Britain, leaving their former land empty. The names 'England' (from Engla land "Land of the Angles") and English (Old English Englisc) are derived from the name of this tribe.

The Anglo-Saxons began invading around AD 449 from the regions of Denmark and Jutland. Before the Anglo-Saxons arrived in England the native population spoke Brythonic, a Celtic language in some parts of England. Although the most significant changes in dialect occurred after the Norman invasion of 1066, the language retained its name and the pre-Norman invasion dialect is now known as Old English.

Initially, Old English was a diverse group of dialects, reflecting the varied origins of the Anglo-Saxon Kingdoms of Great Britain. One of these dialects, Late West Saxon, eventually came to dominate. One of the most prevalent forces in the evolution of the English language was the Roman Catholic Church. Beginning with the Rule of St Benedict in 530 and continuing until the Dissolution of the Monasteries in 1536, the Roman Catholic Church instructed monasteries and Catholic officials like Augustine of Canterbury to preserve intellectual culture within their schools, scriptoria, and libraries.

During the Middle Ages, the Catholic Church exerted great influence on intellectual life and written language. Catholic monks mainly wrote or copied text in Latin, the prevalent Medieval lingua franca of Europe. When monks occasionally wrote in the vernacular, it was common to substitute or derive English-like words from Latin to describe or refer to things in which there was no English word. Extensive vocabulary, a derivative of Latin vocabularium, in the English language largely comprises Latin word derivatives. It is believed that the intellectual elite in British society over the years perpetuated vocabulary that Catholic monks contributed to English; furthermore, they continued the custom of deriving new words from Latin long after the waning of Catholic Church.(citation needed)

Old English vernacular was also influenced by two waves of invasion. The first was by language speakers of the North Germanic branch of the Germanic family; they conquered and colonised parts of the British Isles in the 8th and 9th centuries (see Danelaw). The second was the Normans in the 11th century, who spoke Old Norman and developed an English variety of this called Anglo-Norman. (Over the centuries, this lost the specifically Norman element under the influence of Parisian French and, later, of English, eventually turning into a distinctive dialect of Anglo-French.) These two invasions caused English to become "mixed" to some degree.

Cohabitation with the Scandinavians resulted in a lexical supplementation of the Anglo-Frisian core of English; the later Norman occupation led to the grafting onto that Germanic core of a more elaborate layer of words from the Romance languages. This Norman influence entered English largely through the courts and government. Thus, English developed into a "borrowing" language of great flexibility and a huge vocabulary.

With the emergence and spread of the British Empire, the English language was adopted in North America, India, Africa, Australia and many other regions. The emergence of the United States as a superpower has also helped the spread of English.

Classification and Related Languages

The English language belongs to the Anglo-Frisian sub-group of the West Germanic branch of the Germanic Family, a member of the Indo-European languages. The closest living relatives of English are the Scots language, spoken primarily in Scotland and parts of Northern Ireland, and Frisian. As Scots is viewed by some linguists to be a group of English dialects rather than a separate language, Frisian is often considered to be the closest living relative.

After Scots and Frisian come those Germanic languages which are more distantly related, namely the non-Anglo-Frisian West Germanic languages (Low German, Dutch, Afrikaans, High German), and the North Germanic languages (Swedish, Danish, Norwegian, Icelandic, and Faroese). With the exception of Scots, and on an extremely basic level, Frisian, none of the other languages is mutually intelligible with English, owing in part to the divergences in lexis, syntax, semantics, and phonology, and to the isolation afforded to the English language by the British Isles, although some such as Dutch do show strong affinities with English. This isolation has allowed English and Scots to develop independently of the Continental Germanic languages and their influences over time.

Lexical differences with the other Germanic languages can arise from several causes, such as natural semantic drift caused by isolation, and heavy usage in English of words taken from Latin (for example, "exit", vs. Dutch uitgang) (literally "out-gang" with "gang" as in "gangway") and French "change" vs. German Änderung, "movement" vs. German Bewegung (literally "othering" and "be-way-ing" ("proceeding along the way")). Preference of one synonym over another can also cause a differentiation in lexis, even where both words are Germanic (for instance, both English care and German Sorge descend from Proto-Germanic *karo and *surgo respectively, but *karo became the dominant word in English for "care" while in German, Dutch, and Scandinavian languages, the *surgo root prevailed. *Surgo still survives in English as sorrow).

Although the syntax of German is significantly different from that of English and other Germanic languages, with different rules for setting up sentences (for example, German Ich habe noch nie etwas auf dem Platz gesehen, vs. English "I have never seen anything in the square"), English syntax remains extremely similar to that of the North Germanic languages, which are believed to have influenced English syntax during the Middle English Period (eg., Norwegian Jeg har likevel aldri sett noe I torget; Swedish Jag har ännu aldrig sett något på torget). It is for this reason that despite a lack of mutual intelligibility, English-speakers and Scandinavians can learn each others' languages relatively easily.

Dutch syntax is intermediate between English and German (eg. Ik heb nog nooit iets gezien op het plein). In spite of this difference, there are many similarities between English and other Germanic languages (eg. English bring /brought /brought, Dutch brengen /bracht /gebracht, Norwegian bringe /brakte /brakt; English eat /ate /eaten, Dutch eten /at /gegeten, Norwegian ete /åt /ett), with the most similarities occurring between English and the languages of the Low Countries (Dutch and Low German) and Scandinavia.

Semantic differences cause a number of false friends between English and its relatives (eg. English time vs Norwegian time "hour"), and differences in Phonology can obscure words which actually are genetically related ("enough" vs. German genug, Danish nok). Sometimes both semantics and phonology are different (German Zeit, "time", is related to English "tide", but the English word, through a transitional phase of meaning "period" /"interval", has come primarily to mean gravitational effects on the ocean by the moon, though the original meaning is preserved in forms like tidings and betide, and phrases such as to tide over). These differences, though minor, preclude mutual intelligibility, yet English is still much closer to other Germanic languages than to languages of any other family.

Finally, English has been forming compound words and affixing existing words separately from the other Germanic languages for over 1500 years and has different habits in that regard. For instance, abstract nouns in English may be formed from native words by the suffixes "-hood", "-ship", "-dom" and "-ness". All of these have cognate suffixes in most or all other Germanic languages, but their usage patterns have diverged, as German "Freiheit" vs. English "freedom", (the suffix "-heit" being cognate of English "-hood", while English "-dom" is cognate with German "-tum"). Icelandic and Faroese are other Germanic languages which follow English in this respect, since, like English, they developed independent of German influences.

Many written French words are also intelligible to an English speaker (though pronunciations are often quite different) because English absorbed a large vocabulary from Norman and French, via Anglo-Norman after the Norman Conquest and directly from French in subsequent centuries. As a result, a large portion of English vocabulary is derived from French, with some minor spelling differences (word endings, use of old French spellings, etc.), as well as occasional divergences in meaning of so-called false friends (for example, "library", vs. French "librarie", meaning bookstore) (in French, "library" is "bibliotheque").

The pronunciation of most French loanwords in English (with

exceptions such as mirage or phrases like coup d'état) has become completely anglicised and follows a typically English pattern of stress. Some North Germanic words also entered English because of the Danish invasion shortly before then (see Danelaw); these include words such as "sky", "window", "egg", and even "they" and "are" (the present plural form of "to be").

The English Language 02

From the English Club; lightly edited and formatted:
http://www.englishclub.com/english-language-history.htm

A short history of the origins and development of English

The history of the English language really started with the arrival of three Germanic tribes who invaded Britain during the 5th century AD. These tribes, the Angles, the Saxons and the Jutes, crossed the North Sea from what today is Denmark and northern Germany. At that time the inhabitants of Britain spoke a Celtic language. But most of the Celtic speakers were pushed west and north by the invaders, mainly into what is now Wales, Scotland and Ireland. The Angles came from Englaland and their language was called Englisc, from which the words England and English are derived.

The invading Germanic tribes spoke similar languages, which in Britain developed into what we now call Old English. Old English did not sound or look like English today. Native English speakers now would have great difficulty understanding Old English. Nevertheless, about half of the most commonly used words in Modern English have Old English roots. The words be, strong and water, for example, derive from Old English. Old English was spoken until around 1100.

Middle English (1100-1500)

In 1066 William the Conqueror, the Duke of Normandy (part of modern France), invaded and conquered England. The new conquerors

306

(called the Normans) brought with them a kind of French, which became the language of the Royal Court, and the ruling and business classes. For a period there was a kind of linguistic class division, where the lower classes spoke English and the upper classes spoke French. In the 14th century English became dominant in Britain again, but with many French words added. This language is called Middle English. It was the language of the great poet Chaucer (c1340-1400), but it would still be difficult for native English speakers to understand today.

Early Modern English (1500-1800)

Towards the end of Middle English, a sudden and distinct change in pronunciation (the Great Vowel Shift) started, with vowels being pronounced shorter and shorter. From the 16th century the British had contact with many peoples from around the world. This, and the Renaissance of Classical learning, meant that many new words and phrases entered the language. The invention of printing also meant that there was now a common language in print. Books became cheaper and more people learned to read. Printing also brought standardization to English. Spelling and grammar became fixed, and the dialect of London, where most publishing houses were, became the standard. In 1604 the first English dictionary was published.

Late Modern English (1800-Present)

The main difference between Early Modern English and Late Modern English is vocabulary. Late Modern English has many more words, arising from two principal factors: firstly, the Industrial Revolution and technology created a need for new words; secondly, the British Empire at its height covered one quarter of the earth's surface, and the English language adopted foreign words from many countries.

Varieties of English

From around 1600, the English colonization of North America resulted in the creation of a distinct American variety of English. Some English pronunciations and words "froze" when they reached

America. In some ways, American English is more like the English of Shakespeare than modern British English is. Some expressions that the British call "Americanisms" are in fact original British expressions that were preserved in the colonies while lost for a time in Britain (for example trash for rubbish, loan as a verb instead of lend, and fall for autumn; another example, frame-up, was re-imported into Britain through Hollywood gangster movies). Spanish also had an influence on American English (and subsequently British English), with words like canyon, ranch, stampede and vigilante being examples of Spanish words that entered English through the settlement of the American West. French words (through Louisiana) and West African words (through the slave trade) also influenced American English (and so, to an extent, British English).

Today, American English is particularly influential, due to the USA's dominance of cinema, television, popular music, trade and technology (including the Internet). But there are many other varieties of English around the world, including for example Australian English, New Zealand English, Canadian English, South African English, Indian English and Caribbean English.

Bilingualism in Canada

Excerpt from Globe and Mail 2008/04/05   by Konrad Yakabuski

Where else but in Canada could a straightforward debate about the who and when of French immersion in the third-smallest province send the whole country's official languages intelligentsia into a fit of doomsday ism? Watching the very real passion with which parents have reacted to New Brunswick's decision to end early immersion, it is hard not to think of what U. S. columnist Dan Savage said recently about his own nation's debilitating obsession.

Not, race. The other one: religion. "Australia got the convicts. Canada got the French. We got the Puritans." Mr. Savage evidently meant it as a compliment - to Canada and Australia. And though we should definitely take it as one, the "French fact" has from Durham to Dumont - warped our national psyche, fed our collective neuroses and nearly torn us asunder. Four centuries after Champlain's arrival, we are no nearer, inside or outside Quebec, to reconciling ourselves to his linguistic legacy.

For English Canadians, the question is this: Do they really care enough about the other official language to learn it, not just for the purposes of properly pronouncing *foie gras* and *salade nicoise* on a holiday in Paris, but to understand, appreciate and grow closer to French-Canadian reality? The evidence is fairly conclusive that they don't. Despite the billions spent since the adoption of the Official Languages Act in 1969, the already derisory rates of bilingualism are falling in English Canada. Parents may pine for French immersion classes, but mostly for reasons that have nothing to do with bridging the solitudes.

Francophone Quebeckers have an equally ambivalent relationship with l'autre langue officielle. They are drawn to, yet repelled by it. A case in point: A couple of months ago, the Parti Quebecois leader, Pauline Marois, suggested that history and geography should be taught in English in French public schools as part of a goal of making all Quebeckers bilingual by the time they finish their basic education. But when writer Victor-Levy Beaulieu snapped back at her, warning greater English proficiency would set in motion the "slow genocide" of francophone Quebeckers, Ms. Marois took to the op-eds to proclaim "No to a bilingual Quebec."

The federal policy of official bilingualism was never meant to make Canada a bilingual country. Its primary objective has always been to ensure the protection and survival of the English-language minority in Quebec and the French-speaking minority outside its borders.

It's not working, particularly for francophones *hors Quebec*, who are being assimilated before our very eyes. They now make up barely 4 per cent of Canadians outside Quebec; each new census tracks their decline. In Willow Bunch, Sask, where a francophone majority held the fort as lately as the mid-20th century, the number of people who speak

309

French at home has dwindled to 30 souls, old ones at that, among a population of 300.

The federal public service, which should be a model of bilingualism, appears to be a hopeless cause. English-speaking employees regularly spend more time in language training than doing their jobs. They go off for months or years to get their "C" level bilingual status - the highest attainable - only to come back to work as functionally unilingual as before. Not that it really matters. Ottawa still works largely as it did before 1969: If there's an anglo in the room, the meeting is in English.

Though Ottawa has its hands full just trying to meet the basics of official bilingualism, it has occasionally dreamt bigger. In 2003, the Chretien government adopted a five-year, $810 million plan that aimed, among other things, to make half of young Canadians bilingual by 2013. It is not working. Indeed, the bilingualism rate among anglophones between 15 and 19 - considered the "peak" rate for all cohorts - fell by a fifth to 13 per cent in the decade to 2006.

More early-age French immersion would not reverse that trend. Quality, already dubious due to a lack of truly bilingual teachers, would decline as quantity expands. Even most current French-immersion graduates - the minority who stick with the program until the end - have an astonishingly approximate grasp of the language. It's bad enough that they make basic grammatical and syntactical errors when speaking. (Don't ask about their written French). But plop most of them down in front of *Tout le Monde en Parle* or *Ici Louis-Jose Houde*, and they'd be lost. Current immersion programs seem to leave their graduates almost as completely disconnected from the daily reality of life in French Canada as non-graduates. How can that be nation-building?

If immersion doesn't open the door to the other solitude, why do people get so upset when there's less of it available? It's because parents want their kids immersed all right, just not necessarily in French. "Immersion is like an elitist private school within the public system," one Ontario teacher explained. "It's the highest-achieving kids who get chosen.

Class sizes are generally smaller. One couple told me they were so happy their son was being filtered from the dregs, which was actually how they put it." Immersion students may turn out to be Canada's equivalents to France's *enarques*, the graduates of the elite *Ecole Nationale d'Administration Publique*, who inevitably go on to positions of power and influence in French society.

In this light, New Brunswick's decision to opt for intensive French in Grade 5 and optional immersion later on, is quite defensible. Too many non-immersion kids get left behind because they are squeezed into classes where their numbers overwhelm the ability of the most gifted teachers to meet their needs. The collectivity suffers as a result. Except for the haste with which it seems to have made this decision, New Brunswick's Liberal government does not deserve to be excoriated.

If English Canadians cared about learning French, they would. That is simply human nature. Around the world, everywhere, when people need and want to learn a language, they do. There is no early English immersion in Finnish public schools. Kids don't start basic English classes until they're nine. Yet it is almost impossible to find a Finn under 40 who does not speak crisp, elegant, near perfect English. And it's not as if there's a ton of opportunities to practise on the streets of Oulu or Jyvaskyla. Most Finns master English on top of Swedish, though Finnish has almost no resemblance to Swedish, unlike English to French. But if you're serious about being bilingual or trilingual, you do what you must.

The National Broadcaster

In Canada, we aren't and don't. Claude Dubois knows all about that. The iconic Quebec singer just sold more than 250,000 copies of his latest album and was inducted last month into the Canadian Songwriters Hall of Fame. But when the CBC ran a taped version of the concert featuring the inductees, Mr. Dubois and the other francophone artists were cut. Our ratings obsessed national broadcaster was afraid French content might scare away viewers. It was an insult to Mr. Dubois and Quebec; both took it as one. CBC executive vice-president Richard Stursberg apologized. "Upon reflection," he explained, the network should have tried harder to show "the full diversity of the participants." At the CBC, the other official language is an afterthought.

We've receded. In the 1970S, francophone stars were regularly featured on the CBC; Ginette Reno and Rene Simard had their own variety shows. For a generation of English viewers, this was their first window onto Quebec culture. It may have inspired a few of them to learn French, and certainly raised their consciousness.

Today, the CBC broadcasts Canada's Next Great Prime Minister without even lip service to the other official language. But what is one to expect from a show whose main sponsor is a company (Magna International) whose former and future senior executive once ran for the leadership of a national political party without uttering a single word in French? Months later, when she crossed the floor to the Liberals, the best Belinda Stronach could offer francophone journalists was: *"En anglais, s'il vous plait."*

If learning French is a luxury in English Canada, most people in Quebec consider learning English a necessity. Yet Quebeckers know they are playing with fire. You'd be hard pressed to find a Quebecker who does not feel he or she has been personally and professionally enriched by learning English. But when census data show, as they did in December, that mother-tongue francophones now make up less than 50 per cent of the population on the Island of Montreal, and less than 80 per cent of Quebec's population for

the first time since the 1930S, it gets the people thinking in survivalist terms. It gets a newspaper such as Le Devoir to write this headline: "Historic retreat of French in Quebec." The issue gets framed - more or less - in these terms: Without a thriving francophone metropolis at its core, Quebec will be reduced before long to a Louisiana with sugar shacks.

Each of the solitudes maintains a tortured relationship with the language it doesn't speak first. English Canada needs the French fact to distinguish itself from the United States, but apparently not enough to become truly bilingual. Quebec needs to learn English to thrive in North America and avoid a retreat into isolation, but fears that each step out of its shell might deprive it from the option of going back.

It's has reason to be afraid. That is what has happened everywhere else, from New England to Willow Bunch. Four decades of official bilingualism have done nothing to alleviate that threat. It never could, or can. And so we beat on, to paraphrase F. Scort Fitzgerald, boats against the current, borne back ceaselessly into our mutual unilingualism.

Bilingualism in Governments

From the Ottawa Citizen, 2010/04/10   by Dan Gardner

Most of us need not apply for the top jobs

The hunt is on for Michaëlle Jean's successor at Rideau Hall and Graham Fraser (Commissioner of Official Languages) insists the next governor general must not only be an accomplished and respected individual. He or she must be bilingual.

Those who cannot speak both French and English should not even be considered for the job.

He would say this, of course. Fraser is the official languages commissioner and a passionate advocate of bilingualism. And this sort of talk has become standard fare in Official Ottawa. Supreme Court appointments. Senior civil service positions. Any of the country's top jobs. Whether they're covered by the Official Languages Act or not, any opening at the top prompts Fraser and others like him to pop up and insist that bilingualism is a mandatory qualification.

For the most part, Canadians agree. Or they shrug and say nothing, which is the quintessentially Canadian form of agreement. It is telling that a private member's bill that would make bilingualism a legal requirement for appointment to the Supreme Court recently passed the House of Commons - it's now in the Senate - with little public controversy. But let's take a quick peek at some numbers, shall we?

According to the 2006 census, the rate ofbilingualiSln among francophones was 42 per cent. Among anglophones, it was 9.4 per cent. Among allophones, those whose mother tongue is neither French nor English, it was 12.1 per cent. Bear in mind that as small as these numbers are, they actually exaggerate the real extent of bilingualism in Canada because they measure only people's self reported ability to carry on a conversation in French or English. Not only are people notoriously generous in their assessment of their own abilities, being able to chat about the weather falls well below the standard usually expected when bilingualism is a qualification for employment.

But let's take the numbers at face value. And turn them upside down to reveal the portion of the iceberg that lies below the waterline. The rate of unilingualism among francophones is 58 per cent. Among anglophones, it was 90.6 per cent. Among allophones, 87.9 per cent. Thus, according to the conventional wisdom as enunciated by Graham Fraser, the over whelming majority of Canadians should never be considered for any of Canada's top jobs.

It's an interesting state of affairs, particularly when it is contrasted with one of the traditional arguments in favour of gender equality. Women make up 51 per cent of the population, that argument goes. If they are excluded, one-half the available intelligence and energy is squandered. Thus, a country, corporation, or government that wishes to accomplish all it can must make every reasonable effort to include women in their recruitment pool. Every rational person accepts that argument today.

And yet many of the same people are content to say that for the top jobs in Canada, the overwhelming majority of Canadians are automatically disqualified. No matter how talented and capable they may be. No matter how accomplished. No bilingualism, no job.

Consider what this does for the current search for a governor general.

Thanks to the tradition that vice-regal appointments alternate between French and English Canadian, - which is itself arbitrary and dubious, but let's fight one battle at a time, - making bilingualism a mandatory qualification bars at least 90 per cent of the candidates in the nation before the search even begins. No one would dream of hiring a janitor for Rideau Hall this way and yet lots of people think it's reasonable when deciding who will be in charge at Rideau Hall.

No matter how talented and capable they may be.
No matter how accomplished.
No bilingualism, no job.

The consequence of mandatory bilingualism is as obvious as it is unmentionable in the polite circles of Official Ottawa. The top jobs often won't go to the best people. Former Supreme Court justice John Major - his tongue liberated by retirement - has been blunt about this. Make bilingualism mandatory for Supreme Court judges and you'll still get good people. But you won't get the best.

This is especially true of Canada's court of last resort, where the bilingualism that would be required is not the ability to hold one's own at a cocktail party. It's the fluency needed to hear oral arguments in complex cases and interpret arcane legal texts without the benefit of translators. At the same time as we demand this, we will continue to expect that Supreme Court judges will be among the very most brilliant and accomplished jurists in the country. And we will continue to allocate spots regionally: Three go to Quebec, three to Ontario, two to the West, and one to Atlantic Canada.

In all of Canada, the number of truly elite jurists with the bilingual fluency of a Pierre Trudeau is tiny. How many do you suppose there are in Alberta? British Columbia? Nova Scotia? Right.
Bonne chance, recruiters. Of course there's a standard response to this. If you want the job, get the qualification. But in almost every case, those who are so flippantly dismissive either grew up bilingual, or became bilingual in their youth, and live and work in those small and unusual pockets where bilingualism is the norm. They have no idea how hard it

315

is for a middle-aged person - no matter how intelligent or determined - to achieve bilingual proficiency, particularly if they live in a unilingual environment. The cost in time, effort, and money is enormous. If it can even be done.

The wise employer doesn't expect reality to adapt to his wishes. He adapts to reality. But Official Ottawa has never been keen on reality. And anyway, the top jobs can always be filled, no matter how tiny the recruitment pool, if we reduce our expectations sufficiently. Graham Fraser for Governor General, anyone?

Dan Gardner's column appears Wednesday, Friday, & Saturday. Email: dgardner@thecitizen.canwest.com.
Blog: ottawacitizen.com/katzenjammer

Criticism of Bilingualism

From two anonymous comments:
Re: "Sorry, I Don't Speak French", by Graham Fraser,

Unfortunately Graham Fraser, intelligent and sympathetic though he is, fails to ask a very simple question: Do anglophones want to learn French? Having studied and worked at the University of Ottawa it is painfully clear to me that most do not, and that those who do are woefully unaware of the effort required to acquire a second language. Indeed, if a referendum were organized in English Canada, asking citizens whether they would prefer to live in a genuinely bilingual Canada (including Quebec) or would rather see Quebec secede and live in a monolingual English Canada, I strongly suspect the latter option would gain majority support. . . . Anonymous

Years ago, I left Quebec, believing also that I was leaving the French environment behind. The government's programs in social engineering of French into English society are artificial, pointless and offensive. On the other hand, the Quebec government is systematically trying to suppress English usage via its Fascist language laws. In the greater context of North America, French is irrelevant. Mandarin would be a more useful language to learn. French is a dying language. Government imposition of French is akin to humping a corpse back to life. Lots of perspiration (money) and little gain. Quebec can secede, fine by me. I was born in Canada, but would rather see the country break up than live in one whose social polices make me want to spit on it in contempt and frustration.. . . Anonymous

The French learn English

From the Globe and Mail 2008/12/26

by Anita Elash Levallois, France

English instruction becomes French 'cause célèbre'

France is beefing up its courses in the language of the long despised Anglo-Saxons to improve its rate of bilingual graduates. Yvon Portier begins teaching his sixth grade physical education class at College Jean Jaures with a few simple and increasingly vehement instructions. "Pair up. Choose your partner. Stop running please. Mind the stairs. Don't push your classmate! Be quiet please! Shut your mouth!!"

Mr. Portier's exhortations may sound perfectly normal to anyone who has ever been in a gym class with 11 and 12 year olds. The difference is that Mr. Portier is speaking English at a junior high school in the heart of France - a country that still falls into existential crises over whether musicians who sing in English should be allowed to represent France at the Eurovision song contest.

He is teaching his gym class in English as part of an experiment to try to develop better ways to teach French children the language of the long-despised Anglo-Saxons. The experiment is part of a nationwide effort, announced by Education Minister Xavier Darcos this fall, to ensure that all French children are bilingual when they graduate from high school. "It is a wonderful ambition," Mr. Portier said in French. "I think it indicates an opening of the French spirit."

Education Ministry officials say they do not know how many students in France are bilingual when they graduate from high school. But English programs general inspector François Monnateuil said he is certain most are "not very good at speaking English" and that many who do speak well have wealthy parents who could afford to send them to immersion programs abroad. He said until recently, the French weren't interested in foreign languages. "The unity of our country has been based on the idea that one language keeps us together," he said. "For a long time French people had the idea that a lot of international people spoke French anyway, so it wasn't useful to learn a foreign language."

French teaching methods often demand perfection and emphasize writing rather than speaking in class, and have discouraged students from learning second languages, Mr. Monnateuil said. The French realized the situation must change when a survey of various European countries assessed students' ability to speak English put France at the bottom of the list, on a par with Spain. "The results probably would have been ignored, but they came at a time when, because of globalization, French society was more open to the subject," Mr. Monnateuil said.

Students are now required to learn two foreign languages, the first starting toward the end of grade school and the second starting in junior high. Although English is not mandatory, 86 per cent choose it as their primary foreign language, Mr. Monnateuil said.

This fall, schools began offering two hours a day of after-school English classes for students who need extra help. Starting this winter, they will offer week-long immersion courses that try to mimic immersion courses available abroad. The goal, said Mr. Darcos, is to make sure that all French children - not just those with wealthy parents - have a chance to perfect their English.

Mr. Monnateuil says the key to success will be to overcome the widespread belief that "as a French person I don't speak English well so I should not speak it at all."

In Mr. Portier's class, most of the students have no trouble trying out their English when a foreigner asks to speak to them, even though most admit to having "some difficulties" with vocabulary. "I have 11 years old. It's good to know English because *c'est la language universelle,*" says Remy, adding English is his best subject. Guillaume, 12, says he wants to be a "tennis man," but doubts he can get good a job unless he becomes fluent in English.

Mr. Portier says his goal is not to teach English but to use gym class to reinforce the English his students learn in their formal language class. "I know they are making some progress. I see that if you give an order at this age, there's an immediate argument. If you give an order in English, they want to prove they understand and they fall in line," he says.

One Culture

The Culture of Canada

From Wikipedia; lightly edited and formatted:
http://en.wikipedia.org/wiki/Culture_of_Canada

Canadian culture is a term that encompasses the artistic, musical, literary, culinary, political and social elements that are representative of Canada, not only to its own population, but people all over the world. Canada's culture has historically been influenced by European culture and traditions, especially British and French. Over time, elements of the cultures of Canada's Aboriginal peoples and immigrant populations have become incorporated into mainstream Canadian culture. It has also been strongly influenced by that of its linguistic, economic, and cultural neighbour, the United States.

Canada's federal government has influenced Canadian culture with programs, laws and institutions. It has created crown corporations to promote Canadian culture through media, such as the Canadian Broadcasting Corporation (CBC) and the National Film Board of Canada (NFB), and funds many events to promote Canadian traditions. It has also tried to protect Canadian culture by setting legal minimums on Canadian content in many media using bodies like the Canadian Radio-television and Telecommunications Commission (CRTC).

Canada's culture, like that of most any country in the world, is a product of its history, geography, and political system. Being a settler nation, Canada has been shaped by waves of migration that have combined to form a unique blend of customs, cuisine, and traditions that have marked the socio-cultural development of the nation. Though this article attempts to feature a variety of subjects pertinent to the culture of Canada, it is in no way exhaustive, and to gain a much deeper knowledge of Canada and its culture, one must also consult other articles pertaining to Canada and its peoples.

Development of Canadian Culture

Canadian culture is a product of Canada's history and geography. Most of Canada's territory was inhabited and developed later than other European colonies in the Americas, with the result that themes and symbols of pioneers, trappers, and traders were important in the early development of Canadian culture. The British conquest of Canada in 1759 brought a large Francophone population under British rule creating a need for accommodation and compromise, while the migration of United Empire Loyalists from the Thirteen Colonies brought in strong British and American influences.

Although not without conflict, Canada's early interactions with First Nations and Inuit people were relatively peaceful, compared to the experience of native peoples in the United States. Combined with relatively late economic development in many regions, this peaceful history has allowed Canadian native peoples to have a relatively strong influence on the national culture while preserving their own identity.

Bilingualism and multiculturalism

French Canada's early development was relatively cohesive during the 17th and 18th centuries, and this was preserved by the Quebec Act of 1774, which allowed Francophone culture to survive and thrive within Canada. In 1867, the British North America Act was designed to meet the growing calls for Canadian autonomy while avoiding the overly strong decentralization that contributed to the Civil War in the United States. The compromises made by Macdonald and Cartier set Canada on a path to bilingualism, and this in turn contributed to an acceptance of diversity that later led to both multiculturalism and tolerance of Native culture and customs.

Multicultural heritage is enshrined in Section 27 of the Canadian Charter of Rights and Freedoms. In parts of Canada, especially the major cities of Montreal, Vancouver, and Toronto (for example, in Toronto's Kensington Market area), multiculturalism itself is the cultural norm and diversity is the force that unites the community. In Quebec, cultural identity is strong, and many French speaking Quebec commentators speak of a Quebec culture as distinguished from English Canadian culture, but some also see Canada as a collection of several regional, aboriginal, and ethnic subcultures.

While French Canadian culture is the most obvious example, Celtic influences have allowed survival of non-English dialects in Nova Scotia and Newfoundland. However, the influence of Ulster immigrants to Toronto has had the effect of minimizing Irish influences in Ontario's culture, and highlighting British influences instead, until the 1980s. Canada's Pacific trade has also brought a large Chinese influence into British Columbia and other areas.

Canada has always placed emphasis on equality and inclusiveness for all people. For example, in 1995, the Supreme Court of Canada ruled in Egan v. Canada that sexual orientation should be "read in" to Section Fifteen of the Canadian Charter of Rights and Freedoms, a part of the Constitution of Canada guaranteeing equal rights to all Canadians. Following a series of decisions by provincial courts and the Supreme Court of Canada, on July 20, 2005, the Civil Marriage Act (Bill C-38) received Royal Assent, legalizing same sex marriage in Canada. Canada thus became the fourth country to officially sanction same sex marriage worldwide, after The Netherlands, Belgium, and Spain. Sexual orientation was included as a protected status in the human rights laws of the federal government and of all provinces and territories.

Canadian Identity

Primary influences on the Canadian identity trace back to the arrival, beginning in the early 17th century, of French settlers to Acadia and Saint Lawrence River valley, English settlers to Newfoundland and the British conquest and settlement of New France from the early 18th century. First Nations played a critical part in the development of European colonies in Canada, from their roles in assisting exploration of the continent, the fur trade, European power struggles, and the creation of the Métis people. Through their art and culture, First Nations, Inuit and Métis continue to exert influence on Canadian identity.

The question of Canadian identity was traditionally dominated by three fundamental themes. Firstly, the often conflicted relations between English Canadians and French Canadians stemming from the French Canadian imperative for cultural and linguistic survival. Secondly, the generally close ties between English Canadians and the British Empire, resulting in a gradual political process towards complete independence from the imperial power. Thirdly and finally, the close proximity of English speaking Canadians to the military, economic and cultural powerhouse of the United States. With the gradual loosening of political and cultural ties to the United Kingdom, in the 20th century immigrants from European, African, Caribbean and Asian nationalities have shaped the Canadian identity. That process continues today with the continuing arrival of large numbers of immigrants from non British or French backgrounds, adding the theme of multiculturalism to the debate. Today, Canada has a diverse makeup of nationalities and cultures and constitutional protection for policies that promote multiculturalism rather than a single national myth.

The issue of Canadian identity remains under scrutiny, perhaps more than the identity of the people of any other modern nation. Journalist Andrew Cohen wrote in 2007, "The Canadian Identity, as it has come to be known, is as elusive as the Sasquatch and Ogopogo. It has animated and frustrated generations of statesmen, historians, writers, artists, philosophers, and the National Film Board . . . Canada resists easy definition". In true Canadian fashion, however, even the search for an identity has become itself an object for self criticism.

Good Immigrant Cultures in Canada

From the Globe and Mail 2008/04/03   by Unnati Gandhi, Vancouver

Gathered around a kitchen stove at the Dasmesh Punjabi School in Abbotsford, B. C., Gurbir Brar 14, and his friends are arguing about whether the onions for their vegetarian lasagna are properly cooked. The pasta is boiling away on a second burner. Gurbir said he enjoys cooking just as much he loves to mimic his favourite wrestling stars. The same goes for the other boys, he said, who make up about half of the home economics class. "It's fun. You get to try new things," the Grade 9 student said. That's what gets Sulochana Chand, principal of the 500 student Sikh independent school, to smile. "If we were in India, boys would be running away from the kitchen. Here, there's a real balance in the two cultures." The scene at the Abbotsford school is being played out across urban Canada, as a clearer image of Canada's ever diverse face emerged with newly released census data.

Visible minorities now number more than five million, growing at a rate that is five times that of the rest of the population. They make up a staggering 16.2 per cent of Canadians, and if current trends continue, they could account for roughly one-fifth of the total population by 2017. And for the first time, South Asians slipped past Chinese to become the country's largest visible minority group, with a population of 1,262,900. By comparison, about 1,216,600 people identified themselves as Chinese. Together, the two ethnic groups make up just under half of all visible minorities. But at the same time, Canadians reported ties to more than 200 ethnic origins - everything from Aboriginal to Zulu - confirming the nation's title as one of the most multicultural places in the world.

The numbers tell a new, dual identity story of Canada, one that shows visible minorities integrating more easily into the mainstream while also maintaining strong ties to their own culture and language. Visible minority parents are especially eager to emphasize cultural tradition to their children, who make up a much larger swath of the overall population.

The census shows that 96 per cent of visible minorities live in urban areas, compared with 69 per cent of the overall population. In Toronto and Vancouver, about half of visible minorities are under the age of 15; in Montreal, that figure is about a quarter. Nationally, 17.9 per cent of Canadians are in this age bracket. In Brampton, where South Asians make up 31.7 per cent of the population (the most in any community across Canada), entire shopping malls and community centres resonate with Punjabi, Gujarati and Hindi.

The city's newest hospital, the Brampton Civic Centre, was opened as a result of millions of dollars in donations from the region's South Asian population. "We're living in a very diverse city, a very cosmopolitan and multicultural city, where we embrace our multiculturalism," said Brampton Mayor Susan Fennell. The census is just the statistical evidence of the profile of the city of Brampton. It's no surprise at all."

Nav Bhatia, a prominent Sikh businessman in Mississauga, hopes to see more of the same across the country, saying that the onus to make Canada welcome to immigrants is on the South Asian community now that it is the largest visible minority group. "There's no more excuses. We need to intermingle so that the rest of Canadians know we all have the same interests at heart." Mr. Bhatia, who owns a Hyundai dealership, said the cultural landscape for immigrants was very different as little as a decade ago. "Ten, eleven years ago, the Indian movies only played at the third grade theatres. Now, we see women in shalwar-kameez and saris at AMC with everybody else . . . we might look different - I'm a turbaned Sikh - but we all like watching a quality movie in a quality theatre."

But in a delicate counterbalance to that very diversity, the census data also revealed a decrease in the number of individuals who self-identified as "Canadian." An explanation as to why is a little more nuanced than simply attributing the downward trend to segregated communities or a lack of patriotism, said an analyst at Statistics Canada. "It means different things to different people," said Jane Badets, adding that those who typically identify themselves as Canadian are third or fourth-generation. The majority of South Asians and Chinese are first and second- generation. But some who drop the hyphenated Canadian label from their identities say they do it because the Canadian identity is implied. "If we're talking to someone in Canada, I just say I'm Punjabi," said Sharonveer Sandhu, a Grade 8 student at Dasmesh. "When you go to Germany, you add the Canadian'".

Visible Minorities by Origin

Paragraphs are lightly edited excerpts from:
http://en.wikipedia.org/wiki/Demographics_of_Canada#Ethnic_origin

Multiple responses: Counting both single and multiple responses, the most commonly identified ethnic origins were (2006 census):

Ethnic Origin	%
Canadian	32.2
English	21.0
French	18.8
Scottish	15.1
Irish	13.9
German	10.2
Italian	4.6
Chinese	4.3
N American Indian	4.0
Ukrainian	3.9
Dutch	3.3
Polish	3.2
East Indian	3.0
Russian	1.6

Ethnic Origin	%
Welsh	1.4
Filipino	1.4
Norwegian	1.4
Portuguese	1.3
Metis	1.3
Swedish	1.0
Latin American	1.0
Hungarian	1.0
Jewish	1.0

Visible Minorities [total] by Canadian City from 2006 Census

Toronto	42.9
Vancouver	41.7
Calgary	22.2
Edmonton	17.1
Montreal	16.5
Ottawa	16.2
Winnipeg	15.0
Halifax	7.5
Regina	6.6
St Johns	1.9

Multiculturism Backlash

From the National Post, 2008/04/10   Letter to Editor by Carol Dunn

Re: Turning Self-Hatred Into A State Creed
by Barbara Kay, April 9, 2008.

As Barbara Kay notes, multiculturalism has backfired on us - it has not encouraged tolerance and helped combat hatred, but achieved quite the opposite.

327

My 16 year old son attends a Toronto high school. He is always asked where he is from. He has learned to answer, "Scotland and England" because when he says he's "Canadian" he's told: "There isn't such a thing". My 12 year old attends a junior high school in Toronto. When being held at knife point in the boys' washroom, he was asked if he was Russian. He answered that he was Canadian and was laughed at and called "a white wimp." Thanks to multiculturalism, today's kids have forgotten that they are Canadian first, and are instead focussing on battles their ancestors fought, or are still fighting. Separate national identities tie us to our grisly pasts and hold us all back. Too bad Canada missed such a great and unique opportunity.

Herouxville, Quebec   *Excerpt from National Post 2008/10/31*

Herouxville wins . . . and that's a good thing ! *Others should follow Quebec's example.*

So it becomes official: The tiny town of Herouxville has won the great argument over "reasonable accommodation" of immigrants to Quebec.

In 2007, Herouxville's municipal council passed an official code of "life standards" designed to advise new Quebecers (though there were none in town yet) of the province's culture norms. We do not, the code said, practise polygamy, separation by caste, sex discrimination or segregation or honour killing. Although it is a secular society, Quebec does observe traditional Christian holidays and has buildings and streets named after great Christian figures. Boys and girls play together in our parks and public facilities, and your doctor or lawyer or MP might be a woman. Get used to it.

Herouxville's code is rambling, deliberately provocative and in parts just plain weird. But what mostly made it controversial - in this culturally relativistic age - was the core idea that Quebecers had the right to consciously impose any cultural expectations at all upon immigrants. And that idea has now been taken up by the Government of Quebec, which announced Wednesday that it will require newcomers to sign a declaration promising to participate in the "shared values" of the Quebecois people.

The province's neo-Herouxvillian document is simpler and much less objectionable than the original model - but it surely never would have been adopted in the first place if the little community hadn't thrown down the gauntlet. From now on, immigrants entering Quebec will have to indicate their understanding and agreement that Quebec is a pluralist, liberal- democratic society where French is the official language, the sexes are equal, church and state are separate and secular law takes precedence over religion, though everyone is free to observe his own faith.

If a sign of liberalism's lamentable journey from egalitarian origins to cheap identity politics were needed, one could find none better than the frantic race to object to this motherhood statement of what ought to be liberal fundamentals. The editorial board of the Montreal Gazette, for instance, complains that the declaration is unenforceable, and yet at the same time is "somehow repellent" in its explicitness and clarity and yet again is too "slippery" in its meaning to be of any good.

Elsewhere, we read of the declaration being denounced as a pre-election "political stunt"; this, of course, is what you call a very popular measure when you don't personally like it. Would it be much of a "stunt" if it weren't near-certain to win votes?

Other measures were announced along with the declaration: The province plans to expand French-language education for prospective immigrants, and language-training funding is also to be made available to Quebec employers who hire newcomers. Nobody described these expensive measures as "political stunts", and some critics ignored them completely; only the culturally assertive, low-cost idea of advising immigrants how to integrate was singled out.

Perhaps most extraordinary was the quote from sociologist Victor Armony, in our own pages, to the effect that successful immigrants

"Don't need Quebec society to patronize them." But as we see it, the far more patronizing slight comes from doctrinaire multiculturalism, which refuses to recognize the reality that immigrants are real people with real values - not human props in a feel-good ethnic fun fair - and that oftentimes those values are in conflict with Canada's, especially as regards women, gays and the place of religion in our society. Quebec's government, like Herouxville, at least pays immigrants the respect of recognizing the hard edges on their world views, even as it asks them to bend them as the price of integrating into their new homeland.

That's a fair price - one that millions of Canadian immigrants have paid since the birth of this country. We see nothing wrong with the Quebec government making this trade-off explicit. Indeed, we urge other governments to follow its example.

Honour Killings

From the National Post 2008/11/18   by Marvin Levant

Understanding Honour Killings

An honour killing is the murder of a girl or woman who has allegedly committed an act that has shamed and embarrassed her family. For the family to show its community that it has reasserted control, the woman is killed. "Harm to reputation" is considered a partial or complete defence for murder.

A manual of Islamic law, certified by Cairo's al-Azhar University as a reliable guide to Sunni orthodoxy, says that "retaliation is obligatory against anyone who kills a human being purely intentionally and without right." However, "not subject to retaliation" is a "father or mother (or their fathers or mothers) for killing their offspring, or offspring's offspring." In other words, someone who kills his child incurs no legal penalty under Islamic law. Why does this stipulation appear in a manual of Islamic law if honour killing has nothing to do with Islam?

The most shocking aspect of Aqsa Parvez's murder is not that it was allegedly committed by her closest male relatives in an "honour killing." No, the most shocking thing is that women like Farrah Khan - a member of a group for young Muslim women called Our Collective Dreams - are in a complete state of denial about what motivates these crimes. Instead of showing support for the victims and disgust toward their murderers, Ms. Khan and others end up misdirecting their wrath at those who dare to see the obvious - the religious and cultural underpinnings of these despicable and dishonourable acts.

As for those who decry the "honour killing" label, viewing its use as "racist" and "Islamophobic," I would direct their attention to a headline this past week in the Pakistani newspaper The Daily Star: "1,019 women killed for honour over three years." The article goes on to recount how Pakistan's "National Assembly was told on Thursday that more than 7,000 cases of rape and murder of women were registered between 2005 and 2007, in addition to 1,019 cases of honour killings." If it isn't "racist" to call them "honour killings" in Pakistan, why should it be "racist" to call them "honour killings" outside Pakistan? Isn't the insistence, *"that one set of people are endowed with a right denied to others"*, the very definition of discrimination?

Immigrant Behaviour

From the National Post 20081016   by Stewart Bell

Quebec man urges al Qaeda to attack Canada

A man in Quebec has posted messages on the Internet encouraging al-Qaeda to attack Canada, the latest in a series of similar sentiments that are worrying counterterrorism officials.

The author of the messages, who uses the pseudonym Altar, praised terror leader Osama bin Laden and asked why al Qaeda was focussing its efforts only on Europe instead of Canada. "Allah is great and may Allah bless Sheikh bin Laden. That the sword held by the hand of al-

331

Qaeda hits not only Europe, but that it hits all our enemies. Wherever they are," he wrote in a 25 Sept 2008 posting.

"Me, I live in Canada and the Canadian government supports the Americans. The government of Canada supports Israel. Canadian soldiers are sent to Afghanistan and Iraq." "Now it's Canada's turn." A copy of the message, posted to a French-based Internet forum called Minbarsos, was found by the SITE Intelligence Group, which monitors terrorist Web sites. In his online biography, Altar writes that he is a Sunni Muslim who lives in Quebec and that: "I want to chase the non-Muslims from Canada. Only their deaths will make Islam triumphant. God is Great." The message concludes: "May Allah guide us to always defend our religion. That the Crusaders whether in Iraq or in Ottawa, the sword of Islam will fall on their head. God is Great." This kind of rhetoric has been appearing increasingly on the Internet, often the work of young radicals who join online forums that promote al-Qaeda.

"Don't forget, these al-Qaeda sites, normal people can't get onto them," said terrorism expert Bruce Hoffman, a professor at Georgetown University's Edmund A. Walsh School of Foreign Service. "They're password protected; you have to be vouched for personally. So the access is controlled, so you have to take something like this somewhat seriously."

The RCMP in Quebec could not be reached for comment yesterday. Canadian counterterrorism police have already investigated several similar cases involving online activities. The RCMP arrested a Moroccan man in Trois-Rivieres, Que, last September for allegedly posting messages on the Web threatening terror attacks in Germany and Austria.

In January, the National Post revealed that the RCMP was investigating a Toronto university student who had repeatedly posted messages on the Internet supporting attacks on Canadian soil. Another young Islamist identified by the Post in April had posted messages online referring to bin Laden as a "hero" and "champion of Islam," urging people to support the Taliban and calling for the deaths of moderate Canadian

Muslims. Altar writes in French, but he is not further identified. He lists his occupation as "organizer." In an earlier posting, circulated in June, he criticized Canada for double standards in Afghanistan.

"When a government gratuitously kills women and children . . . they call it an 'operation to maintain the peace' and when the men defend themselves . . . they call it terrorism. Real terrorism is the oppression of an entire state. Fighting in the path of Allah is not terrorism, it is a door to paradise."

Prof. Hoffman said it was sometimes not difficult for authorities to identify those using the Web to incite terrorism. But extremists continue doing it. "They still believe they are cleverer than the government operating against them are. For them, it's the thrill and the rush of taking part in this. "For some of them, the possibility of being harassed is a mark of distinction, it's something that is appealing."

Muslim Beliefs and Laws

Paragraphs are lightly edited excerpts from:
http://www.breakthechain.org/exclusives/rickmathes.html

This is a true story and the author, Rick Mathes, is a well known leader in prison ministry. The man who walks with God gets to his destination. If you have a pulse, you have a purpose. The Muslim religion is the fastest growing religion per capita in the United States, especially in the minority races! Last month I attended my annual training session that's required for maintaining my state prison security clearance. During the training session there was a presentation by three speakers representing the Roman Catholic, Protestant and Muslim faiths, who explained each of their beliefs.

I was particularly interested in what the Islamic Imam had to say. The Imam gave a great presentation of the basics of Islam, complete with a video. After the presentations, time was provided for questions and answers. When it was my turn, I directed my question to the Imam and asked: 'Please, correct me if I'm wrong, but I understand that most Imams and clerics of Islam have (Ed: issued a fatwah and) declared a holy jihad (Holy war) against the infidels of the world and, that by killing an infidel, (which is a command to all Muslims) they are assured of a place in heaven. If that's the case, can you give me the definition of an infidel?'

There was no disagreement with my statements and, without hesitation, he replied, 'Non-believers!' I responded, 'So, let me make sure I have this straight. All followers of Allah have been commanded to kill everyone who is not of your faith so they can have a place in heaven. Is that correct?'

The expression on his face changed from one of authority and command to that of a little boy who had just been caught with his hand in the cookie jar. He sheepishly replied, 'Yes.' I then stated, 'Well, sir, I have a real problem trying to imagine Pope John Paul commanding all Catholics to kill those of your faith or Dr. Stanley ordering all

Protestants to do the same in order to guarantee them a place in heaven!'

The Imam was speechless!

I continued, 'I also have problem with being your friend when you and your brother clerics are telling your followers to kill me! Let me ask you a question: Would you rather have your Allah, who tells you to kill me in order for you to go to heaven, or my Jesus who tells me to love you because I am going to heaven and He wants you to be there with me?'

You could have heard a pin drop as the Imam hung his head in shame. Needless to say, the organizers and/or promoters of the Diversification' training seminar were not happy with Rick's way of dealing with the Islamic Imam , and exposing the truth about the Muslims' beliefs.

In twenty years there will be enough Muslim voters in the U. S. to elect the President! I think everyone in the U. S. and Canada should be required to read this, but with the ACLU (American Civil Liberties Uion), there is no way this will be widely publicized, unless each of us send it on! This is your chance to make a difference.

English Common Law & Islam Are Incompatible

From Romanian National Vanguard News; lightly edited and formatted:
http://news.ronatvan.com/2009/07/08/in-england-girls-vulnerable-to-islamic-law-incompatible-with-british-laws/

In England, Girls are Vulnerable

In March of last year a severely autistic man with the mental age of three married a woman in Bangladesh, via the telephone. Three of Britain's most senior judges intervened, ruling the marriage could not be legal under English law, as the man was unable to give his consent. This marriage, said Lord Justice Thorpe, was "sufficiently offensive to the conscience of the English court that the court should refuse to recognise it and should refuse to give effect to the law of Bangladesh and sharia law." Only six months later, sharia courts that had formerly operated illegally in Britain were reclassified as "tribunals" under the Arbitration Act, allowing them to pass effectively legally binding judgments in many civil matters.

However, with sharia law incompatible with English law and modern human rights norms, concerns were rightly raised that the sharia court system in Britain would grow into a parallel legal system. The disparity between English and sharia law was highlighted only a month later, as the House of Lords passed judgment in the case of a Lebanese woman who had claimed the right to remain in the UK with her son. An earlier Lebanese court decision, under sharia law, meant that, despite a history of abuse, her former husband would get automatic custody of the child when he turned seven.

Lord Hope of Craighead observed that under the sharia judgment, " .

. . there is a real risk of a flagrant denial of their article 8 rights (of the European Convention on Human Rights) if the appellant and her child were to be returned to Lebanon." Lord Bingham of Cornhill added, rather triumphantly, that her case was supported "(...) by Justice and Liberty." Justice and liberty, Lord Cornhill appeared to say, are not supported by sharia. Not even in civil cases. For in sharia, the rights of the man supersede the rights of the woman and children, Muslims are privileged over non-Muslims, and where sharia is the dominant or sole form of law, cruel punishments, including death by stoning, hanging, etc., are meted out for homosexuality, adultery, apostasy, etc.

Although it has generally been thought that five sharia courts were operating in Britain, just over a week ago Civitas revealed that there are now at least 85 sharia courts operating across the country. It is troubling, Civitas says that some sharia rulings it looked at, "(...) advise illegal actions and others that transgress human rights standards as applied by British courts," and that, "(...) for many Muslims, sharia courts are in practice part of an institutionalised atmosphere of intimidation, backed by the ultimate sanction of a death threat."

In other cases, a lack of ability in spoken English, or lack of familiarity of British society, law, police, etc., will undoubtedly mean that many Muslim girls and women in particular are left vulnerable to a court system that is biassed against them. The Daily Mail newspaper reported a few days ago that, for example, Muslim women have to pay two and a half times as much as a man in seeking a sharia divorce in Britain, because her word has to be corroborated. In other words, the burden of proof is on the woman, and her evidence is not admissible by itself.

There were up to 8,000 forced marriages reported last year in England, with the Forced Marriage Unit dealing with an 80 percent increase from the previous year. Most of the victims are teenage girls from Pakistan and Bangladesh, with some as young as 13 forced to marry to preserve "family honour," or to allow foreign nationals to emigrate to Britain as a spouse.

With the problem increasing, a Forced Marriage (civil) Act was passed in November 2008, making forced marriages unlawful and allowing them to be annulled. However, the act does not make forcing someone to marry against their will, or aiding forced marriage, a punishable offense. Public funds are also unavailable to those who have been married in Britain for less than two years, meaning that victims who flee an abusive marriage often find themselves destitute. "The situation," according to Kate Wareing, director of Oxfam's UK Poverty Programme, "is so extreme that the police turn to the Home Office to detain the women so they have somewhere else to go."

Nevertheless, even if a victim of forced marriage does escape, and even if the marriage is annulled under English law, the problem for any Muslim girl or woman may not end there. In February of last year, a 15 year old Pakistani girl was forced to marry a forty year old man with the mental age of five, again via the telephone. When she arrived in England from Pakistan she was forced to work as a prostitute by her new family, who invited men to their house to rape her. "This marriage," Victoria Golshani on Islamist Watch observes, "was not recognized by the Home Office but was and is still recognized by the Sharia courts that flourish in the UK," having been approved by the Islamic Sharia Council in Britain, despite the minimum age for marriage being 16 under English law.

Should she have a boyfriend at some point in the future, though doing nothing abnormal in the eyes of English society, she will be committing adultery in the eyes of Britains 85 sharia courts, and, as such, in the eyes of many Muslims in England and her home country, Pakistan. Such a thought would undoubtedly make any Muslim girl rightly fearful for her safety.

In 2003, Abdulla Yones was found guilty of murdering his 16 year old daughter, Heshu. The father had discovered that she was in a relationship with a Lebanese Christian, and later received an anonymous letter accusing his daughter of being a "slut" and a "prostitute." "Disgusted and distressed" by her relationship, Abdulla beat her for six months, before stabbing her eleven times and cutting her throat open in a frenzied attack. In his decision Judge Neil Denison nevertheless suggested that, "It is arguable that Heshu's conduct provoked her father," adding in his concluding remarks that the situation had arisen out of "irreconcilable cultural differences between traditional Kurdish values and the values of western society."

Sharia law and Western norms of law and human rights are indeed irreconcilable. Britain's sharia courts, as they have proven, have no respect for English law, or the rights of girls and women, but seem only to facilitate their abuse. If the Forced Marriage Act had made aiding or abetting forced marriage a criminal offense then members of the Islamic Sharia Council in Britain would be standing trial for recognizing, and continuing to recognize, the forced marriage of a minor, and one suspects this is precisely why it was made only a civil offense.

The desire of sharia judges to extend their reach, and to introduce harsh punishments, such as the chopping off of the hand for theft, shows that their vision of a future Britain is medieval and barbaric. Britain needs to have the courage of its convictions, and stand up for the human rights of girls and women, and the liberty of its citizens. The longer the sharia courts are allowed to operate the more these unalienable rights will be sacrificed.

Western Feminism & Islam Are Incompatible

From Deborah Young's Blog:11/12/2009; lightly edited and formatted:
http://paltalknewsnetwork.com/node/664

In 2004 Theo Van Gogh was murdered in the street of his beloved Amsterdam by an Islamic man furious at the movie "Submission" Van Gogh had produced with Ayaan Hirsi Ali, a former Muslim woman from Somalia. The movie was about defiance, about Muslim women and the oppression and abuse they suffer under the precepts of the Quran. Muhammad Bouyeri shot Theo and after Theo begged, "Can't we talk about this?" Bouyeri shot him 4 more times and sawed Theo's throat with a knife, then stabbed a 5 page letter onto the dying man's chest. The letter threatened Western Governments, Jews and Ayaan who had to go into hiding. Van Gogh was the great grandson of Theo Van Gogh, the artist Vincent Van Gogh's brother.

The moment was a defining one for Holland. They finally realized that their western values were incompatible with the Islamic faith practised by the many Muslims in Holland. It set the country on fire. As Hirsi Ali says, "Opinion makers were now saying that it was irresponsible and indeed morally wrong to pretend that appeasing Islamic leaders would magically lead to social harmony. Dutch society was churning with discussion over how to best integrate Muslims, and Muslims in Holland also seemed largely aware now that they needed to choose between Western values and the old ways."

The freedom of expression that liberated Hirsi Ali once she moved to Holland is unknown in most if not all theocratic Islamic countries. Theo's murderer and others like him don't realize how deeply people in the West are committed to the idea of an open society, she points out. Even though open societies are vulnerable, they are stubborn. It is the place where she ran for safety and freedom and she wants to keep it that way: safe and free.

Hirsi Ali grew up in a culture of death in Somalia, Saudi Arabia and Kenya. She wrote in her book "Infidel" that "death lures many to take their own lives to escape the dismal reality. For many women, because of the perception of lost honour, death comes at the hands of a father, brother or husband. Wishful thinking about the peaceful tolerance of Islam, she points out, cannot interpret away this reality: hands are still cut off, women still stoned and enslaved.

Ayaan has made this her life's purpose: to educate those of us who are free that we in the West would be wrong to prolong the pain of transition unnecessarily, by elevating cultures full of bigotry and hatred toward women to the stature of respectable alternative ways of life. The fact is that hundreds of millions of women around the world live in forced marriages, and six thousand small girls are excised every day. As was Hirsi Ali. With a pair of scissors wielded by a local religious man while being held down by adults.

The apologists for militant Islam do the West no favours when they run in with their politically correct mega-phones directing us all on what to think when another Muslim commits terror and murder in the name of his religion. The apologists for militant Islam do the Muslim faith no favours when they tamp down much needed discussion on how we in the West are to cope with a population that has gone through no reformation and often does not seek to assimilate in the country that opened its doors to them, but instead to take it over. The next time you see a woman in a burqa shopping, ask her if she was excised as a girl. Ask her what level of education she was allowed to achieve. Ask her if she was forced into her marriage. The women of the West have fought too hard and too long to be "free" to throw it all away by calling the oppression and abuse of millions of women in the name of religion just another lifestyle choice.

It is oppression and abuse.

We in the West are a tolerant people. Freedom of speech is protected by our constitution. Religious freedom in protected by our constitution. And women have been liberated, to run their own lives. All three of these are in direct conflict with strict Islam. You are not allowed to criticize or even question Islamic precepts. They tolerate no religion but their own. And women are subjugated with no voice or power either within the religious arena or at home. Peaceful Muslims are just as victimized as the rest of us by strict Islamists. (Writer Heather Michon points out that Islamic feminism is on the rise in the Muslim world and Europe is going to play a huge part in that development.)

Even American Muslims who have grown up in America enjoying the perks and benefits of an open society, such as Major Hasan and his Imam, dare to embrace the belief that Islamic law trumps the U.S. Constitution. This sets up a dangerous conflict because we are not a theocracy. The goal of a global Islamic Government is incompatible with religious tolerance.

Ayaan Hirsi Ali made her mark in Holland. She pushed through legislation that caused the Dutch government to register murders in that country based on honour killings and to register the domestic violence, sexual abuse and incest and the number of excisions of little girls taking place every year on Dutch kitchen tables. The Dutch government registered the number of drug-related killings and traffic accidents every year but not the number of honour killings because no Dutch official wanted to recognize that this kind of murder happened on a regular basis. Once these figures were clear, the facts alone shocked the country and helped her reach the goal of eliminating the complacent attitude of moral relativists who claimed all cultures are equal. She took away the excuse that nobody knew.

The creeping in of sharia law is incompatible with Western values. It is mainly Muslim men in England who stridently demand to follow only Sharia law instead of the laws of England, much to the horror of Islamic women who have fled brutal theocracies to escape Sharia so they might attend universities, and not marry if they wish, and not be killed for being raped. And part of that creeping Sharia law that is marking itself in free countries is the criminalization of religious talk and discourse if it involves Islam. That is Sharia law. In our country Christians and Jews, Catholics and Baptists (and Hare Krishna's) are routinely debated, ridiculed and admired at various times and by various factions. Islam does not get a pass in a free society, which becomes un-free once freedom of speech is suppressed.

As a free society it is our duty to engage in vigorous discourse on the violence in our country being perpetuated on the innocent in the name of Islam. We are not the ones who are bringing up religion. When you shout "Allahu Akbar" before engaging in murder, you bring religion to the table. Now is not the time to apologize or wish away the realities. Now is the time to confront and hold feet to the fire: we have shed literal blood, sweat and tears to form a more perfect union, an open society that relishes its freedoms. And we won't be held hostage to the notion we must tolerate the intolerable.

There are times when silence becomes an accomplice to injustice. Or as Winston Churchill put it: "The malice of the wicked is reinforced by the weakness of the virtuous." Unfortunately, Theo Van Gogh learned that the hard way.

European Court of Human Rights (ECHR)

Paragraphs are lightly edited excerpts:
http://en.wikipedia.org/wiki/European_Court_of_Human_Rights

The European Court of Human Rights (French: Cour européenne des droits de l'homme) in Strasbourg is an international judicial body established under the European Convention on Human Rights of 1950 to monitor respect of human rights by states. The European Convention on Human Rights, or formally named Convention for the Protection of Human Rights and Fundamental Freedoms, is a convention adopted by the Council of Europe. All 47 member states of the Council of Europe are parties to the Convention. Applications against Contracting Parties for human rights violations can be brought before the Court by other states, other parties or individuals.

Relationship to the European Court of Justice (ECJ)

The Court of Justice of the European Union (ECJ) is not related to the European Court of Human Rights. However, since all EU states are members of the Council of Europe and have signed the Convention on Human Rights, there are concerns about consistency in case law between the two courts. Therefore, the ECJ refers to the case-law of the Court of Human Rights and treats the Convention on Human Rights as though it was part of the EU's legal system. Even though its members have joined, the European Union itself has not, as it did not have competence to do so under previous treaties. However, EU institutions are bound under article 6 of the EU treaty of Nice to respect human rights under the Convention. Furthermore, since the Treaty of Lisbon has taken effect on 1 December 2009, the EU is expected to sign the Convention. This would make the Court of Justice bound by the judicial precedents of the Court of Human Rights and thus be subject to its human rights law, resolving this way the issue of conflicting case law.

Some notable cases - Refah Partisi v Turkey (2003)

In upholding the Turkish Constitutional Court's dissolution of The Welfare Party (Refah Partisi) for violating Turkey's principle of secularism (by calling for the re-introduction of religious law) the court held **"that sharia is incompatible with the fundamental principles of democracy."**

The Court justified the breach of the appellants' rights by reasoning that a legal regime based on sharia would diverge from the Convention's values, "particularly with regard to its criminal law and criminal procedure, its rules on the status of women and the way it intervenes in all spheres of private and public life in accordance with religious precepts."

Muslim Majority Countries

Paragraph are lightly edited excerpts:
   http://en.wikipedia.org/wiki/List_of_Muslim_majority_countries

Of the 48 countries with more than 50% of the population classed as Muslim, only five are listed as being parliamentary democracies, including Iraq. Saudi Arabia is listed as an absolute monarchy, Iran and Pakistan as parliamentary republics, Afghanistan as presidential republic.

Minarets in Switzerland

From the National Post 2009/11/12
                              by Alaa Al-Aswany, Zurich, Switzerland

Switzerland's "Battle of the Minarets"

On the occasion of the publication of my book, "Friendly Fire" in German, the Swiss publishing house Lenos invited me to hold a number of seminars in Switzerland and Germany. As soon as I arrived in Zurich, I found that Swiss public opinion was preoccupied with an interesting and important matter: what they call here the battle of the minarets.

The story began with the Schweizerische Volkspartei (SVP; Swiss Peoples' Party), a strong right wing party that for years has proposed laws hostile to foreigners and immigrants. Switzerland has a population of about seven million people, of which about 300,000 citizens are Muslims. The Muslim community in Switzerland is peaceful and quiet, and has not given rise to any incidents of violence whatsoever. But SVP has gathered more than 100,000 signatures on a petition that calls on the government to ban minarets. If the referendum triggered by this petition passes, Muslims would have the right to set up mosques as they wish, but without minarets.

In SVP's opinion, Islam is a religion that advocates murder, violence and the oppression of women, and the minaret is an emblem of war rather than a religious symbol. To support the argument, SVP cited a rhetorical remark by Turkish Prime Minister Recep Tayyip Erdogan, who said in a speech: "The minarets are our lances, the domes our helmets, the mosques our barracks, and the faithful our army." SVP also claimed that many Muslim states prevent Christians from performing their religious rites, so Switzerland should treat Muslims in the same manner.

SVP chose for this campaign a horrible poster showing the Swiss flag with a woman in a complete face veil standing on it, and many minarets breaking through the flag as though they are bombs or missiles. Some Swiss cities refused to permit distribution of the posters on the grounds that they incited racism and hatred of Muslims, while others allowed them on freedom of expression grounds.

So far, the story is familiar to any Western observer: a right wing political party incites hatred of Islam and Muslims, and tries to restrict and persecute them. But the reaction of the Swiss has been interesting. Independent intellectuals, left, and centre parties, the Greens, and

344

Christian, Jewish and Muslim organizations all mounted a big counter campaign defending the right of Muslims to build minarets, and called SVP's proposal a violation of the right of Swiss Muslims to freedom of worship and belief.

Thomas Wipf, head of the Swiss Council of Religions, said: "We are strongly in favour of enabling Muslims to worship in freedom and dignity, and if minarets are a requirement of their religion we call on them to explain that to Swiss public opinion. Even if some Muslim states deprive Christians of their religious rights, that does not justify Switzerland persecuting its Muslim citizens, because we should never answer one injustice with another injustice.

Swiss Justice Minister Eveline Widmer-Schlumpf, a former member of SVP, has strongly condemned the campaign to ban minarets, saying it would violate the Swiss constitution, which guarantees freedom of belief and worship for all citizens without exception. The Swiss parliament has strongly recommended that people vote against the initiative, as has the Federal council. In fact, the Swiss government has given permission for a new minaret, which would bring the total number in Switzerland to five.

But the battle was not yet over. On 29 Nov 2009, there was an official referendum in which people could vote on whether to impose the ban. Opinion polls showed that 53% of Swiss support the right of Muslims to build minarets, versus 34% who opposed, and 13% who had not yet taken a final position. Swiss voters have supported a referendum proposal to ban the building of minarets, official results show. More than 57% of voters and 22 out of 26 cantons (provinces) voted in favour of the ban

Firstly, these events make it clear that not all Westerners are hostile to Islam, as some extremist sheikhs repeatedly say. In fact, a large section of them continue to defend the rights of Muslims in the West. Yet, as the SVP campaign showed, Western xenophobic movements are acquiring more supporters . . . largely because Westerners are afraid of the bloody and retrogressive image that some Muslims present of their religion.

Those who signed the petition to ban minarets are not necessarily racists who hate Islam, but they are afraid of an unfamiliar religion that is always linked in their minds with killing, blood and the oppression of women. We Muslims have to imagine the reaction of a Westerner when he sees Osama bin Laden on television advocating the killing of as many Christians and infidels as possible, or the reaction of a Western woman when she hears some extremist sheikh saying that Muslim women should wear face veils with just one eye hole.

What happened in Switzerland that month is important for all of Europe, and indeed for the entire world. As SVP won the referendum, then Islam has become, officially and legally, a second class religion.

Dutch MP Geert Wilders

From Wikipedia; lightly edited and formatted:
http://en.wikipedia.org/wiki/Geert_Wilders

Geert Wilders:
" . . . He believes that all Muslim immigration to the Netherlands should be halted and all settled immigrants should be paid to leave. Referring to the increased population of Muslims in the Netherlands, he has said: "Take a walk down the street and see where this is going. You no longer feel like you are living in your own country. There is a battle going on and we have to defend ourselves. Before you know it there will be more mosques than churches!"

In a speech before the Dutch Parliament, he stated: "Islam is the Trojan Horse in Europe. If we do not stop Islamification now, Eurabia and Netherabia will just be a matter of time. One century ago, there were approximately 50 Muslims in the Netherlands. Today, there are about one million Muslims in this country. Where will it end? We are heading for the end of European and Dutch civilisation as we know it. Where is our Prime Minister in all this?"

Excerpt from the National Post 2010/02/08   by Paul Russell

Letters to the Editor (re Muslims in Holland)

Women's Studies programs have very real supporters. And we heard many of these voices last week as nearly three dozen letter rolled in, critical of a Jan 26 editorial titled "Women's Studies is still with us." These correspondents spared no quarter in expressing their anger.

Allowing this article to be published was completely irresponsible, and violated many of the rights and freedoms guaranteed under the Charter,' wrote Robyn Caplan. "The entire article is an incitement of hatred toward the female sex." "This editorial is the most ridiculous piece of newspaper writing I have ever seen," agreed Ana Lukatela. "You all look like cretins".

"(The editorial) was, without a doubt, the most misinformed piece of ignorant drivel I have ever read," added Chris Russell (who pointed out that he is a man). "Not everyone is a fan of Women's Studies, and some people think feminism is no longer needed . . . but to claim that almost any of the radical view points (mentioned in the editorial) are commonly held by feminists or Women's Studies is just outlandish."

Not everyone, though, was upset by the editorial's viewpoint. "I just wanted to congratulate the editorial board,' wrote Jana Esdale. "It takes an immense amount of courage to tell the truth sometimes. "Feminists are not looking for equality; they're looking for dominance," she continued. "As a woman, I find myself continuously frustrated by the likes of feminists who set back what should be a shared cause. Men are not the enemy, and neither is the National Post. So, thanks for having the balls to write the article. I'll be defending it to the best of my ability in my feminism class come Monday morning."

Dutch politician Geert Wilders who has likened the Koran to Hitler's Mein Kampf and who has called for a ban on immigrants from non-Western countries has been roundly criticized by many in the press. So when Post contributor Daniel Pipes last week referred to the far right MP as "the most dynamic political force in the Netherlands," letter writers angrily responded.

"It would be an utter calamity if his ideas were to be embraced," one published letter stated. But other readers let us know that Mr. Geert's ideas have merit.

"It is indeed an 'utter calamity' when presumably rational people wilfully forget real events in favour of head-in-the-sand debating-society rhetoric," wrote Norman L. Roth.

"What is the alternative to restricting Muslim immigration to Western countries?" added Frank Hilliard. "If we don't do something while we still can, the growing Muslim minority will demand shariah law, first for itself and then for everyone."

Other letter writers said Mr. Wilders' provocative statements cloud the real issue: censorship. "It's all right not to agree with Geert Wilders; personally, I do," wrote Anita Kern. "However, the point is whether he is allowed to speak his views. Do we have freedom of speech any more in the West or don't we?"

Re: "It Would Be An Utter Calamity If His Ideas Were To Be Embraced."

Letter writer Jennifer Waterman sides with her overseas relatives who view Dutch MP Geert Wilders as "a divisive force in a country known for its enlightened common sense." No doubt it is lovely to be recognized for such a quality, but unfortunately, Muslims in Holland remain generally unimpressed. For example, in 2007, Imam Ahmed Salam refused to shake the hand of Rita Verdonk, the Dutch minister of immigration at that time, because she was a woman, and then he called on Muslims to not pay taxes.

And last November marked the fifth anniversary of the murder of Dutch filmmaker Theo van Gogh, at the hands of a Muslim man. Ms. Waterman says, "It would be an utter calamity if his ideas were to be embraced" in Holland. If she were to spend a few hours browsing the Web for Islamists, jihad and militant Muslims, she would very quickly learn that it will be an utter calamity if Mr. Wilders' ideas are not embraced.

Gerry Porter, Ottawa.

Bad times for Burqas

From Macleans Magazine 2010/02/22   Editorials

French Prime Minister François Fillon announced this week he'll deny citizenship to a Moroccan national who forces his French born wife to wear a burqa. "If this man does not want to change his attitude, he has no place in our country," he said. Meantime, President Nicolas Sarkozy's call for a law banning full burqas is gaining steam. He has declared the full veil and body covering "not welcome" in France and inconsistent with the country's values. It's certainly not welcome in Paris post offices. Two burqa clad robbers walked into a post office in the Paris suburb of Athis Mons, an area with a large immigrant Muslim population. They pulled out handguns and stole the equivalent of $6,000.

France & the Burqa Ban

Paragraphs are lightly edited excerpts:
        http://www.abc.net.au/news/stories/2010/02/07/2812378.htm

Burqa clad robbers hold up post office

Two burqa-wearing robbers have held up a French post office using a handgun concealed beneath an Islamic-style full veil, court officials said. Officials said postal office staff let the pair through the security double doors of the banking branch near Paris, believing them to be veil-wearing Muslim women. Once inside, the pair flipped back their head coverings and pulled out a gun. They made off with 4,500 euros ($7,100) seized from the staff and customers of the branch in Athis Mons, just south of Paris, according to the online edition of Le Parisien newspaper. Police have opened an investigation.

France is seeking to restrict use of the head to toe Islamic veil on the grounds it is incompatible with French values, after a parliament report called for a ban in schools, hospitals, government offices and public transport. President Nicolas Sarkozy's right-wing party has already presented a bill to make it illegal for anyone to cover their faces in public on security grounds. Mr Sarkozy has declared the burqa "not welcome" in secular France and favours legislation to outlaw it, though he has warned against stigmatising Muslims. According to the interior ministry, only around 1,900 women wear the burqa in France, which is home to Europe's biggest Muslim minority.

A Tale of Two Rapes

From About.com; lightly edited and formatted:
  http://middleeast.about.com/b/2007/11/27/a-tale-of-two-rapes.htm

About 18 months ago in Qaif, a Saudi Arabian city in the eastern part of the country, a 19 year old woman ran into an old boyfriend who'd promised to give her back an old photograph of her. She wanted the photo back because she was to marry someone else. She went to the old boyfriend's car. Both were stopped by seven men. Both were gang raped by the men, several times over. One of the seven men filmed the rapes on his mobile phone. Police got hold of the footage. That should have been enough to put away the rapists.

Not in Saudi Arabia. The prosecution and judge presiding over the case ignored the footage. Four of the rapists were sentenced to one to five years in prison, with up to 1,000 lashes, not for rape but for kidnapping. The rape charges, the court claimed, could not be proved.

And the woman who was raped? She was sentenced to 90 lashes. Her crime: riding in a car with another man not her husband. The woman was incensed naturally enough. She protested. "At the first session, (the judges) said to me, 'what kind of relationship did you have with this individual? Why did you leave the house? Do you know these men?' They asked me to describe the situation. They used to yell at me," she told Human Rights Watch. "They were insulting. The judge refused to allow my husband in the room with me. One judge told me I was a liar because I didn't remember the dates well. They kept saying, 'Why did you leave the house? Why didn't you tell your husband?'"

And for that, the court doubled her lash sentence to 200, and added six months in prison for good measure. The court also suspended her lawyer's license to practice law. The reason: "Judges of the Qatif General Court," the Times reported, "have accused him of trying to tarnish the court's image by talking to the media." Lashes, the Times notes "are meted out in increments because offenders could not survive hundreds of lashes at once. The administrator of the punishment is supposed to hold a Koran under his arm so he cannot swing the whip too fiercely; lashes are not supposed to leave permanent scars. The sentence is frequently delivered in public, often at the entrance to a jail."

Not that those qualifiers diminish the brutality of the practice, or its misogyny, or the court's sadism. But that's Wahhabism in Saudi Arabia, where it wouldn't even be accurate to compare the law to something Medieval—unless the comparison was with Christian Medieval law. In Medieval Islam, none of this would have been tolerated, and even less so in the Prophet Muhammad's time. Muhammad would have regarded as barbaric and unacceptable such treatment of women, who were, in his eyes, on equal footing with men in all matters moral, social or commercial. (On Tuesday, the Saudi Justice Ministry, bowing to the embarrassment of international outrage, agreed to "review the case.") But Saudi Arabia is far from the only outpost of Byzantine barbarism when it comes to reviling women, punishing the innocent, and excusing rapists.

Hop over to allegedly modern and snazzy Dubai in the United Arab

Emirates, that rich city state doing so much to attract investors, tourists, foreign labourers and celebrities to bask in its immense riches and supposedly western-friendly environs. Alexandre Robert, 15 years old, was enjoying himself there last summer when, taking a ride with a friend, he found himself surrounded by three adult Arab men, Emiratis, who proceeded to kidnap him, strip him, rape him, then dump him with a threat that they'd kill his parents if he talked.

Robert talked anyway, and the men were apprehended. But the Egyptian doctor who examined Robert (and found the men's semen inside him) dismissed Robert's claim that he was raped and accused him of being a homosexual. The authorities lied to Robert's family, saying at first that the two assailants were medically clean, when one of them had tested positive for HIV when imprisoned on a prior offense. And for good measure, Robert was threatened with prosecution and prison—for engaging in homosexual acts.

Places like Dubai pretend that homosexuality doesn't exist by banning it, then re-branding it an aberrance and casting it off, literally, when it happens to appear: foreigners, who make up three-quarters of the population of the Emirates, are deported when outed, although Emirati homosexuals are generally treated gingerly.

Where does that leave Robert? In the safety of Switzerland for fear that had he stayed in the Emirates, he might have ended up in prison. But his case carries on. He returned to Dubai in early November just to testify in the case. His mother has started a web site, boycott dubai. com, dedicated "to all the children of the world whose wounds were never recognized, their words never heard and their suffering never known," and dedicated "to all the mothers of the world even the ones of my son's aggressors." The Arab Peninsula is awash in a certain kind of riches. Justice is not among those. The renaissance of Islam has been stimulated strongly through a repeated increase in the price of oil since 1973. With this has come a new awareness of legislation in the Islamic states.

The legal basis of Islam is the Sharia, Islamic law, that controls and orders all areas of life. It is not a moral law for the sensitising of conscience but is a penal law, requiring the punishment of violators through an instrument of the state. Islam demands a religious state as an executor to enforce the law. A Muslim is not free to believe or do what he wishes. He is under Islamic law, which was derived and assimilated from the Qur'an, the example of Muhammad (sunna), the final analogy (qijas) and consensus (idjmaa).

Islam describes Muslims as worshippers and slaves of Allah (ibaad Allah). They have submitted themselves to him and are therefore his possession. The word Islam means, "surrender, devotion and submission".

Whoever falls away from faith in Islam commits, from an Islamic perspective, an unforgivable sin. He takes himself away from Allah, his owner, which is theft, and weakens the Islamic state, an action branded as revolt or insurrection. He who falls away from Islam must according to the Sharia, be prosecuted, taken into custody by force, and called on to repent. If necessary, his return is to be "helped" along with torture. He who does not embrace Islam again has, according to the Sharia, forfeited his life and is to be put to death by the state. According to the daily paper, Al Alam, King Hassan II of Morocco, who is also the imam of his country, presented the following state of affairs before a human rights commission on May 15, 1990:

"If a Muslim says, 'I have embraced another religion instead of Islam,' he, before he is called to repentance, will be brought before a group of medical specialists, so that they can examine him to see if he is still in his right mind. After he has then been called to repentance, but decides to hold fast to the testimony of another religion not coming from Allah, that is, not Islam, he will be judged."

Such thinking abounded in Christian churches during the Middle Ages, too. The Inquisition took on violent proportions and carried out the governmental functions of punishment. However, this madness in Church history was in direct opposition to the law and spirit of Christ. Indeed, the New Testament upholds the teaching of eternal punishment for the godless and for those who fall from living faith in Christ; but with the Parable of the Lost Son (Luke 15:11-24), Jesus teaches that the father waited for the rebellious son until he returned, and then he rushed out to meet him. The father did not have him searched for, kept under surveillance, followed, locked up, tortured, starved or killed. The spirit of Christ grants freedom and does not kill. But the revelations of Allah in the Qur'an require the death of all apostates. The grace and love of Christ are greater than the hate and law of Islam; this grace and love oppose the efforts of all inquisitors. Whoever follows Christ loves apostates and does not condemn them.

Islamic states are presently renewing their legislation, replacing it with earlier Islamic structures, and are trying to rid themselves of the influence of colonial powers. In most of the Islamic countries, endeavours are underway to make the Qur'an and the Sunna the basis of modern legislation.

Not all Muslims agree with this retreat into the Islamic Middle Ages of earlier times. Our world has become smaller through modern travel and telecommunication. The influences of humanism, rationalism, technology and modern living have left their mark on many Muslims. One-third to one-half of the Muslim population in Algeria, Egypt, Turkey, Pakistan and Indonesia resists the introduction of the Sharia. They do not wish to come under the yoke of oppression again -- one which would demand that thieves have their hands and feet amputated, adulterers be whipped, and converts be killed.

However, one-fourth to one-third of the Islamic population passionately demands the immediate introduction of the Sharia and is prepared, in some places, to enforce it with the help of terrorism and revolutions. In each Islamic country, fundamentalists and liberals wrestle over the Sharia. In Syria, these differences led to a civil war in 1982 -- one in which the army brutally defeated the uprising of the Muslim Brotherhood. Turkey was already rid of the Sharia by 1926, emerging as a secular state. But in other countries a re-Islamisation is underway -- especially in Morocco, Libya, Sudan, Saudi Arabia, Iran and Pakistan, where the Sharia or the Qur'an have been legally introduced as fundamental law.

Until now, the enforcement rulings have not been enacted in detail, nor have they been abandoned. The establishing of the Sharia and its enforcement is subject to a continual developmental process in all Islamic countries.

The punishment of apostates from Islam is being demanded again and again by Islamic jurists and fundamentalists who stimulate public opinion; individual converts are persecuted by fanatics or placed under pressure by their own families. The slander against these witnesses of Jesus Christ and their subsequent imprisonment have been an acknowledged and ever recurring fact during the last 20 years in Morocco, Egypt, Turkey, Iran and Pakistan. Many have been tortured. Some have died during their imprisonment. Parents have locked up their daughters in storage chambers, letting them die of thirst. Islam is an intolerant spirit. According to Western ideas of freedom of religion, Islam consistently resists basic human rights.

The frequent reprinting of this book which, since 1934, has undergone eight revisions, makes the often bitter clashes over the Sharia and its implementation in individual countries even more apparent. The translator of the following extract, who is a graduate from an Islamic school of law, has translated similar texts from the Arabic -- texts which present and explain the penalty for apostasy in Islam.

Those responsible for harbouring refugees should not let themselves be deceived by Muslim translators who claim that there is no religious persecution in their countries; rather, they should study the legal demands of the Sharia explained in this book. Liberal theologians and everyone who is concerned with establishing peace among religions should consider this discussion of law, not remaining imprisoned by the ideas of the Enlightenment. Responsible Christians must realise that Islam is an anti-Christian religion that never allows the conversion of a Muslim to Jesus, for the fundamentals of Islamic law demand his death.

This translation is not intended as a Christian apologetic but serves to clarify the discussions between the religions objectively, leading the reader to a foundational legal understanding of Islamic law, free from mystical speculation and humanistic wishful-thinking.

Muslim Killers Who Need No Motive

From The Ottawa Citizen: ~2008/11/27

The news reports out of India, filled with scenes of carnage and horror, concluded with some variation of: "the motive for the attacks was not immediately known." This is not surprising.

Terrorists who kill in the name of Islam don't need "motives." They kill because, in their view, they have a religious duty to do so. The hijackers who orchestrated the 9/11 attacks on the U.S. never issued demands. Killing, for them, was an expression of faith. Oh sure, the Islamist organizations that train and send killers might eventually articulate a political "motive," but often these have the ring of post facto rationalizations.

This is something Israel has understood for many years. Islamic radicals would kill Israeli civilians to protest, say, Israel's presence in Lebanon. So Israel withdraws entirely from Lebanon and . . . the killing continues. Or perhaps the Islamists say they're killing civilians to protest Israel's presence in Gaza. Israel withdraws entirely from Gaza and . . . the killing continues. Israel builds security barriers and then suddenly the "humiliation" of the barrier becomes the reason to kill Israeli civilians. And on it goes.

Islamist terrorists who kill civilians in Madrid will offer one rationalization; Islamist terrorists who kill civilians in New York, London or Bali will offer others. No doubt the killers who attacked tourists in India this week will come up with a justification of their own. Maybe even several justifications, since they seem to have been targeting a range of people, particularly Americans, Britons and Jews.

But at some point one starts to wonder whether it will ever be possible to address the multiple, shifting and often contradictory grievances that the radicals harbour, at least to the point that they'll stop killing people.

Were the terrorists who attacked India affiliated with the so-called Indian Mujahideen? Or were they from Lashkar-e-Taiba? Maybe al-Qaeda sent them. Each of these groups might have different "motives" depending on the day of the week. The one thing they share is a belief that Islam is the supreme religion whose adherents must defend and promote it by force. Whoever committed the atrocities in India this week are both religious warriors and political actors.

This poses a difficult problem for the Indian government, and indeed for governments of all countries that are confronting this scourge. The Palestinians, for example, have legitimate political grievances, most notably the lack of an independent state, but can the West assume that the creation of a Palestinian state will end the religious war against Israel?

The approach of the late Israeli prime minister Yitzhak Rabin was to "fight terror as though there were no peace process, and to pursue the peace process as though there were no terror." This is a difficult needle to thread, however.

The 9/11 attacks forced the US to reflect seriously on how its foreign policy up to that point had contributed to the jihad against America. Yet a review of US foreign policy showed that in many ways the Americans had sided with Muslim concerns. The US helped the Mujahideen in Afghanistan defeat the Soviets, the US lost soldiers trying to feed starving people in the Muslim country of Somalia, the US intervened to help Muslims in Bosnia and Kosovo and the US had liberated the Muslim country of Kuwait from a bully who was intimidating the whole Muslim Middle East. If it takes a long time for Indian authorities to identify what the terrorists were hoping to accomplish in Mumbai, it could be the terrorists are still working on their reasons.

The Taliban in Afghanistan & Pakistan

From The National Post 2008/11/17   by Matthew Fisher

There is nothing yet in Pakistan to rival the Afghan Taliban's notorious Ministry for Ordering What is Right and Forbidding What is Wrong - also known as the Ministry for the Enforcement of Virtue and the Suppression of Vice.

But there is much nervous talk here today about the Talibanization of Pakistan and how the current war in Afghanistan, which followed six yea of Taliban rule, has contaminated the politics and threatened the security of this country. With equal conviction, many Afghanis accuse their neigbours of having poisoned the country by giving the Taliban sanctuary and by allowing them to rearm and recruit. There is much truth in both arguments.

Despite a stepped-up US campaign of Predator drone strikes against Taliban and al Qaeda targets just inside the Pakistani border, or perhaps because of them, the security situation across Pakistan's North West Frontier Province has continued to deteriorate. Violent incidents are now so common that it is impossible to keep track of them. What is certain, is that it is now extremely dangerous for outsiders to go anywhere in Pakistan's North West.

In separate attacks that took place in the space of just 72 hours in Peshawar last week, gunmen shot dead an American aid worker, kidnapped an Iranian diplomat after killing his Pakistani guard, and shot and wounded a Japanese journalist and his colleague who has been a correspondent for Newsweek for seven years.

The brazen ambush of Newsweek's Sami Yousafzai who survived three bullets fired into his body from short range, will have a particularly chilling effect on reporters trying to chronicle the explosive growth of the Taliban in Pakistan. The dapper, irrepressibly genial Pasthun is generally considered the most well-connected of the small band of brave, unheralded local journalists who crisscross the Afghani - Pakistani frontier.

The targeting of Yousafzai is part of an emerging pattern. A jihadi magazine known as Tora Bora recently published a death list naming five Pakistani journalists whose writings supposedly abetted the CIA, according to the New Yorker's Web site. Among those threatened was Ahmed Rashid, a highly regarded author who has done more than anyone else to explain to his countrymen and to the world what the Taliban is, and the kind of Islamic dominion it seeks to establish in Afghanistan and parts of Pakistan.

The Afghan influence over events in Pakistan began during the mujihadeen's war against the Soviet Army in the 1980s. Several million Afghani Pashtuns fled to Pakistan, bringing their medieval and strict interpretation of Islam to the sprawling camps that were established in northwestern Pakistan. Over time, many of the refugees left the camps where their economic opportunities were limited. Some returned to Afghanistan. Others joined Pakistani Pashtuns who were seeking their fortune elsewhere in the country.

Twenty years on, 2.5 million Afghani and Pakistani Pashtuns have congregated 500 kilometres from their traditional homelands in the slums of Karachi. At the same time an inexhaustible supply of Pakistani and Afghani boys have been growing up in Saudi-funded religious seminaries (Madrasas) in Pakistan where they have been force-fed the Taliban and Saudi-based Wahabi ideologies which are based on the principle that there has not been a single good new idea since the 10th century. It is these young fanatics - both Afghani and Pakistani - who have been carrying out many of the suicide attacks here and against the NATO backed Karzai government in Afghanistan.

One of the many reasons it has been impossible for the governments of Afghanistan and Pakistan and their allies to gain an accurate fix on who they face has been that the Taliban is not monolithic. There are

Afghan Taliban and Pakistani Taliban factions, as well as tribes, clans, and sub-clans whose allegiances, aims, and territorial ambitions are not always the same. What they share, however, is a deep distrust of modernism and everything Western. These zealots - and there are now many, many thousands of them - seek to establish an Islamic caliphate in Afghanistan and parts of Pakistan or die a glorious martyr's death trying. Their numbers are still growing . . . and so is their confidence.

One People

The People of Canada

From Canadian Cultural Tours; lightly edited and formatted:
http://www.culturaltours.ca/en/a_can.html

Canada, which occupies almost the entire northern part of the North American continent, is the second largest country in the world, after Russia. Despite its vast expanses, extending over 4 million square miles, Canada has a relatively small population of just under 31 million people. The majority of Canadians are concentrated in the southern part of the country, near the border with the United States. Most of the good agricultural land is found in the more densely populated southern areas, while the rest of Canada is dominated by enormous wilderness regions that are inhospitable for farming, but rich in natural resources. Although a century ago, the majority of Canadians lived in rural areas, today over 80% of the country's population lives in urban centres of 10,000 or more.

The country is made up of five distinctive regions, including ten different provinces and three territories: British Columbia with its stunning mountains and Pacific coastline, the prairie provinces of Alberta, Saskatchewan, and Manitoba, the central heartland areas of English Ontario and French Québec, the Atlantic provinces of New Brunswick, Nova Scotia, Prince Edward Island, and Newfoundland, and the Arctic territories of Nunavut, the Northwest Territories, and the Yukon. Culturally and physically, Canada is a very diverse and complex country.

The first inhabitants of Canada arrived via the Bering Strait, at least 20,000 B.C., and reached the eastern areas of the country by about 10,000 B.C. As the ice of the glaciers melted, other waves of migrants entered the regions of the high Arctic about 4,000 years B.C. At the time of the arrival of the Europeans, it has been estimated that the native population of Canada was about 250,000 people. Most of these native groups were semi nomadic Algonquian speaking peoples, with large pockets of Iroqoian speaking peoples located in the East, the highly sophisticated Northwest Coast tribes, with their own complex linguistic patterns, and the Inuit in the Arctic areas.

While the first permanent European occupation started with the French and the founding of Québec City in 1608, Basque fishermen and whalers had plied Canada's eastern shorelines long before this period. The French created a colony of farmers and fur traders in the St. Lawrence River Valley, which by the time of the English Conquest in 1759, had reached a population of 60,000 people. During the English colonial period, 1759 - 1867, large numbers of immigrants came to Canada from the British Isles and settled in the areas of the Canadian Maritimes and what is now Ontario. Still today, these two eastern regions have strong Scottish, English, and Irish traditions among their populations.

In 1867, Canada became a semi-independent nation and set about the populating of its western regions. In 1885, Canadian Pacific Railway completed the country's first transcontinental railway, and by 1914, over 2 million settlers had poured into the prairies and the western coastal areas. Almost half of these settlers came via the United States, while many of the others came from the United Kingdom, or Eastern Europe.

World War I and World War II were both major turning points for Canada as a nation. Closely linked with the United Kingdom, Canada made tremendous contributions to the Allied war effort. These sacrifices helped mature the young nation and prepared it for a gradual transition to full sovereignty. Canada obtained control of its foreign policy in 1931, and then brought home its constitution (which had originally been an Act of the British Parliament) in 1982. Today, Canada is a vibrant and sophisticated country, with one of the highest living standards in the world. Its riches include a highly educated population, vast natural resources, and the extraordinary beauty of its wilderness areas. During the last thirty years, Canada has opened its doors to immigrants from around the world, and by 2005, it is calculated that 12% of our population will be made up of visible minorities. The future looks bright for Canada.

Immigration & Languages

National Post 2009/03/24   by Rudyard Griffiths

Jason Kenney, the federal Minister of Citizenship, Immigration and Multiculturalism, should be commended for kick-starting a much needed public discussion about the language skills and civic literacy of aspiring Canadian citizens.

For too long, Canada has avoided the kind of common sense dialogue about immigration policy that Minister Kenney is galvanizing. The reality is the "quietism" of successive federal governments about all things related to immigrant selection and recruitment is a public policy debacle of historic proportions: tens of thousands of newcomers languishing in dead-end Jobs, the out-migration of up to 40% of professional male immigrants in the last decade alone and the justifiable hardening of attitudes among visible minority groups who rightly feel they are being exploited economically.

Minister Kenney is spot on in his assertion that the ability to speak one of Canada's two official languages is fundamental to an immigrant's economic success and overall social integration. In fact, detailed multi-decade research shows that language proficiency outstrips job experience, educational background, gender and age as the factor which has the greatest positive impact on a newcomer's ability to settle successfully in Canada.

That said, making proficiency in reading, writing and speaking either official language a prerequisite for every person applying to come to Canada is only part of the solution. Of the 250,000 newcomers Canada welcomes each year only a quarter have their language abilities assessed in the process of becoming permanent residents.

The majority of newcomers begin the path to full citizenship as dependents of a "primary applicant" or citizen and do not have to demonstrate they can speak French or English. Canada needs to redouble its efforts to ensure that this much larger group of permanent residents attains basic language proficiency as quickly as possible.

Basic language proficiency is especially important for immigrant women. Having entered Canada as spouses of primary applicants, and therefore not pre-screened for language proficiency, women are significantly more likely to lack a working knowledge of French or English. This situation must be addressed so that every female newcomer attains the basic fluency needed to participate in civic life.

The federal government should also put special emphasis on second-language training for school age children, particularly in the country's major cities. In Toronto, the city that attracts the majority of newcomers to Canada, the percentage of elementary schools with English as a second language (ESL) instructors has declined from 41% to 29% in the last decade while the number of students requiring such instruction has doubled. The federal government should find ways to work with the provinces to get more funding for language instruction into urban classrooms to relieve overburdened ESL instructors.

We would also do well to revamp our citizenship exam. According to Dominion Institute research, immigrants take the exam seriously. Let's build on this dedication by designing a much more comprehensive exam that covers a range of subjects related to Canada's history, political systems and the responsibilities of citizenship.

Few, if any, of Minister Kenney's predecessors have propelled public debate over how to make immigration work for newcomers and Canada in such positive ways. Those of us hankering for more common sense citizenship and immigration reform look forward to seeing what sacred cows this creative policy thinker will choose to startle next.

Credits: National Post: Rudyard Griffiths is the co-founder of the Dominion Institute and the author of Who We Are: A Citizen's Manifesto (Douglas & McIntyre Books).

Immigration & Refugees

From National Post 2009/03/25   By Steven Edwards

Refugee claims in Canada spike 30%

United Nations   The Minister calls it abuse of Nation's generosity.

Immigration Minister Jason Kenney spoke yesterday of "wide scale and almost systematic abuse" of Canada's refugee system after a United Nations report showed a 30% increase in the number of people seeking refugee or asylum status in Canada. Much of the increase came from a major rise in the numbers of Mexicans, Haitians and Colombians claiming they will face persecution if Canada sends them back to their respective countries, the UN says.

But the world body also says the United States saw a three per cent drop in the number of people asking for asylum in that country last year. Overall, the percentage increase for Canada is almost three times the average for 51 countries studied in Asylum Levels and Trends in Industrialized Countries 2008 by the UN High Commissioner for Refugees.

"This is clearly an abuse of Canada's generosity" Mr. Kenney said during an interview. "It is a violation of the integrity of our immigration system." One difference between the United States and Canada is that the US operates a detention system in which applicants can be effectively jailed pending review of their cases, while applicants in

Canada are often eligible to apply for a temporary work permit. "It discourages people from making a claim if they have to stay in jail," said David Matas, a refugee lawyer in Winnipeg.

Show 'bogus claimants' the door: Kenney

Canada received 36,900 new applications last year, according to the UN report, whereas the United States, whose population is 10 times larger, received an estimated 49,000.

"Canada has witnessed a steady increase in new asylum seekers in the past years, and in 2008 was the second largest recipient of applications" says the report's commentary. "On average, every 10th application in the industrialized world was made in Canada." Applicants in Canada go before the Immigration and Refugee Board, which puts the application figure for 2008 at 34,800 - slightly lower than the UN's finding. The board's case-approval rate for the past several years has varied between 42% and 46%; but rejected applicants have a slew of appeals and other options available to them.

"People . . . whose initial claims are rejected are able to stay in Canada, sometimes for several years, making serial appeals," Mr. Kenney said. "In some cases, it would seem their objective is to stay long enough that they can make a compelling case that it would be uncompassionate for them to be deported." Mr. Kenney noted the Immigration and Refugee Board rejects up to 90% of claims made by Mexicans. "That would suggest wide scale and almost systematic abuse,' Mr. Kenney said.

Canada sometimes delays deportation of rejected Haitian applicants, meanwhile, because Ottawa lists the Caribbean country, the Western hemisphere's poorest, among those as potentially unstable or susceptible to other forms of disaster. "That may be acting as an incentive for false claimants,' Mr. Kenney added. He spoke of a "broad political consensus" that Canada's inland refugee system was "broken". "I have asked my parliamentary colleagues at the immigration committee and in the Opposition parties to begin a dialogue on ways we can reform the inland refugee system to make sure there is a fair process that complies with the principles of natural justice, but ensures that bogus claimants are shown the door, and quickly," he said. Mexicans are exempted from a US - Canada agreement that gives both countries the right to refuse an application already rejected by the other's refugee review system - possibly leading to "double-dipping".

But Mr. Matas suggests Canada may be also more "receptive" to reasons Mexicans may have for seeking to leave. "The problem in Mexico is less the government (persecution) than the government's inability to protect people from gang warfare and drug cartels," he said. "People may also feel safer in Canada, since anyone being pursued by gangsters would be more susceptible if they were just across the border."

In addition to the 7,554 refugee and asylum claimants approved by the Immigration and Refugee Board last year, the government and private sponsors of refugees overseas who've already fled from their countries of origin brought in more than 11,000, according to Citizenship and Immigration Canada statistics.

From the Ottawa Citizen 2009/03/25   by Steven Edwards

UN report shows increase of 30 percent for refugee claims

United Nations - Spike in refugee claims shows "abuse" of system Kenney says.

Immigration Minister Jason Kenney spoke Tuesday of "wide-scale and almost systematic abuse" of Canada's refugee system after a United Nations report showed a 30per-cent increase in the number of people seeking refugee or asylum status in Canada. Much of the increase comes from a major rise in the number of Mexicans, Haitians and Colombians claiming they'll face persecution if Canada sends them back to their respective countries, the UN says.

However, the world body also says the United States experienced a three-per-cent drop in the number of people asking for asylum in that country last year. Overall, the percentage increase for Canada is almost three times the average for 51 countries studied in Asylum Levels and Trends in Industrialized Countries 2008 by the UN High Commissioner for Refugees.

"This is clearly an abuse of Canada's generosity," Kenney said Tuesday. "It is a violation of the integrity of our immigration system." The US operates a detention system in which applicants can be effectively jailed pending review of their cases, while applicants in Canada are often eligible to apply for temporary work permits. "It discourages people from making a claim if they have to stay in jail," said David Matas, a refugee lawyer in Winnipeg.

Canada received 36,900 new applications last year, whereas the US, whose population is 10 times larger, received an estimated 49,000. "Canada has witnessed a steady increase in new asylum seekers in the past years, and in 2008 was the second largest recipient of applications," the report's commentary says. "On average, every 10th application in the industrialized world was made in Canada." Applicants in Canada go before the Immigration and Refugee Board, which puts the application figure for 2008 at 34,800. The board's case-approval rate for the past several years has varied between 42 and 46 per cent, but rejected applicants have appeals and other options available to them.

"People . . . whose initial claims are rejected are able to stay in Canada, sometimes for several years, making serial appeals," Kenney said. "In some cases, it would seem their objective is to stay long enough that they can make a compelling case that it would be uncompassionate for them to be deported." Kenney said the Immigration and Refugee Board rejects up to 90 per cent of claims made by Mexicans. "That would suggest wide scale and almost systematic abuse," Kenney said.

Canada sometimes delays deportation of rejected Haitian applicants because it lists the Caribbean country, the Western hemisphere's poorest, among those as potentially unstable or susceptible to other forms of disaster.

Canadian Citizenship & Caregivers

Excerpt from the 7 April 2010National Post 2009/06/08
by Martin Collacott

The Live-in Loophole & Citizenship

The very public dispute over the treatment of foreign workers in the household of MP Ruby Dhalla raises questions about how well the live in caregiver program CLCP) is working, both in terms of the best interests of those coming here under its provisions as well as the welfare of Canadians in general.

The program is a peculiar hybrid since people who would not normally qualify for immigration apply to stay here permanently after completing two years of service as a live in caregiver. Why is this possible?

The short answer is that many applicants, particularly from lesser developed countries, are prepared to work long hours for low wages in order to obtain permanent residence in Canada. What this means, in effect, is that the relatively small number of affluent Canadians who can afford to bring in live in caregivers from overseas are being underwritten by the taxpayers of Canada. While few data are available on the downstream social and economic costs of the LCP, given the fact that the earnings of those who come to Canada through this program continue to be low even after obtaining permanent status, it is likely that the ultimate expense to the taxpayer considerably exceeds the benefits to the employers who brought them here.

The LCP, moreover, is rife with problems. Two of the immigration offices where many of the applications are made - Manila and Chandigarh - have seen a major proliferation of local caregiver schools that exist either in name only or have questionable standards.

Many appear to have been created solely for the purpose of getting people into Canada as live in caregivers (or "nannies" as they are often called). The office in Chandigarh, for example, has identified 69 "nanny schools" in the city of Jalandar alone and 160 altogether in Punjab province. Many of their graduates moreover, are young men, which is odd in a society where care giving is seen as women's work. Many are destined to work for relatives in Canada and it is suspected they are applying through the LCP because they would not qualify under any other immigration category.

As a result of all this we have seen not only a dramatic increase in applications but also in the numbers actually admitted through the LCP - rising from 6,741 in 2004 to 13,840 in 2007, with the number of males increasing by more than 150% in the same period. In parallel with this, the total of live in caregivers and family members granted permanent residence status in Canada climbed from 1,988 in 2002 to 10,510 last year. Clearly the live in caregiver program needs a major overhaul.

The most obvious correction would be to admit only those who could qualify for permanent resident status in accordance with the standards used for skilled immigrants in general. If someone coming through this channel wants to work as a live in caregiver and can find an employer, there would be nothing to prevent them from doing so. Since they have already been granted permanent residence status, they could not be coerced into working excessive hours or abused in other ways for fear of losing employment and their chance to stay here.

Such a change could, of course, result in a reduction in the number of people coming from overseas to work as live in caregivers. Would this necessarily be a bad thing? For some employers perhaps it would - particularly those with large enough houses to accommodate a nanny and have them close at hand and available for service any time of the day or night. An internal government document obtained through access to information indicates, however, that there are sufficient Canadian caregivers willing and able to meet the demand for live out home care. One must, therefore, ask why we need to bring in so many live in caregivers from overseas. Caregivers should come to Canada only as temporary workers.

In the event that the government decides to continue with a program of live in caregivers from abroad, two fundamental changes should be made. First, the caregivers should come in strictly as temporary workers and be required to leave the country when their contract is completed. It makes no sense to allow people to stay here permanently who cannot meet normal immigration requirements. Secondly, the government should put in place more explicit standards and guidelines to ensure that such temporary workers are not exploited and receive reasonable treatment from employers while in Canada.

National Post: Martin Collacott is a senior fellow at the Fraser Institute in Vancouver and former Canadian ambassador in Asia and the Middle East.

Canadian Citizenship & Immigration

Excerpt from the National Post 2009/03/28   by Kevin Libin

Some call it intolerant, others like the Minister's muscular multiculturalism

Caught in a rare moment inside his Parliament Hill office, Immigration and Multiculturalism minister Jason Kenney has finished his interview with Fox News to talk about American military deserters seeking refuge in Canada. And an interview with a BC television station to discuss the case of a Chinese grandmother needing a special permit to visit Canada to tend to an injured grandson. And a TV reporter wanting to talk about Croatian visa policy. At the same time, his communications staff was fielding calls from reporters about the government's decision to ban British MP George Galloway from visiting Canada, as well as the latest turn in a public battle with the Canadian Arab Federation, and reports on abuses in Canada's refugee system finally managing to put aside, for now, the media and political fallout from the minister's comments days earlier about strengthening language proficiency requirements for new citizens.

For the past few weeks, and despite pressing matters in portfolios related to the economy, Mr. Kenney has arguably been the most public face of the federal Conservative government, daily stick handling everything from tricky, politically charged issues, with accusations of racism and unethical political interference, to local-interest immigration sagas. It is, Mr. Kenney admits, an "emotionally draining . . . tough position." But, for Mr. Kenney, a full-fledged Cabinet minister for not quite six months, the most challenging and politically perilous work planned for his portfolio - reshaping Canada's approach to immigration and multiculturalism - has scarcely begun.

The higher profile matters - the Galloway issue, the scuffle with Arab groups, the language abilities of immigrants - form the early marks of a pattern of what is to come. Rejecting the CAF's support for Islamic terrorists and arguably anti-Semitic messages, Mr. Galloway for financially supporting Hamas, calling for newcomers to better integrate: These are of a piece with efforts to fortify what the Conservatives would call The Canadian Identity.

It is, Mr. Kenney makes clear, a vision for a country that stands up for its pluralism, but also for its core liberal traditions of tolerance, democracy and secularism. "We can't afford to be complacent about the challenge of integration," he says. "We want to avoid the kind of ethnic enclaves or parallel communities that exist in some European countries. So far, we've been pretty successful at that, but I think it's going to require greater effort in the future to make sure that we have an approach to pluralism and immigration that leads to social cohesion rather than fracturing.

For a country with the highest average per capita immigration rate on the planet - roughly 250,000 new residents arrive yearly from nearly every region and creed - maintaining such philosophical hygiene will take great energy, audacity and support from within Canada's ethnic communities, where immigration reform is personal. It will take, also, someone able to absorb repeated accusations of racism or xenophobia, which are already flying Mr. Kenney's way. When he advocated to the Calgary Herald recently a limited federal role in promoting multiculturalism - "I think it's really neat that a fifth-generation Ukrainian Canadian can speak Ukrainian - but pay for it yourself," he said - Liberal MP Borys Wrzesnewskyj complained the minister was jettisoning sacred tenets.

"He's the minister in charge and he fundamentally disagrees with the intent of the (Multiculturalism Act) legislation that supports his portfolio," Mr. Wrzesnewskyj says. Liberal MP Jim Karygiannis this week called Mr. Kenney "intolerant" for raising the issue of enhanced language requirements. The Arab Federation painted him a Zionist lackey.

But there are those, many of them within Canada's ethnic pockets, who support such a muscular approach. "What is different with him is, with previous (Conservative) immigration ministers, both have been pussycats; this guy is a tiger," says Tarek Fatah, an author, prominent Liberal supporter and founder of the Muslim Canadian Congress. "He's standing up for Canadian values. I would like every politician to stand up for this country the way Jason Kenney has."

Before being elevated to Cabinet last fall, Mr. Kenney spent two years shuttling between community halls, temples and church basements, building support networks in Sikh, Hindu, Korean, Japanese, Chinese, Jewish and Arab communities, as Secretary of State for Multiculturalism and Canadian Identity. His mission: to break a near lock his Liberal opponents have had on ethnic support since Trudeaumania.

Come last October's election, the payoff arrived: The Tories upset numerous Liberal strongholds surrounding Vancouver and Toronto by converting Asian, East Asian and Middle Eastern voters from red to blue. Mr. Kenney's predecessors, including Diane Finley and Monte Solberg, were ministers of Immigration. When Mr. Kenney got the job in October, the Prime Minister added the "and Multiculturalism."

Multicultural maven is a curious role for a pale, Reform party pioneer raised in Saskatchewan, educated by Jesuits, deeply socially conservative, who came to politics primarily with an agenda for fiscal restraint (Before becoming a Reform MP in 1997, he headed the Canadian Taxpayers Federation). But political opponents looking to brand him as too redneck for the sensitive immigration file find it hard to land a punch. In his diverse Calgary Southeast riding, families speak fondly of Mr. Kenney's efforts, long before he became the minister in charge, in helping them sort out immigration issues; his key staffers, including a Tibetan, a Muslim and an Armenian, resemble the dessert lineup at the UN cafeteria.

He spearheaded the government's efforts to recognize the Ukrainian Holdomor, its apology to the East Indian community for the Komagata Maru incident, he has defended Chinese Uyghur Muslims and paid his respects at the Mumbai Jewish centre attacked by terrorists. On his office wall hang portraits of abolitionist heroes William Wilberforce and Abraham Lincoln. A few years ago, Mr. Kenney boarded an entire family newly arrived from India in his Calgary home while they settled into Canadian life. "It gave me, for the first time, a real view of the immigration experience from the eyes of a family that's landed without any previous connections in Canada," he says. "I benefited from it more than they did." Today, the kids call him Uncle Jason.

"The irony is that as a white Catholic kid, he's very cosmopolitan person. Maybe the most cosmopolitan minister we've had," says Mr. Solberg, now an advisor for government relations firm Fleishman-Hillard in Calgary.

If Mr. Kenney is to succeed in reshaping his sensitive file, he will likely need his solid ethnic-friendly credentials and deep community networks. It helps, too, that he has the confidence of his boss, Stephen Harper. Mr. Kenney has become a key member of the Prime Minister's inner circle after years out of favour for his loyalty to Canadian Alliance leader Stockwell Day. Everything he does today comes clearly with the Prime Minister's blessing, says Tom Flanagan, the University of

Calgary political scientist who served as Mr. Harper's chief of staff and strategist.

The minister is dealing now with "probably the most difficult issues," Mr. Flanagan says. "Charges of racism are always just one syllable away." And increasingly powerful statements denouncing anti-Semitism ("Peaceful and pluralistic Canada sees signs that this evil is newly resurgent," Mr. Kenney recently told a European summit on the issue), criticizing Muslim-led attempts to censor blaspheming Canadian writers through human rights commissions, and slamming certain groups that would stoke ancient and modern Middle East enmities here, have led to accusations in Arab communities, and in some corners of the media, that the minister has abandoned an unprejudiced approach and made Canada a stooge for the so-called Israel lobby: The CAF called him a "professional whore," the Toronto Star a "professional fool." (The CAF announced this week it will take the government to court over its failure to renew the group's immigration settlement contracts.)

For Mr. Kenney, these things, and more, are part of preserving the Canadian way. Immigrants, he says, should come prepared to accept our national standards, or stay out. "My job is in part to ensure that we successfully integrate newcomers into Canadian society and that our particular Canadian model of pluralism remains a success," he says.

"There's always a danger that political correctness can dissuade us from making clear distinctions between what constitutes legitimate political debate, and on the other hand, extremism and the promotion of hatred and violence. We cannot allow political correctness to cloud our ability to make those basic distinctions."

This is an approach that has taken hold more firmly elsewhere since Al Qaeda opened Western countries' eyes to the risks of careless multicultural policies, but has not yet made progress here. It is, says Mr. Solberg, a trend toward a more "melting pot" approach, rather than the Liberal concept of a multi cultural "mosaic" where immigrants are encouraged to retain their separateness. "I think Canada has really gone beyond that; I think the immigrant communities have gone beyond

375

that, too. They're more self-assured," he says. "This old model of needing (government) to preserve their culture no longer exists."

The Conservatives have keen most influenced by reforms in Australia, a country with remarkably similar economic features that has reshaped its approach to both integration - better matching newcomers to the labour market's needs, increasing their job-finding success rate by 38% - and cultural integration. Former Aussie prime minister John Howard famously announcing "we will decide who comes to this country, and the circumstances in which they come," would rename the Department of Immigration and Multicultural Affairs the Department of Immigration and Citizenship, declaring the shift from "altruism to pragmatism." His successor, Kevin Rudd, although a political adversary, has stuck with the program.

Mr. Kenney said he believes it does immigrants no favour to bring them here seeking work in fields that do not need them, or with unrecognized credentials. It might even harm their loyalty. He was stunned, he says, recently sitting in an Immigration Canada interview with a thirty-something citizen who arrived in Canada over a decade ago but who was unable to understand questions in English or French.

Canada has not yet gone as far as Australia in enforcing a cultural and economic compatibility from its immigrants, but Mr..Kenney seems to be headed in a similar direction (He also acknowledges following recent British moves to delegitimize Arab and Muslim groups involved with radical elements, while the Netherlands, France and even Quebec have experimented with methods of preserving traditional standards).

"The idea that we are a happy mosaic and we can continue to let people do anything they want, short of breaking the law, is short-sighted," says Martin Collacott, a former Canadian ambassador who studies immigration for the Fraser Institute; a country must select its immigrants carefully to ensure they are fit to become productive, dedicated citizens. The Liberals, dependent on ethnic support, were politically unable to take such steps, Mr. Collacott points out. Liberal prime ministers, for instance, would not list the Tamil Tigers a terrorist group (even today, Liberal MPs are still routinely spotted at events supporting the Tigers), and they appointed Hezbollah and Hamas supporters to the Immigration and Refugee Board. Last year, Tory plans under then immigration Minister Finley to raise qualification levels for immigrants to work down an 800,000 application backlog had the Liberal opposition, roused by outraged ethnic groups, threatening to bring down the minority government.

Mr. Kenney, having built from the ground up his own simpatico Conservative base in Canada's ethnic pockets, has a freer hand to move more aggressively. Since his appointment, the minister has yet to bring forward any legislation, though it's true that the opportunity to do so has so far been limited. But he promises an "ambitious policy agenda" coming soon. When it does, it will almost certainly prove at least as divisive as anything Mr. Kenney has done in recent days, and will likely take all the political and ethnic goodwill he has spent years accumulating to succeed - presuming, by then, he has a sufficient stock of the stuff left.

Canada's Tolerance is Misplaced

Excerpt from The Calgary Herald 2009/03/30   By Mahfooz Kanwar

Canada's Immigration Minister Jason Kenney is getting flak from the usual suspects, but he deserves praise instead. Recently, Kenney pointed out that while at a meeting in Toronto, members of Canada's Pakistani community called on him to make Punjabi one of Canada's official languages. It makes me angry that such an idea would enter the minds of my fellow and former countrymen, let alone express them to a Minister of the Crown.

A few months ago, I was dismayed to learn that Erik Millett, the principal of Belleisle School in Springfield, New Brunswick, limited playing our national anthem because the families of a couple of his students objected to it.

As a social scientist, I oppose this kind of political correctness, lack of assimilation of new immigrants to mainstream Canada, hyphenated Canadian identity, and the lack of patriotism in our great nation. Increasingly, Canadians feel restricted in doing things the Canadian way lest we offend minorities. We cannot even say Merry Christmas without fear of causing offence. It is amazing that 77 per cent of the Canadian majority are scared of offending 23 per cent of minorities. We have become so timid that the majority cannot assert its own freedom of expression. We cannot publicly question certain foreign social customs, traditions and values that do not fit into the Canadian ethos of equality. Rather than encouraging new immigrants to adjust to Canada, we tolerate peculiar ways of doing things. We do not remind them that they are in Canada, not in their original homelands.

In a multicultural society, it is the responsibility of minorities to adjust to the majority. It does not mean that minorities have to totally amalgamate with the majority. They can practise some of their cultural traditions within their homes . . . their backstage behaviour. However, when outside their homes, their front stage behaviour should resemble mainstream Canadian behaviour. Whoever comes to Canada must learn the limits of our system. We do not kill our daughters or other female members of our families who refuse to wear hijab, niqab or burka which are not mandated by the Qur'an anyway. We do not kill our daughters if they date the "wrong" men. A 17 year old Sikh girl should not have been killed in British Columbia by her father because she was dating a Caucasian man.

We do not practise the dowry system in Canada, and do not kill our brides because they did not bring enough dowry. Millions of female fetuses are aborted every year in India, and millions of female infants have been killed by their parents in India and China. Thousands of brides in India are burned to death in their kitchens because they did not bring enough dowry into a marriage. Some 30,000 Sikhs living abroad took the dowries but abandoned their brides in India in 2005. This is not accepted in Canada.

In some countries, thousands of women are murdered every year for family or religious honour. We should not hide behind political correctness and we should expose the cultural and religious background of these heinous crimes, especially if they happen in Canada. We should also expose those who bring their cultural baggage containing the social custom of female circumcision. I was shocked when I learned about two cases of this barbaric custom practised in St. Catharines, Ontario a few years ago.

I have said it on radio and television, have written in my columns in the Calgary Herald, and I have written in my latest book, Journey to Success, that I do not agree with the hyphenated identity in Canada because it divides our loyalties. My argument is that people are not forced to come to Canada and they are not forced to stay here. Those who come here of their own volition and stay here must be truly patriotic Canadians or go back.

I am a first generation Canadian from Pakistan. I left Pakistan 45 years ago. I cannot ignore Pakistan, because it is the homeland of my folks, but my loyalty should be and is to Canada. I am, therefore, a proud Canadian, no longer a Pakistani Canadian. I am a Canadian Muslim, not a Muslim Canadian.

I do not agree with those Canadians who engage in the fight against the system in their original countries on Canadian soil. They should go back and fight from within. For example, some of the Sikhs, Tamil Tigers, Armenians and others have disturbed the peace in Canada because of their problems back home. Recently, a low level leader of MQM, the Mafia of Pakistan, came to Canada as a refugee and started to organize public rallies to collect funds for their cause in Pakistan. On July 18, 2007, the Federal Court of Canada ruled that MQM is a terrorist group led by London based Altaf Hussain, their godfather.

As a member in the coalition government of Pakistan, this terrorist group is currently collaborating with the Taliban in Pakistan. That refugee was deported back to Pakistan. Similarly, I disagree with the newcomers who bring their religious baggage here. For example, Muslims are less than two per cent of the Canadian population, yet in 2004 and 2005, a fraction of them, the fundamentalists, wanted to bring sharia law to Canada. If they really want to live under sharia, they should go to the prison like countries where sharia is practised.

I once supported multiculturalism in Canada because I believed it gave us a sense of pluralism and diversity. However, I have observed and experienced that official multiculturalism has encouraged convolution of the values that make Canada the kind of place to which people want to immigrate in the first place.

Here, we stand on guard for Canada, not for countries we came from. Like it or not, take it or leave it, standing on guard only for Canada is our national maxim. Remember, O Canada is our national anthem which must not be disregarded by anybody, including the teacher in Springfield, New Brunswick.

Mahfooz Kanwar, PHD, Is A Sociologist And An Instructor Emeritus At Mount Royal College.

Canada Coddles Minorities

From Globe & Mail 2008/04/17   by Brian Laghi

The majority believes Canada coddles minorities

A majority of Canadians says their country bends too much in trying to make visible minorities feel at home, even as voters pat themselves on the back for being a welcoming society.

Results of a new survey for The Globe and Mail/CTV News also show substantial national fault lines on immigration, with urban Canadians more likely to support the growth of visible minority groups than their rural cousins are. According to the poll, 61 per cent of those surveyed believe that Canada makes too many accommodations for visible minorities. In Quebec, 72 per cent of those surveyed feel that way. At the same time, 88 per cent of Canadians believe that their community is welcoming to members of visible minority communities.

As the Conservatives move to amend Canadian immigration laws to clear a backlog, the party's base is apparently less positive about the increasing numbers of newcomers who call themselves visible minorities. "On the one hand, there's a bit of self satisfaction in terms of our record," said Peter Donolo, a partner with the polling firm The Strategic Counsel. "But there's also this kind of anxiety that's most pronounced in certain groups."

Mr. Donolo said some of the unease might stem from a spate of recent issues. They include whether Islamic sharia law should be recognized, and a Tory proposal during last year's Ontario election to extend public funding to all faith-based schools. In Quebec, the government called public hearings into the "reasonable accommodation" of immigrants. The poll also found that 45 per cent of those surveyed believe new Canadians hold on to their customs and traditions for too long, only two percentage points below those who feel newcomers integrate into Canadian life at a natural and acceptable pace.

Mr. Donolo noted there were substantial differences among Canadians on the issue, depending on their age, their education, the size of their community and other factors. For example, on the matter of whether accepting new immigrants of diverse ethnic and religious backgrounds is an enriching part of the Canadian identity, 65% living in cities of more than one million agreed, compared with 53 % of Canadians in communities of fewer than 30,000.

And on the matter of whether new Canadians hold on to their customs for too long, 54 per cent in small communities said they felt they did, while 42 per cent in the large centres said they did not. "People who tend to feel strongest about this are people who live in the smaller communities, where there would be less contact with members of minorities," said Mr. Donolo. "Whereas, the intensity of this feeling is much reduced in larger communities." Supporters of different political parties also had differing views.

When asked to characterize the fact that five million Canadians are visible minorities, 55 per cent of Liberal supporters said it was a positive development, compared with 38 per cent of Conservative backers. By contrast, 53 per cent of NDP backers, 56 per cent of Bloc Quebecois backers and 59 per cent of Greens found the numbers a good thing. Asked whether, at 16 per cent, visible minorities make up too much of the nation's population, 55 per cent of Canadians said it doesn't matter. Only 9 per cent said the proportion was too large, while 10 per cent said it was too small.

Mr. Donolo said some of the poll's results might help to explain policy decisions made by various governments. For example, the Conservative initiative to ban face veils at voting booths may stem from the fact that 82 per cent of Bloc Quebecois voters believe the country has yielded too much in making accommodations.

"They understand that there's some potential, particularly with switching Bloc voters," he said. "At the same time, though, they have to be on guard because there's a history or tendency of the media to brand them as outside the mainstream on these issues." He added that Conservatives want to grow their base, and have made efforts to court visible minorities. The poll of 1,000 Canadians was conducted from last Thursday to Sunday, and is accurate to within 3.1 percentage points, 19 times out of 20.

From the 2006 census:

Five million Canadian citizens are members of visible minority groups. Do Canadians view this as positive or negative?

Age	18 - 34	35 - 49	50+
Positive	54%	51%	41%
Negative	5%	6%	14%
Not sure	39%	40%	44%

Visible minorities now comprise 16% of Canada's population. Do Canadians feel the proportion is too small or too large?

Age	Canada	18 - 34	35 - 49	50+
Too small	10%	8%	12%	11%
About right	22%	18%	22%	25%
too large	9%	5%	8%	13%
Doesn't matter	55%	69%	55%	46%

Is the acceptance of new immigrants of diverse ethnic and religious background a defining and enriching part of our Canadian identity?

Age	Canada	18 - 34	35 - 49	50+
Weakens sense of national identity	30%	20%	33%	35%
Strengthens sense of national identity	67%	75%	61%	53%

Do Canadians feel that new immigrants hold on to their customs and traditions for too long?

Age	Canada	18 - 34	35 - 49	50+
Hold on too long to customs	45%	37%	42%	52%
Integrate at an acceptable rate	47%	55%	51%	40%

Do Canadians make too many accommodations to visible minorities in Canada ?

Age	Canada	18 - 34	35 - 49	50+
Agree	61%	53%	60%	68%
Disagree	36%	47%	37%	28%

Canada: Take It . . . or Leave It

From the Calgary Herald, 2008/03/10   by Naomi Lakritz:

As a fairly new Canadian citizen, I have one thing to say to Charles Roach, the Toronto lawyer who is battling to have the oath to the Queen removed from the citizenship ceremony. What I want to say is this: If you don't want to fulfil this country's requirement for becoming a citizen, there is another country you once called home and you can return there. You don't come here and demand that the citizenship ceremony be changed because you don't like it.

Shame on the Ontario Court of Appeal, which has ruled that Roach's case can go to trial. Double shame on Associate Chief Justice Dennis O'Connor, who said: "There's nothing, quote, 'citizenshippy' about it." Speaking as someone who has been a Canadian citizen only since 2005, I say there is everything 'citizenshippy' about it, Your Honour.

Roach came to Canada from Trinidad in 1955, and 53 years later, he still has not become a citizen. His petition to the court was a joke. It read in part: "The Applicant does not enjoy the right to stand for public office or the right to vote in federal, provincial, or municipal elections, and the right to be employed as a public employee." Roach also complains that his four children, born in Canada, "have attained full political rights and have not had to take the citizenship oath."

Sorry, Charles, but that last bit is just plain dumb. I have no patience with this claptrap.

You choose to come to Canada, to become a Canadian and to make this country's traditions and heritage proudly your own. I consider it the highest privilege to call all things Canadian my own, since becoming a citizen. I come from a country, the US, that hasn't had much to do with monarchs since we had that little matter of a tea party in the Boston harbour 235 years ago.

But Canada's traditions and history are bound up with the Queen and when in Canada, you do as Canadians do. If you can't stomach this country's citizenship ceremony, then find some other country to immigrate to whose citizenship ceremony is more palatable. Meanwhile, don't expect to be able to vote, run for office or be considered for federal government posts that require citizenship. If you're only a permanent resident, those rights are not yours.

You take Canada the way it is and you make it your country . . . or you don't. And if you do, then you take the oath, in which you vow to: "be faithful to Her Majesty, Queen Elizabeth the Second, Queen of Canada, her Heirs and Successors."

I recall that oath as being a lovely part of my citizenship ceremony. I'm no fan of the present dysfunctional clan of Windsor, but I'm a huge fan of Canada and very proud to be a Canadian citizen, and to show respect for this country's history and traditions by taking that oath.

Does Roach avoid driving on Queen Elizabeth Way in his home province of Ontario? If he wins his case, what's next? Demanding that the name of the Court of Queen's Bench be changed, because it offends?

Roach claims that forcing black people to take an oath to the Queen is like forcing Jews to take an oath to Hitler, because of the monarchy's past connection to slavery. Every time someone doesn't like something, they compare the situation with the Nazi regime, thus further discrediting their cause with extremist and nonsensical analogies. The oath refers to the present Queen, who has never enslaved anyone, and to her heirs, who never will . . . not to her antecedents.

It is bad enough that there are Canadian born citizens trying to undermine majority culture here by insisting that Christmas trees be hidden away from the sight of those of other faiths. But now, we have someone who's not even a citizen insisting that a secular ceremony be changed so as not to offend permanent residents, whom nobody coerced into coming here. How much more will we allow Canada to be deconstructed, before we say we've had enough?

There are plenty of people suffering under tyrannical Third World regimes who would give anything to say an oath to the Queen in exchange for the precious freedom to vote, to practise their religion and to live in peace. I'm sure they'd all be happy to trade places with Roach in an instant.

In a letter to his backers and supporters, Roach wrote: "If we win this class action, a centuries old tradition would begin to unravel." Good work, Charles. Why don't you just keep unravelling everything until there's nothing left of Canada but some tattered threads?